John Miller has previously collaborated with John Gielgud on his memoirs for radio and television, and their two subsequent books – *An Actor and his Time* and *Acting Shakespeare*. He has also written the authorised biographies of Ralph Richardson and Judi Dench, the latter now in its third edition. He has worked for the BBC, UNESCO and TVS, and broadcasts regularly on theatrical and historical subjects. For the Millennium celebrations he wrote and produced *Men in Scarlet* – a *son et lumière* history of the Chelsea Pensioners presented at the Royal Hospital. In 2001 he collaborated with John Mills on his updated autobiography, *Up in the Clouds, Gentlemen Please*.

By John Miller

An Actor and his Time (*with John Gielgud and John Powell*)
Acting Shakespeare (*with John Gielgud*)
An Englishman's Home
Broadcasting: Getting In and Getting On: A Careers Guide
Ralph Richardson: The Authorised Biography
Judi Dench: with a crack in her voice
London Theatre Walks (*with Jim De Young*)
Up in the Clouds, Gentlemen Please (*as editor*)
Peter Ustinov: The Gift of Laughter

PETER USTINOV
THE GIFT OF LAUGHTER

John Miller

ORION

An Orion paperback

First published in Great Britain in 2002
by Weidenfeld & Nicolson
This paperback edition published in 2003
by Orion Books Ltd,
Orion House, 5 Upper St Martin's Lane,
London WC2H 9EA

Third impression 2004

Copyright © 2002, 2004 John Miller

A CIP catalogue record for this book
is available from the British Library.

ISBN 0 75284 262 5

Typeset by Selwood Systems, Midsomer Norton

Printed and bound in Great Britain by
Clays Ltd, St Ives plc

For Judi Dench
In gratitude

Contents

Contents

Illustrations

The author and the publishers offer their thanks to the following for supplying photographs and drawings:

1 Tamara Ustinov
2 Sir Peter Ustinov
3 Author's Collection

4 Mander and Mitchenson Collection
5 Hulton Getty Archive

The author and publishers have done their utmost to contact copyright holders. In the event of omissions or errors they will be happy to make proper acknowledgment in any future editions.

Preface

This book came into being in front of a thousand people in Cheltenham Town Hall. I was asked to interview Sir Peter Ustinov in October 1999 about his new novel, *Monsieur René*, at the Cheltenham Festival of Literature. Naturally I leapt at the opportunity and for good measure reread his volume of memoirs, *Dear Me*. I noticed that it was first published as long ago as 1977 and that he had never updated it, although it was still available in paperback, unlike the two previous biographies of him, which are both out of print.

We had an hilarious hour together on stage, when I only got through a fraction of the questions I wanted to ask him; I learnt long ago never to interrupt a great raconteur in full flow. Over dinner afterwards I asked him whether he would permit me to write his biography, and he said yes without a second's hesitation.

A month later he flew in from Switzerland to talk about his novel again at the Guildford Book Festival, this time with Michael Billington of the *Guardian*. So I arrived early at the Yvonne Arnaud Theatre that Sunday, and the two of us had an hour to discuss how best to proceed before Michael arrived to prepare for their evening encounter.

I told Sir Peter I would like the chance to question him whenever he was in this country, which to my great delight was far more often in the subsequent two and a half years than I had ever dared to hope. When I said I wanted to talk to as many of the family as possible, he put on a mock-elderly voice and replied, 'Well, all those who are not locked away.'

Since then, he has helped me track down his old friends and colleagues in many parts of the globe, and I soon discovered the enormous affection in which he is held by all of them, as well as their awe of his many talents.

The latter presented me with the first problem of how to structure the narrative of his life and career, which I have attempted to make coherent by the use of the occasional flashback and flashforward, where a project may have been staggered over quite a long period. Again and again, it was Sir Peter who gave me the clue, sometimes only obliquely, as to how one event led to another and what has shaped his view of life.

War service was a formative experience for most of his generation, but in his case his army years were hugely influential on his outlook and his work. When I read all his plays in chronological sequence, and all his other books too, it was very clear to me how those experiences as a private throughout the war informed his view of the military mind and of the Establishment in general. They also provided him with some of the models on which he based his most inspired comic performances.

He will probably be best remembered for the latter, but there are many other elements in a career that has now entered its seventh glittering decade, and I have tried to reflect them all. At one point, when we were discussing his King Lear, I asked him about the difference between playing tragedy and comedy. For him, he said, 'Tragedy is a greater strain than playing comedy. Sometimes to keep a straight face is difficult in tragedy. You have to find a degree of self-pity for tragedy, which is very difficult for me. I'm not a self-pitying kind of person, I don't think I've got that time to waste.'

Wasting time is not an accusation easily proved against a man with such prolific talents, as I hope the following pages will show. I hope, too, that they will reveal a man who is not just a uniquely gifted artist but one of the truly great men of our time.

John Miller, 2002

Prologue

It is 7 November 2000. Arundel Castle is a hive of activity. It is standing in for Windsor Castle in the BBC's big new historical drama, *Victoria and Albert*. Lights and cameras are being rigged in the dining room, while the set is arranged for a royal banquet; in adjacent rooms extras are being made up and having their wigs dressed.

It is nine o'clock in the morning, and I am in search of Sir Peter Ustinov. This is the first of his two days' filming as the elderly King William IV, and I am keen to watch him at work. I ask one of the production team where I can find him, and one of the stand-ins takes me down the hill to his trailer. He greets me in full make-up and costume, except for his coat; he seems in high spirits, despite telling me that he only got to bed at 1 a.m. after the costume fitting and was collected from the hotel at ten past seven this morning.

He is fairly immobile now because of his diabetes, so we are driven up the hill to the castle, where the first assistant director is waiting for him. 'Welcome, Sir Peter, I'm Mark Egerton,' he says and takes him off to meet the other actors in the first scene. It is the King's seventy-first birthday dinner, and the Duke of Wellington (John Wood) rises to propose the toast 'to the health and long life of His Majesty'.

The first take is the master-shot, favouring Ustinov, and is held throughout his long speech, in which he savagely criticises Victoria's mother, the Duchess of Kent, for keeping the Heiress Presumptive away from the Court. The speech is a powerful one, delivered flawlessly, and when the director John Erman calls, 'Cut,' the whole crew applaud. On the reverse angle of the Duke's toast, as soon as the King repeats his first three words, 'I thank you,' the director calls, 'Cut,' and without a pause Peter says, 'I still thank you,' which brings a laugh from cast and crew.

The rest of the morning is spent shooting this scene from several other angles. Just before Penelope Wilton's close-up for the Duchess of Kent's furious reaction to the King's attack, she is in fits of laughter at one of Peter's stories during the wait. I noticed that even this consummate actress took a few seconds to switch from amusement to a glare of outrage by the time we heard the call of 'Action'.

Peter is clearly hugely enjoying himself as the crusty old monarch, and between takes the atmosphere on set is one of great good humour. Lunch is provided separately for Peter and myself in one of the castle bedrooms, reachable by lift, to spare him the journey down to the catering trailer. I can't resist commenting to Peter, 'I see you're playing the King at seventy-one as rather older than yourself at seventy-nine.'

'Ah, you noticed that, did you? Of course they were much older in those days.'

The afternoon scene is the King's arrival at Windsor. Because of his gout he is carried by four footmen on a chair slung between two poles. The extras don't appear to have been cast for their strength, and to conserve their energies between takes, four of the most muscular members of the crew carry the chairbound King back to the entrance-point. The first time they do this, the assistant cameraman says, 'Charing Cross, sir?' The royal personage responds in the Ustinov East End accent, 'Anywhere you like, but not 'ere.'

During one long wait he entertains the four footmen standing around him by singing several different national anthems.

By now Peter has the whole company eagerly awaiting his next quip or impression, and several of them ask me quietly, with studied casualness, 'When's this book coming out then?'

'Well, I'm not halfway through my research yet, so it should be out in 2002.'

By happy chance Peter is not flying back to Switzerland until Saturday, so we spend most of Thursday and Friday in his suite at the Berkeley Hotel in London, working through more of my long list of questions. Over lunch at the Garrick Club with Ion Trewin, my publisher, I ask Peter what plans he has to celebrate his eightieth birthday in 2001.

'None at all really. I believe the Germans are planning a programme, and the French are talking about it but don't seem to be able to raise the finance. As far as I know, nobody is doing anything in this country at all.'

Ion and I exchange glances, and within days the Garrick Club is planning its own tribute to one of its longest-serving members, dating back to the Second World War.

It is a salutary reminder that Peter Ustinov has been a name in his profession, or in his case professions, for over six decades, on a truly international scale. He has been a hugely successful actor, director, and producer in all the performing media. Even more importantly to him he has also been a writer of plays, screenplays, novels and short stories, television documentaries, opera libretti, history, an autobiography, and a host of articles.

A close study of that prolific output reveals a man who is not only witty, imaginative, and profound, but who has a deeply serious side that is much less well known to his legion of fans. He has frequently said, 'I act for a living, I write because I must.'

The latter may well be the greater compulsion, but having watched him in action on the stage and film set, and having now shared two platforms with him before packed houses at literary festivals, I also believe that he performs because he must. Peter and I were in the middle of a very serious discussion at my home, when my wife entered the room to say that lunch was ready; he responded in a perfect imitation of her Nottingham accent and launched into a story for her, which delayed that meal for several minutes. A telephone call from his agent would be answered in a corresponding American accent; and when we went to one of my favourite restaurants in London, the Como Lario, his Italian backchat with the waiters had the place in an uproar – they begged me to bring him back on his next visit to England.

His mimicry is so brilliant that his cod-Swedish or cod-Swahili sound absolutely convincing unless you happen to speak those languages, and his command of German, French, Italian, and Russian has enabled him to work easily in all those countries.

The accident of birth entitled him to a British passport but, as he often gaily points out, not a drop of British blood runs through his veins. His lineage is wonderfully complicated, as befits such an extraordinary man, and he is very proud of his forebears. He bears a Russian surname, but several other nations have contributed to his genetic make-up, and this rich ethnic mixture has produced a man of uniquely prolific gifts.

One

Before Peter:
The Benois-Ustinov Dynasty

The earliest mention of the family name in Russia appears during the reign of Peter the Great (1672–1725), when the Tsar commissioned a trip abroad by an architect, Ivan Oustinoff. In 1777 one Peter Oustinoff was registered in Moscow as a nobleman. The first traceable ancestor is Adrian Mihalovitch Oustinoff, who made his fortune in the Siberian salt industry in the time of Catherine the Great (1729–96).

His son Mihail Andrianovitch became a merchant in St Petersburg and a landowner with a huge estate around Saratov. When he died in 1838 at the age of 108, he bequeathed 240,000 hectares of land and 6000 serfs to his children, and he was buried in one of the sixteen churches he had built in his lifetime.

Half of this legacy was inherited by his son Grigori Mihalovitch, who conspicuously lacked his father's virtues. His wife Maria Ivanovna bore him four children – Mihail, Grigori, Lydia, and Platon (the youngest born in 1840) – but husband and wife separated when the children were still small. Platon never really forgave his father for this breach, nor for his behaviour after it. The children lived with their mother in the same street in St Petersburg as their father and had to visit him every morning, passing on the way a group of young serf girls, none of them older than sixteen, from one of his villages. They were lined up for him to choose from for his post-breakfast pleasure. Platon reacted against this debauchery by becoming puritanical in his own life, to the extent that he never again spoke to his eldest brother after discovering that Mihail had spent the night with one of his lady friends.

The malign hand of his father also led indirectly to Platon's exile. In 1857 he passed out of St Petersburg Cavalry School with honours, aged seventeen, and was commissioned in the Guards Uhlan Regiment. To celebrate this triumph his father gave him a thoroughbred horse, which fell during the first night-manoeuvres, crushing him and injuring his spine so badly that he was paralysed for months. The loss of his career, and his enforced immobility, pushed him into wide reading and deep introspection.

His estate administrator, a German Protestant, helped him to procure the books he wanted, and after many discussions Platon decided to abandon the Orthodox religion and become a Protestant. Such a step was forbidden by the State, under penalty of confiscation of all estates and exile to Siberia. When he announced his conversion, that punishment looked inevitable. He was saved by the intervention of his uncle, Mihail Mihalovitch Oustinoff, the Russian Ambassador to Turkey and a close friend of Tsar Alexander II, whom he persuaded to mitigate the sentence by allowing Platon to sell his lands and go into exile abroad.

His first port of call was Württemberg, whose queen was a Russian princess, and through her influence he was granted Württemberg nationality and nobility, becoming Baron Plato Von Ustinov. His former administrator shortly returned to his native country with his beautiful daughter Maria; soon she and Platon were married. But on their honeymoon in Italy he discovered that she was not a virgin and their marriage was thus short-lived. After many wanderings, he was drawn to Palestine and settled in Jaffa. He refused for years to divorce Maria, until a failed plot to kill him implicated her, which finally convinced him to sever all their ties.

Now, aged forty-eight, Platon Grigorievitch chose to remarry. He had become friends with the large German colony and especially with Frau Hall, wife of a Protestant missionary to Africa, who was half Portuguese and half Ethiopian. Her eldest daughter Magdalena married Platon in 1888, and four years later she bore him a son. Their religious convictions led them to choose an unfortunate name for him – Jonah, since Jaffa was where God commanded the whale to land that Biblical prophet after swallowing him for three days, though in German it is spelt Jona.

The endless teasing at school led Jona to hate his name, and he could not forgive his parents for choosing it. When his wife later nicknamed him 'Klopik', Russian for 'little bug', later 'Klop' for 'big bug', he gratefully adopted it in preference to his given name.

Baby Jona was lucky to survive infancy. Small and delicate, he nearly died from influenza in his first year and later caught severe malaria. These illnesses led his parents to spoil him, and he grew up into a wilful young boy, indulged far more than any of his three younger brothers and sister. He went first to the German colony's school in Palestine and in his early teens to a school in Düsseldorf, so his first language became German; then he went on to study French at Yverdon in Switzerland and at Grenoble University, followed by a brief spell at Berlin University to read law.

In 1913, when he came to London with the rest of the family, his father decided to sell his collection of antiques to a European museum. Platon successfully petitioned Tsar Nicholas II to permit his return to Russia. At this point war was declared between Russia and Germany, and as Jona and Peter, the two eldest boys, were German subjects they considered it their patriotic duty to travel to Germany and join the army. Two days later Britain was at war. Platon left for his homeland to offer his services to the Russian Army but was told he was too old. He was joined later by his wife and daughter, Tabitha; the two youngest boys, Platon and Gregory, aged eleven and seven, stayed in England with friends.

Jona and Peter were soon in the trenches as private soldiers, but when they were offered commissions they applied for training in the air force. Jona narrowly escaped death, but his brother Peter was not so lucky. Early on the morning of 19 July 1917, Jona woke to find Peter by his bed, already dressed for action. He was off to drop the mailbag from British prisoners of war over the enemy lines and had come to say goodbye. Jona wished him luck, adding, 'Don't be too long.'

'No, it's not my intention. I am so very tired today, I don't know why. When I return, I'll go to bed again, and I'll sleep, and sleep, and sleep. I could sleep for ever.'

It should have been a routine flight. The humanitarian nature of such drops was signalled by flying white streamers from the wing-tips, but the bright sun that morning half-blinded the British anti-aircraft batteries and they opened fire. They later apologised for their mistake. Jona led a volunteer party into No Man's Land and found the body thrown out on the wing of the crashed plane.

The loss of his brother deeply affected Jona, but he carried no grudge against the country that had killed him, and later eagerly adopted its nationality when he was in peril from the Nazis.

The armistice of 1918 provoked revolution in Germany, and Jona was happy to become correspondent for the Wolff Büro news agency in Amsterdam, with the promise of a posting to London as soon as Britain granted permission. But first he was anxious to find his parents in the turmoil of post-revolutionary Russia.

He entered the country with a group of Russian prisoners of war being repatriated and nearly found himself immediately conscripted into the Red Army. In a series of extraordinary adventures in that chaotic time, he traced his mother and sister, but discovered that his father had died of dysentery.

In Leningrad Jona met and fell in love with Nadia Benois, whose forebears had fled from the French Revolution. Jules-Cesard became 'Maître de bouche' to Tsar Paul I and married the royal midwife, Fräulein Concordia Groppe. Besides running the imperial household, they managed to raise seventeen children of their own. One of his sons, Nicholas, married Camilla, the daughter of the Italian composer Catterino Cavos. In 1797 Cavos became Director of the Imperial Theatres, and when the mad Tsar banned Italian opera the following year, Cavos turned his attention to writing operas on Russian subjects.

Camilla's brother Albert, also an architect, built the Maryinsky Theatre (later the Kirov) in St Petersburg and then rebuilt the Bolshoi in Moscow after it burnt down in the 1860s.

Architecture, music, and painting ran strongly in the veins of the Benois family. Nadia's father Louis was an architect who became Principal of the Academy of Arts in St Petersburg, and his oldest brother Albert was a leading member of the Russian watercolour school; but the most famous member of the family was the youngest brother, Alexandre, who fell in love with the ballet and who, with Sergei Diaghilev and Leon Bakst, founded the influential journal *Mir Iskoustva* (*The World of Art*). He collaborated in the creation of the Ballets Russes and designed decor and costumes for many of their productions.

It was Alexandre who wrote to his great-nephew Peter to congratulate him when he first went on stage: 'For centuries our family has been sniffing around the theatre. We have built them, decorated them, written scores for them, conducted in them, directed in them. Now, at last, one of us has the courage to leap on to the stage himself.'

Before we leave this ethnic melting-pot that produced the genes of Peter Ustinov, there is one final element, which he only discovered himself as recently as 2000. It concerned his grandmother, Magdalena.

He told me, 'I knew she was half Ethiopian, but I had no idea her father was a Polish Jewish Christian. It came out at Basel University, from Professor Alex Carmel of the university in Haifa, who was doing research into all this. So it burst on me, and I had to face an audience made up almost entirely of Jewish intellectuals and rabbis, an audience I'm very unused to in Europe, treating the whole thing as though I'd been welcomed into the fold. I said to them, "Look, I've got such mixed blood it doesn't seem to matter very much to me one way or the other. I'm delighted to have found this out, because it means I am one sixteenth of Polish Jewish ancestry, but one sixteenth doesn't really justify your excitement, and I treat it as any other blood, because I believe them all to be equal." They were very appreciative of my toughness in that respect, but they all asked for my autograph, though not in Hebrew, thank goodness.'

At this stage in his life Peter was no longer surprised to learn of yet another gene in his make-up, but he has never ceased to wonder at the extraordinary series of chances and travels that united his various ancestors and eventually led his father to meet his mother.

In his autobiography *Dear Me* he describes it in a very Ustinovian way.

It needed the precipitate action of a Serbian student in Sarajevo, the sabre-rattling of the Austro-Hungarian war party, the limitless ambitions of the Kaiser, the French desire for revenge, the immense speed of the Russian mobilisation, the war at sea, in the air, on land; gas, revolution, humiliation, and conquest to bring them together. I can never hope to repay the immense war-debt which I personally owe to millions of people, whose concerted egotism, self-sacrifice, stupidity, wisdom, bravery, cowardice, honour, and dishonour made it possible for my parents to meet under the least likely of circumstances and with the most far-fetched of pretexts. There is no alternative but humility for me.

If the pace of world change was quickening, the personal story of those parents was now unfolding at whirlwind speed. Two weeks after their first chance meeting through a mutual friend in Leningrad, Jona and Nadia were engaged to be married. In her memoir, *Klop and the Ustinov family*, Nadia recounts how everything moved much faster than they originally intended. Two days before their wedding Klop (as Jona was known from now on) said to his fiancée, 'You know, Nadia, I have been thinking and I have decided not to start our married life until we are out of Russia. We don't know how much longer we shall have to stay here. The conditions are bad and certainly will deteriorate even more. It would be irresponsible to risk starting a family here.'

'Yes,' she replied, 'you're quite right. Why should we hurry? The main thing is to be legally married so that when the time comes for us to go – we're ready.'

So they agreed that Klop would continue living with his friend, Nicolai Nicolaievitch, after the wedding. Neither of them realised the dangers of such a simple domestic arrangement until they were alerted by a friend of Nadia's parents, who had contacts with the Commissariat for Foreign Affairs, that they were being closely watched. He warned them, 'If you don't live together after your wedding, you'll be arrested. You,' he said to Klop, 'will be accused of trying to export bourgeoisie! So, whatever your plans, you must at least live under the same roof after the wedding.'

After he had gone, Klop said, 'It is a sign from above. I'll have to move into your flat after all. But promise, we'll try not to . . .'

'Yes, of course.'

Nadia's conclusion of this story is brief: 'So a bed was quickly prepared for Klop in the little drawing room next to my room. And that is how Peter was started earlier than intended.'

The wedding took place on 17 July and baby Peter arrived nine months later, almost to the day, on 16 April 1921. Although he was conceived in Leningrad, there was some uncertainty throughout Nadia's pregnancy as to which country would be the scene of his birth. Klop once again just escaped being conscripted into the Red Army. A month later the German Embassy got them on a train out together with an echelon of German prisoners of war who were being repatriated. After a journey via Narva, Stettin, and Berlin, the couple reached Amsterdam, where Klop immediately resumed work at the Wolff Büro. They remained there for four months, awaiting permission to go to London. On 22 December they disembarked at Harwich, but an omission on Nadia's visa meant that Klop had to travel to London alone, and when she was finally permitted to join him she underwent a nightmarish journey before they were reunited.

Klop was soon working long hours as the Büro's only representative in London, telephoning detailed and lengthy reports to Berlin. His insistence on completing one such telephone report when Nadia's birth-pains had started meant that they only just reached the nursing home at Swiss Cottage in time.

When Nadia came to after the delivery and watched the nurse washing the baby on her lap, she was astonished to see him lifting his head, as if he wanted to survey the room. The nurse caught her eye and exclaimed, 'Yes, he is a very strong little chap, aren't you, my precious? Yes, you are, my little Blessing!'

This first indication of Peter's strength and curiosity was to become even more marked over the next few months and years.

Two
_____

1921–1937
Enter Peter

The birth of Peter brought a stability to his parents' existence that they had not experienced since they first met. For Nadia it was 'as though an anchor had been cast', even if rather too spherical a shape for an anchor, as baby Peter was very chubby, already showing that tendency to corpulence that has never left him.

He was initiated into the joys of travel within weeks of his arrival, when he was taken off to Germany for his christening. Klop's mother and sister had managed to get out of the Soviet Union, and Magdalena was now resting in the Sanatorium Schonblick at Schwäbisch Gmünd near Stuttgart. The ceremony was also attended by Klop's two younger brothers and two of his aunts. Platon was named as godfather to his nephew. Nadia recounts how Klop asked Trudl Weiffenbach to be godmother, a girl he met in Munich during the war who had hoped he would marry her, so he thought this was the least he could do as a substitute. This, however, seems to be a less than full account of Klop's premarital relationships, as Peter later found out: 'I discovered when I went to the place where I was christened in Württemberg that in the registry there were eight godmothers and one godfather, and I think that is to do with my father's amorous proclivities. The godfather was my uncle, but most of the godmothers I'd never heard of. These were goodbye gestures to various mistresses, Casanova-style, very generous.'

It is perhaps understandable that Klop should have been a bit vague about his previous relationships with these godmothers, as the christening took place on the couple's first wedding anniversary. Klop was highly amused when the pastor conducting the baptism named the baby 'Petrus Alexandrus'. Magdalena, on the other hand, was so moved that she wept throughout the ceremony. She was easily carried away on religious occasions, which her grandson recalls vividly: 'The story of the crucifixion was enough to set her off, as though it were not so much a monumental tragedy as a personal misfortune. When it came to the two robbers, the sobbing began. It was her habit to capture me and place me on her knee for the evening recital, pressing me to her ample bosom, and I still remember my striped flannel pyjama-tops dampened by tears, which soon grew chill against the skin. At times I asked for some more conventional story at bedtime, but even if it began with wolves and piglets and fairies, Gingerbread Street quickly changed to Calvary, and I was left with the mystery of the Passion to fret over in my sleep.'

Not that Peter seemed to need as much sleep as other children, right from the very beginning, which worried his parents who thought he needed rest more than food, because he was almost too mentally advanced for his age. He was only nine months old when he astonished his mother once again. The inventor Nicolai Nicolaievitch, with whom Klop had stayed in Leningrad, came to call when he got to London. He was in full spate, talking Russian very fast and waving his arms about, describing his latest inventions, when Nadia was alarmed to feel Peter shaking on her lap. When she looked at his face, he was convulsed with tears of laughter pouring down his face. She had never seen a baby laugh like that, and after the cause of it had left Klop remarked that it showed Peter had a very keen sense of humour.

At about the same age he also demonstrated his precocity for reading. Sitting on top of a bus with his mother, he suddenly got very excited and, pointing to a huge advertising hoarding, he called out, 'Oxo! Oxo! Oxo! Oxo!' to the amazement of the other passengers.

By the time he was two years old Peter had added considerably to his vocabulary, and with his father's active encouragement he had mastered his first impersonation as a party turn: 'I am Lloyd George and you are rascals!' In 1924 he was got out of bed to perform his little cabaret act before an audience comprised of Haile Selassie and the sizeable entourage that had accompanied the Emperor to London. Other such precocious two-year-olds might have developed into little monsters, but for Peter there was one saving grace: 'and that was that I was irrevocably betrothed to laughter, the sound of which has always seemed to me the most civilised music in the universe.'

By now Peter's ear for mimicry was apparent. On holiday in Scheveningen with his parents, he was playing on the beach when a little local boy stopped and began talking quickly to him in Dutch. After a moment's bewilderment Peter rattled back a stream of what sounded like Dutch but made no sense at all; the other little boy was so put out by this incomprehensible new game that he ran off at high speed.

The gift for re-creating sounds authentically extended to machinery. He has always loved motor cars, and at about the age of four he pretended to be one, an Amilcar, driving all over the flat with the noises of changing gears, accelerating and braking, only stopping when he reversed into bed and cut the ignition. After a while this drove his parents to distraction at home, and when he did it in the street, startled pedestrians would leap out of the way, imagining that a real car was right behind them.

Peter's highly developed imagination meant that he was quite happy by himself, reading and drawing, and did not really miss having other siblings to play with when he was growing up. In fact, his mother had another baby on the way but lost it by lifting Peter off a bus; he now feels guilty about that, 'because I only found out about the miscarriage very much later in life. I found nearly everything out very much later in life.' This was especially true regarding his family.

His first regular contacts with other children began at the age of six, when he started at Mr Gibbs' Preparatory School for Boys in Sloane Street, Chelsea. He did not take to compulsory games – the cricket ball was far too hard for his taste, and he usually found himself in the goalmouth at football because of his lack of speed with the ball; the assumption was that, being large, he might keep the ball out of the net with his body.

Because he was known as 'von Ustinov' he was teased about Germany having lost the Great War, which he says was 'a rather heavy burden to carry if you were six'; but when the racing driver Caracciola won a race in his Mercedes-Benz, Peter was bemused to be congratulated as if he had himself been in the driving seat.

His foreign background led him to react strongly against some of the imagery he encountered, particularly a huge oleogram in the classroom of Christ, holding a Boy Scout by the hand and with the other hand showing him the extent of the British Empire on the map. This left no doubt in the mind of the viewer as to which side Jesus was on, which offended Peter on both aesthetic and political grounds.

His first experiences of acting here were not calculated to render him at all stage-struck. 'I played a pig and had to wear a pig-mask, and I still remember the awful smell of size inside the mask; and I played a nymph, luring Ulysses on to the rocks by singing a song, 'Oh Ulysses, weary and wise', written by Mr Dunlop, one of the masters. I quite understood it when Ulysses just sailed by.'

Peter says that it was at Mr Gibbs' School that he learnt how to survive by emphasising the clumsy and comic aspects of his character, and on the whole this worked. He was generally happy there and although he had difficulty with mathematics, particularly algebra, and with Latin, he was nearly always top in geography, French, history and English.

These relatively carefree days were about to change, on both the personal and the international front. In 1933 Peter was due to leave preparatory school. Just before he left he travelled to Berlin with Nadia to visit her mother and her sister Olga. The Nazi demonstrators were much in evidence, and Peter was just as appalled by the anti-semitism expressed by a boy his own age who was found to keep him company. Klop regarded Hitler as a nonentity and refused to take him seriously at first, but events were soon to change his mind.

The personal change in Peter's life came with the choice of his next school. Neither of his parents wanted to send him away to board, so they settled on his being a day boy at either St Paul's or Westminster. They let Peter decide which by asking him whether he would prefer to wear a straw hat or a top hat. He settled on the latter but came to regret it.

Just as he was about to start there, the family was dismayed to learn that there were no vacancies at Westminster for day boys, so he would have to be a boarder after all. Peter hated it, 'because it had a sense of values that I don't understand. I was a boarder for a year and a half. I have no knowledge of English protocol; it all absolutely baffled me. When I became a day boy and went to another House, my boarding Housemaster wrote a very bitter report, saying, "He never came and said goodbye." But I was eager to leave, I didn't want to linger.'

Peter found most of the staff extremely eccentric. Mr Claridge, who taught French, would look at him and say, 'Mr Ustinovkins, you are looking at me with the expression of a cod which has just slid off a marble slab,' or, 'You look at me with the eyes of an early Lithuanian adventurer.' He says he would not have remembered these remarks if they had been more apt.

Science was taught by a Professor F.O.M. Earp, so he was naturally known to the boys as 'Foam', which seemed an appropriate nickname in his case. He had invented a bicycle with eight gears, which was very advanced for its time, except that the rider had to stop to change gear; it could not be done while the bicycle was in motion. On one occasion the Professor was demonstrating a scientific experiment when there was a tremendous explosion and he disappeared from sight. There was smoke and broken glass everywhere. Suddenly he rose from the ground behind the desk, coal-black, with his clothes ripped apart. He was very short-sighted, so that when he pointed to the space between Peter and another boy and said, 'Now, what did I do wrong, you?' neither of them answered.

Because of the shortage of staff at the time 'Foam' was forced to teach Divinity as well. 'He didn't really know much about it, and he made us divide our pages with a ruler downwards, then attempted to explain most of Christ's miracles scientifically – I remember the water into wine as being probably due to the formation of permanganate of potash crystals, which might have blown into the water and discoloured it.'

This view of Biblical miracles as a series of conjuring tricks had less impact on Peter's view of religion than a particular sermon in Westminster Abbey by the Headmaster, Mr Christie, a lay preacher who enjoyed the sound of his own voice in the pulpit just a little too much. All the stained-glass windows had been taken out for cleaning, and a bitterly cold wind was blowing through the open spaces.

Even now Peter's eyes glint with rage at what happened. 'Christie was an abomination, and I shall never forget that day. A small bird flew in the window and started fluttering around while he was preaching, taking our attention away. He must have got irritated with this small bird, which flew inadvertently into one of the open gas-brackets and flew out again with its wing on fire, circling the aisle like a 1914 aeroplane. As it circled in panic several boys made a gesture to try and rescue it, and from the pulpit Christie said, "Leave it alone ... And Jesus went up into a high place ..." I remember my fury at that, I thought it was absolutely scandalous.'

The world of politics also figured strongly in Peter's experiences at Westminster. His father had moved to the German Embassy in London, to become the press attaché, but he found his position increasingly untenable after the Nazis came to power and von Ribbentrop was appointed as the new ambassador. When his son Rudolf was refused admission to Eton, the British Government pressured Westminster into accepting him. His traditional school uniform was adorned with the diamond-shaped badge of the Nazi Youth, complete with swastika.

Soon after his arrival he entered the school art competition, with a triptych in watercolours of a Wagnerian group of warriors, with shields and crossbows, and horns on their helmets, under the title 'Armed Strength'. This prompted Peter to earn his first writer's fee. He wrote a piece about the young Ribbentrop's artistic creation and posted it off to the Londoner's Diary of the *Evening Standard*. They printed it, with a few alterations, which Peter thought ruined the effect he intended, and wrote to him, asking whether seven shillings and sixpence would be an adequate reward. Now the budding author discovered the value of procrastination. When he forgot to answer, the newspaper sent him a pound instead.

'Then the Housemaster had me in, because he said he knew my father was a journalist, and could I find out where the leak had come from? The Headmaster wanted to know because the German Embassy was furious. After two weeks I went back to the Housemaster and said, "I'm sorry, I've tried every avenue, nobody seems to know where it came from."

'Mr Bonhote said, "I can't help feeling whoever is responsible will go far in life. Damned clever."

'I agreed. "Still, one doesn't want to encourage that sort of thing, does one, sir?"

'He said, "No," and then after a pause, "Of course some people don't need encouragement." '

At the same time, for more serious reasons, Klop decided to sever his connections with von Ribbentrop Senior. For some time his superiors in Berlin had been growing irritated by his straight reporting of the British scene, leaving them all the trouble of having to make up their own distortions. Klop just walked out of the embassy one day and, with the help of Sir Robert Vansittart, Permanent Under Secretary at the Foreign Office, he was granted British nationality almost immediately. Since this had to be published, Vansittart arranged for it to be done in a Welsh-language newspaper in Swansea, so that the Gestapo would not catch on. The Germans, furious at his resignation, told him to go to Berlin and report, an invitation he naturally declined.

In these troubled international times a German-turned-Briton was in a special position. A couple of years later Klop received a call from the German military attaché, telephoning from a callbox. General Geyr von Schweppenburg said, 'Ustinov, I appeal to you because we are completely out of touch. This idiot Ribbentrop has made such enemies in London that all the good work you were doing is now destroyed.' He asked if Klop could arrange a meeting between members of the British General Staff and members of the German General Staff, to try to reach agreement on how to put a stop to Hitler's progress. Schweppenburg added, 'If this goes on we have no means of restraining him.'

Peter's first inkling of this highly secret plot was when his father uncharacteristically asked him to go to the cinema.

'When I asked why, I was told it was none of my business and was given sixpence. I had to tell him that the cheapest seat was ninepence.

' "Are you sure?"

' "I'm positive."

'So he called to my mother, "Nadia, have you got threepence?"

'We lived in a flat on the fourth floor with no lift, and as I started going down the stairs some very old gentlemen were climbing up, reeking of cigar smoke. I never asked what that was all about then, but during an air raid early in the war he told me. The German officers had all taken leave at the same moment and had gone off to different destinations, from where they had taken commercial airliners to London. The British were led by the Chief of the Imperial General Staff, General Sir Montgomery Massingberd. The Germans were adamant that this was the last occasion on which they could put a stop to Hitler if Britain stood firm, but the British feared it might be a trap. My father was appealed to by all these people and played his part, yet at the same time he couldn't get a job.'

The adult divisions over appeasement were echoed at Westminster School in mock elections, instigated by the Headmaster as an education in citizenship. He was a little alarmed by the emergence of a leftish grouping calling itself the United Front of Progressive Forces, or Uffpuff. When he called the leaders to meet him for an assurance that they were not undemocratic, he discovered that their motivation was anti-Conservative and anti-appeasement. Some of Uffpuff's leading lights, like Francis Noel-Baker and, later, Tony Benn, were to continue their political interests across Parliament Square as Labour MPs.

Peter's political sympathies had been decided much earlier than this. When he was about four and a half years old he suddenly enquired of his father at breakfast, 'Please tell me, what is Conservative, Liberal, and Labour?'

His father tried to put it in the simplest terms to one so young.

'Well, you see, Peter, the Conservatives are people who don't want any change at all, Labour are people who want a very quick change, and the Liberals are those who also want change, but a slow and gradual one.'

Peter pondered this explanation for a moment and made his first political choice.

'Then I am Liberal.'

'Why?' asked his father.

'If you make a quick change it will be a mess, but if you have no change at all you will have no history.'

His political knowledge, opinions, and activities have all increased considerably since that infant pronouncement, but his basic stance has remained much the same in the following seven and a half decades.

Perhaps because of Peter's eager intellectual curiosity, his father treated him as more adult emotionally too, which had a less happy effect on their relationship. When the two of them were sitting at a café in France, Klop looked at a woman passing their table and remarked, 'She has wonderful breasts, don't you think so?' Peter was not yet of an age to appreciate such an observation and found himself becoming furious with his father. 'Then he took me to my first nude show in Paris, which was frighteningly unpleasant; it was really hideous. The nudes were shaved, and they had elastoplast over vital bits, it looked as if they had been wounded in the wrong place. I'm sure he only invited me, not to see my reaction, but to give him an excuse to go. I was frightfully ignorant about all that, and I must say I reacted against it, perhaps a little too long. My father was an inveterate flirt, which turned me into a tiny puritan.'

So the family pattern of rejecting paternal behaviour repeated itself – Grigori's libertinism producing Platon's puritanism, followed by Klop's hedonism generating a similar reaction in Peter to that of his grandfather. This meant that Peter became, and remained, closer to his mother than his father throughout their lives: 'She was the most unpossessive woman I can imagine. She never interfered with my life at all, she never tried to guide me. She was sometimes a mother, sometimes a sister, and as often as not a daughter.'

She was, however, not only sympathetic to his career ambitions but most influential in ensuring that he could realise them. In retrospect, it seems curious that Peter never appeared on any stage at Westminster, as most leading actors first found their vocation treading the boards at school. Nadia had long thought that was his destiny. When he was eight, he came home after seeing a gangster film and demonstrated one of the fights so brilliantly that she said to Klop then, 'I think Peter should be an actor. His performance just now was quite remarkable.'

The prospect did not please Klop. 'Yes, it was remarkable, but I think he would make an even better diplomat or KC than an actor.'

They agreed to let him decide himself when the time came, but when it did Nadia gave her son more than a nudge in the right direction. She had become a successful painter and gradually moved into stage design, especially for the ballet. Michel Saint-Denis brought the celebrated Compagnie des Quinze to London, and Nadia spent some time backstage, doing sketches from the wings. She so admired the French director's work that when he set up his drama school, the London Theatre Studio, she thought that this was where Peter should go. Neither he nor his mother thought he would pass his School Certificate as, unlike the later O levels, examinees were required to pass in a spread of subjects, both arts and sciences, and the latter were still a mystery to Peter.

He went along with his mother's suggestion, as the prospect appealed to him more than the alternatives, but it was hardly a burning desire: 'It was my mother's idea. I wasn't really drawn to the theatre, because I never understood how actors remembered all those lines. I've now played King Lear twice, and I still don't understand how it's done.'

At the age of sixteen he had not yet understood the nature of auditions either. Candidates were instructed to choose a major play and learn a page by heart. Peter interpreted this to mean the whole page, not just one character's lines, so he played all the parts. This amused and impressed Saint-Denis, but there remained one reservation. He said, 'We would like to take him, but he is rather too young; he is only sixteen, and we think that is too young.'

Nadia had the answer to that: 'He's very eager to come, and incidentally he has eyes very similar to yours.'

Saint-Denis looked at Peter, puffed on his pipe for a moment, and said, 'He has good eyes. All right.'

He must have seen something more promising than just his eyes to accept Peter at a younger age than all the other students bar one, but it was to be a while before that promise was realised.

Three

1937–1941
From drama student
to dramatist

Peter had been eager to leave behind the curious constraints of the English public-school system, but now he found himself forced to engage in equally incomprehensible exercises that were of doubtful value to him. He was not alone in his reaction; Peter Daubeny joined the Studio in the same year, and he was much more caustic about the exercises they were required to perform than Peter Ustinov ever was.

Daubeny wrote in his memoirs, *My World of Theatre*, that the converted chapel in Islington 'looked like a gymnasium, and its curriculum, it seemed to me, was one more suitable for a seminary of psychiatric therapists than students of drama'. They were asked to do bizarre improvisations, like a dinosaur in labour, or a bush in a snowstorm.

The two Peters discovered that they were both born on the same day in 1921 and soon formed a close friendship. They used to travel on the same bus to Islington every morning, and Ustinov had great fun imagining what new fantasies might be required from them. Sometimes his foresight was very canny.

For a whole term they each had to adopt the persona of an animal of their choice, and while some of them raced around as an elk, or an okapi, the Ustinov careful choice was a salamander, who 'just dozed comfortably in the sun for three whole months, occasionally tilting a quizzical eye at the members of the faculty and darting out my tongue to ensnare an unwary fly. This exercise certainly revealed more about my character than it did about what goes on in the heads of lizards.'

GEN. SIR AUGUSTINE DAUBENY

GEN. SIR HUBERT DAUBENY

FIELD-MARSHAL SIR ADHEMAR DAUBENY

GENERAL SIR RUPERT DAUBENY

GEN. CONFORMITY DAUBENY

GEN. SIR LAMBERT DAUBENY

SIR ALARICK À DAUBENY

SIR PIRBR DAUBEN

DAUBENFREED BONETOOTH

SIR GUILLAUME À D'EAU BENIT

DAUBINIUS PRAETOR

PILTDAUBENY

Are you really worthy of the Tradition?

The family tree created by Peter Ustinov for Peter Daubeny when he
published *My World of Theatre* in 1971

Saint-Denis's character was so dissimilar to that of his youngest student that it was hardly likely they would achieve any rapport. Peter found him a most untypical Frenchman. 'He was not quick, he was ponderous in his attitude. We rehearsed *Alcestis* by Euripides, and he suddenly stopped during rehearsal and said, "I'm sorry, I've got you off on the wrong foot. It isn't like that at all, I'm rehearsing it as though it's Sophocles, and it's Euripides of course. There should be a comic element, which makes people laugh." It was awfully difficult. He had a French class too, and that was more indicative of the fact that he represented a side of France that one hardly knew, very Northern. He said to me, "Ustinov, you must express here fear, do you know how to express fear? By contracting your buttocks."

'I tried once or twice and said, "I can't walk that way." I now don't know whether I was always taking the mickey out of that kind of absurdity.'

His fellow students shared none of those doubts at the time about Peter's satirical intentions. James Cairncross, in the year ahead of him, immediately spotted his talents: 'It was patently obvious that no drama school was going to be able to teach him anything. He was a brilliant mimic and could do many, many different voices – a wonderful gibberish Russian, and also a wicked impression of Michel Saint-Denis, not in front of him, of course. He could also do all sorts of musical instruments brilliantly.'

Peter's own attention was caught on his first day at the Studio by a girl who 'wasn't obviously pretty or beautiful. She belonged to no particular type. She held mystery for me, and that was enough to cause indescribable confusion in my thoughts and feelings. I found myself planning to sit close to her, or in her eyeline, or behind her. Eventually we just drifted into one another's company.'

Her name was Isolde Denham, daughter of the playwright Reginald Denham by his first wife, the actress Moyna MacGill. After their divorce, Moyna married Edgar, the son of the leading Labour politician George Lansbury, and bore him twin sons and a daughter.

Angela Lansbury was thirteen years old in 1938 and took a

great interest in her sister's first real boyfriend. The impression he made on her then remains as vivid more than sixty years later. 'Peter was a little bit overweight at that time, but a fascinating person. He had a very unusual way of dressing, he didn't follow the norm in any sense whatsoever. He was full of voices and characterisations and personalities, all of which spilt out of him with such abandon and excitement, I found it quite catching. As a very young aspiring actress I was tempted to spar with him. We would share moments of speaking absolute gibberish to each other, in strange languages that had no meaning.' Angela thought it was wonderful that Peter would take the time to have some fun with her, even though she was only thirteen and he was madly in love with her sister.

In the summer vacation at the end of his first year, Peter gained his first experience before a paying audience, in the little Barn Theatre at Shere, in Surrey. Appropriately for his debut, it was as a Russian, Waffles, in *The Wood Demon*, Chekhov's first version of *Uncle Vanya*. Peter was nervous almost to the point of panic on the first night, but came through it. 'By the second night, I felt I had done it most of my life.'

His new-found confidence was severely tested in the next play, Lorca's *Mariana Pineda*, in which he played a lecherous Spanish Chief of Police who behaves rather like Scarpia in *Tosca*. The director, John Burrell, tried to explain Lorca's symbolism to the actors, but Peter felt way out of his depth and could not understand why lust should be so garrulous. This production was the play's English première, so *The Times* sent its drama critic, who pronounced that 'Peter Ustinov gave the part of Pedrosa a sinister restraint which was acceptable.' This first notice in a national newspaper is treasured even more in retrospect, as its subject reflects that 'Never since have I been called either sinister or restrained.'

It was during the fortnight's run of this play that he first met Charles Laughton, who brought his wife Elsa Lanchester to the Barn and then invited all the cast for tea. *The Sign of the Cross*, in which Laughton played Nero, had just been released in London. Peter went to an early-afternoon screening, finding the film over-melodramatic for his taste. Walking across Green Park, to his astonishment he suddenly bumped into Laughton who, to Peter's even greater surprise, remembered him, and they fell into conversation.

The famous film star then promised the young actor a treat, which, to the latter's dismay, turned out to be one of the most expensive seats for *The Sign of the Cross*. He was too tactful to tell either Laughton or the cinema manager that he had just sat through it once already that day. For the sake of his future relationship with that unique actor, it was just as well, or he might have found the making of *Spartacus* twenty years later even more fraught with clashing temperaments.

Peter persevered through his second year at the Studio but felt he was making little progress and decided to leave at the end of it. Saint-Denis's response to this news would have discouraged many less resilient personalities. He warned Peter that not only had he come to the school early, he was leaving early, with very limited prospects.

'With your looks,' he said, 'and the way you're built, I don't know what your future is. Perhaps Shakespearean clowns, but one doesn't see them every day.'

When Peter declined his advice to stay another year, he was dismissed with a prediction that rankled. 'You will – if by some chance you succeed – fall into the world of tricks, like Charles Laughton.'

The French director was gifted in stagecraft, but his temperament was the antithesis in every respect of Ustinov's. 'There was something about Michel's whole attitude towards his art, which took it down a peg. He hated the idea of success, because it was suspect. It was very indicative that when I suddenly had a success as a playwright he never came and saw the play. I said to a former member of the Compagnie des Quinze that he always makes me feel as if we're going to win because we're weaker than the others. He said that it was worse than that: we will win because we are poorer than the others. I thought that if his companies don't last, it's for that reason.'

His 1939 company folded for a different reason. He planned a new production of *The Cherry Orchard*, starring Edith Evans, Peggy Ashcroft, Gwen Ffrangcon-Davies, Ronald Squire, Alec Guinness, and George Devine. Saint-Denis offered Peter the chance to understudy George Devine, who had been one of his tutors at the London Theatre Studio; the two other male understudies were James Cairncross and James Donald.

On 1 September the rehearsal was broken off, and everyone trooped down to the stage door to hear the latest news on the stage doorkeeper's wireless when, James Cairncross remembered, 'It was announced that Hitler had marched into Poland. There was one of those appalling silences when you knew that the ground had been wrenched from under your feet, and God knows what the future would hold.'

Peter was too young for the call-up, but now achieved his first great success in the guise of two ancient and very different characters. He auditioned for Leonard Sachs, who ran a Victorian cabaret at the Players' Theatre. For his audition piece he created the Bishop of Limpopoland, based on a real colonial bishop who had preached to him and the other schoolboys in Westminster Abbey, describing his mission to convert the heathen in Darkest Africa. Whenever he quoted Swahili to them he assumed that his audience understood and never bothered to translate for their benefit; after a stream of Swahili he would pause and say to the boys, 'So what was I to do? Naturally I took the second course.'

Peter developed this experience into a richly comic performance, although he says now, 'I've felt ashamed ever since.' (When I got him to reprise part of that act at the Cheltenham Literature Festival sixty years later, it brought the house down, apart from the man with no sense of humour who came up to me afterwards to point out that what we'd heard wasn't real Swahili; he knew because he spoke the language. Peter sighed resignedly when I repeated this to him and said, 'Oh, there's always one.')

The second of these creations was also very loosely based on a real person – Madame Schumann-Heink, a leading contralto of the time. This incarnation he named Madame Liselotte Beethoven-Fink, an ageing Austro-German lieder singer, for whom he created passages of mock Schubert and a fractured English in which she explained Schubert's complicated background as having 'a little bit of insect in that family'.

These two monologues brought him instant success, though his father was not impressed, saying sorrowfully, 'Not even drama ... vaudeville.' This dampening response was more than offset by the acclaim of James Agate, Ivor Brown, and the then-critic of the *Tatler*, Herbert Farjeon, himself a writer of revue sketches, who said that it might have been Edmund Kean doing a party turn. This prompted even Klop to come and see what was attracting such acclaim, after which he brought a number of friends on several occasions.

The Players' Theatre attracted both established stars and promising new talent, including Alec Clunes, Bernard Miles, and Rosalind Atkinson; she was in the pantomime where Peter played Alderman Fitzwarren, and the writer in him still winces at her lines:

> Courage, Harlequin, do not despair,
> You shall have fairy aid in this affair.

When Leonard Sachs was called up a little later on he asked Jean Anderson to take over the running of the theatre, which she did for the rest of the war, with occasional guest appearances from former stars, which she much appreciated. 'All those people who had worked for Leonard, and were now in uniform, would write to me whenever they got leave to ask if there was any chance of getting in the bill during that leave, and that was very rewarding. Peter used to come and do his two wonderful turns, the oldest diva and the oldest bishop in the world, and they were magic.'

Jean Anderson remembered a particular night at the height of the buzz-bomb attacks, when one rocket came very close. 'It was a packed house as usual, and nobody moved. Peter was doing the Bishop of Limpopo. Everybody just froze. We just waited until we heard the blast very near. Bits of plaster came down, and a few things fell off walls. Peter just said, "Ah, I see the Wright Brothers have gone wrong again." It brought the house down, and then he went on with his performance.'

But his earliest appearances there were only intermittent and not very well paid, so he jumped at the chance to go to Aylesbury Repertory Theatre, for the princely sum of £2 10s a week. (It says a lot about the financial state of the theatre that every actor I have met can always recall precisely their very first salaries.)

He made a convincing start in *White Cargo*, as the doctor struggling to cope in an outpost of the empire, covered in sweat and killing imaginary mosquitoes; he was so convincing that he received a letter saying, 'I was so moved by your appeal for medical magazines that I herewith enclose the latest copy of the *Lancet*.'

With only a week to rehearse each play, sometimes preparations were cut a little fine. Peter just made curtain-up for the opening night of *Rookery Nook*, in which he played Harold Twine, the part played famously by Robertson Hare, as he had been waiting anxiously on Aylesbury Station for the arrival of a bald wig.

His facility for languages came in useful for the French Professor in Terence Rattigan's *French Without Tears*, the German seal-trainer in Robert Morley's *Goodness How Sad*, and that epitome of the English upper class, Colonel Pickering, in Shaw's *Pygmalion*.

In the early summer of 1940 Peter returned to the world of revue for his first appearance in the West End, now coming back to uncertain life after the theatre closures on the outbreak of war. Norman Marshall, who had made his name running the little Gate Theatre, asked him to join the company of *Swinging the Gate*, at the Ambassadors' Theatre. It was led by Robert Helpmann and Hermione Gingold; she had a reputation for being eccentric and Peter rapidly discovered why. 'When I first saw her, she said, "Come in," and she was relieving herself sitting astride the sink!'

But it was at her initiative that he was brought into the show, after she saw him at the Players'. 'I was enchanted by him and insisted on his being in the revue. We gave him two spots that were supposed to last a maximum of three minutes each, but Peter ended up making each last for ten.'

This generous gesture was seasoned with her characteristically acerbic wit, when she persuaded Ronald Millar to fill the remaining vacancy by enumerating the company as 'a cast of nine supporting me (my dear, if only they were!)'

She could not have been best pleased when James Agate in his *Sunday Times* column used her young protégé's previous success against her, despite his disappointment with one of his current creations: 'Mr Peter Ustinov appears as a dilapidated and unsuccessful operatic composer reduced to describing Mascagni as "small beer". But, alas, Signor Marcantonio Sostenuto's own beer turns out to be so small that one can hardly perceive it. And I invite Miss Gingold graciously to drop her "Queen of Song" and allow Mr Ustinov to retrieve his losses with that Lieder-singer in decay which has so often delighted the Players' Theatre, but which cannot be known to the general public, although it is one of the minor masterpieces of the day.'

Peter's West End salary meant that at last he could afford to leave home, and he found a tiny penthouse flat in Dover Street. Surprised by its cheapness, he rapidly discovered that its large area of glass roof was only too vulnerable to German bombers and needed a lot of blackout protection.

Disappointed that his new material for *Swinging the Gate* had not quite hit the mark, he invented a new character, an old Russian professor who was jealous of Chekhov and attacked his imagery. 'I want to be a seagull! ... For me ... physical impossibility.'

He seemed to be specialising in foreign parts at this time, spending a lot of his time buying French plays in Harrods, which then had a whole French section. He translated a French play, *Fishing for Shadows*, which was presented briefly in October 1940 at the little Threshold Theatre Club; he also acted in it. The author of *Fishing for Shadows* was Jean Sarment, who was also an actor. Peter had to put on the play without his permission, since there was no way of reaching him in Occupied France. The two of them did actually make contact after the war, but there was never any question of royalties, even retrospectively, as hardly anyone came. 'Very often there were more people on the stage than there were in front, and there were only five of us. I translated it and produced it very quickly, because we had a nucleus of actors who were out of work.'

One of the few people to see the play was Herbert Lom, who had met Peter when they were both acting at the Barn Theatre in

Shere, though in different plays. He wrote him a letter after the performance, offering some criticisms of the production, and received a two-page reply, hotly defending his intentions against his friend's disappointed expectations:

You suggest that we had nothing to say. Oh yes! We have a lot to say. Some of it is going to be said now. It is not out of cowardice that I put on a play which had nothing to do with war, social conditions, capitalism, oppressed minorities, or whatever topicality you hoped to find dramatised. It perhaps needed added courage to present a play which is 'mounted' in the space of one week with a cast which is so young ... The 'mother', whatever you or I think of her, joined us five days before the play opened. I did the translation in two days. You saw the finished product (finished!), and left because you failed to find your message, but there is a week's hard work, in which insurmountable difficulties were overcome, and two shillings spent on the set! We do not pretend to be good. It is a first exploration into a corrupt and wealthy world. We do not ask for congratulations, but we also disown any responsibility towards the 'complications' of life. Life has enough complications at the moment to prevent people from coming to the theatre at all ... No, really, Herbert – you blame us for the intentions of the author! One must be faithful to an author's text once one has agreed to play it. No psychological (or more often journalistic) web may be woven across it ... If this is strongly said, it is because it is warmly felt.

The youthful passion with which he defended this very small-scale wartime production reveals the depth of his feelings for the theatre and his respect for the craft of writing; he has often expressed those views since in more measured terms, but they have, if anything, become more strongly held over the years.

Peter had continued seeing Isolde Denham after leaving the London Theatre Studio, and now both aged nineteen, they plunged into marriage. Isolde's mother was taking a group of evacuee children to America, including her own offspring. Peter now thinks that if they had not got married at that moment they never would have, as Isolde would probably have crossed the Atlantic too, and he recognises that they were really both too young to embark on married life at such a time.

To complicate their introduction to life together, Peter had given Isolde a cocker-spaniel puppy named Ophelia, soon shortened to Pheli; it started having fits and was not yet house-trained, so it left its mark all over their basement flat in Redcliffe Road, which was quite near his parents' home. The bombing had begun, and whenever there was an explosion nearby at night, Klop and Peter both ran out to see if the other's house was still standing.

Swinging the Gate came off, and Peter put his first toe into the world of films. He played Van der Lubbe, the Dutch halfwit framed for burning down the Reichstag, in a dramatised documentary, *Mein Kampf – My Crimes*; then he performed one of his monologues and climbed a star-spangled rope-ladder in a ludicrous short film about young people, called *Hello Fame!*

After these unfortunate beginnings he found himself working under a major director, Michael Powell, in *One of Our Aircraft is Missing*. The cast included Godfrey Tearle, Eric Portman, Hugh Williams, and Robert Helpmann. His revue appearances with the latter did little to prepare him for coping with his performance here. 'Robert was playing a Quisling, saying, "Save me from them," and digging his nails into my arms. It was really extremely painful. He couldn't equate acting with reality at all. I flinched a bit but continued acting as I'd been told to.'

Peter was trying to emulate the relaxed playing of Gerald du Maurier and Leslie Howard, until he became aware of the beady eye of Hugh Williams watching him. Eventually Williams came over and asked politely, 'Excuse me, young man, but what are you going to do in this scene?'

'Well, I thought I'd do almost nothing.'

'Oh no you don't, *I'm* doing nothing.'

Peter took that as an awful warning to do something.

He was cast as a Dutch priest and was eternally grateful to the two real Dutch priests who were employed as technical advisers on the film. They hated each other and were consequently never present on the set together. On Peter's first day of shooting one of them came up to him and said, 'Excuse me, but where is your crowse?'

'My what?'

'We wear around our necks a crowse.'

'Oh, well, I didn't think I'd need one.'

'During the occupation in Holland I never went out in the street without my crowse, in order to show people I was a priest; it became a symbol of resistance, and always you had to wear your crowse.'

'Well, you'd better tell the director that.'

'I will tell him. Mr Powell . . .'

So they shot the scene again, by which time the first Dutch priest had gone to the canteen, and the second one came on to the floor. He immediately stopped the shooting.

'What's he doing with a crowse on?'

'Well, the other man told us that he wouldn't go out without it during the war.'

'On the contrary, it's too dangerous to go out with the crowse, because there were all sorts of symbols like Stars of David and crowses, and ignorant Germans could easily mistake one for the other, and then you are in the hot waters. I would never be seen in the street with a crowse on.'

To be on the safe side, the compromise reached was that all of the scenes with the priest were shot twice, once with Peter wearing the cross and once without (the latter were finally used in the film), thus requiring the Ustinov presence for twice as long and doubling the payment he received. This was irritating for everyone except the actor concerned. 'I've always been very grateful for Dutch dissension and democracy, even within the restricting confines of the Church.'

He assumed another nationality in a screen adaptation of J.B. Priestley's *Let the People Sing*, playing an elderly Czechoslovak professor. Then for once he played someone younger than himself, a brilliant pupil in a Nazi spy-school, in *The Goose Steps Out*, a farce starring Will Hay.

The old and famous comedian failed to impress the newcomer. 'I couldn't see what made people laugh. Everything had to stop while he had his tea, he was very Edwardian in that respect.'

In between these varied film experiences, Peter was rescued from poverty by Herbert Farjeon, who offered him a daytime revue called *Diversion*, with Edith Evans, Dorothy Dickson, and Bernard Miles.

Peter heeded Agate's earlier advice to bring back Liselotte Beethoven-Fink, which the critic hailed in the *Sunday Times* as a portrait of complete authenticity: 'Creaking, bedizened, grotesque, the Mrs Skewton of the old Viennese stage, this scarecrow is pathetic because she has not passed away, but is still of this world if indeed there is any life at all under that powder, paint, false hair, and all the other cloaks to decay. She is like an Empire in ruins, and there is one of these great seventeenth-century sermons in the libidinous cackle which falls from these senile lips. True? Anybody who has known any old ladies belonging to a regime which is ceasing to endure will recognise Mr Ustinov's Hogarthian veracity.'

Diversion was such a success in wartime terms that its original run of five weeks was extended to nine, and it was followed later by *Diversion No. 2*. The new members of the company included Joyce Grenfell and another young actor born the same day as Peter, with whom he shared a dressing room. In 1941 he was still calling himself Derek van den Bogaerde.

Peter wrote a couple of sketches, including one on three different producers of *King Lear*. The first was based on Michel Saint-Denis; the second on Herbert Marshall, a Communist; the third on Rupert Doone, who, Peter thought, 'was very precious and had insisted in one play on everyone putting sequins on their upper lids'. When Peter came to play Lear himself many years later, it is hardly surprising that he wanted no directorial gimmicks to be imposed on his conception of that play.

There were two, and sometimes three, performances of *Diversion No. 2* each day, which had to finish before the air-raid warnings began to sound between 5.30 and 6 p.m. This left the actors free in the evenings, so Peter did an act at a small basement nightclub called, imaginatively, The Nightlight.

As if this were not enough, he began to work on his first full-length play, *House of Regrets*. Unlike many writers, who require peace and quiet to be creative, Peter was able to write surrounded by visitors and the hubbub of conversation, a facility he has never lost. Dirk Bogarde was astonished by his energy, as he watched him passing sheet after sheet to an entranced Joyce Grenfell sitting on the floor.

He wrote the story in pencil in school exercise books. He has never learnt to type and could not then afford to have the manuscript typed, so he gave the only copy to Herbert Farjeon, who took it away to read. After some weeks with no response from the man he now regarded as his benefactor, Peter began to lose faith in the play. However, this was to be restored in the most dramatic manner possible.

Peter was already exploring other avenues in addition to writing and performing. In 1941 he directed for the first time, a Russian play by Valentine Katayev, adapted by Charlton Morton and E.B. White, and given the English title of *Squaring the Circle*. Its West End production at the Vaudeville did not cause a great stir, but *The Times* was encouraging, saying that 'Mr Ustinov's production is neatly invented and sets a lively pace.'

But his greatest ambition was to succeed as a writer, and his frustration with Farjeon's evasiveness he now discovered to be unjustified.

Peter was visiting his parents in Gloucestershire, where his mother had moved to escape the blitz. Klop was now doing secret and dangerous work for MI5 but joined his wife when he could at weekends. The three of them were together on 22 June 1941, when the news broke that Hitler had invaded the Soviet Union, so they devoured the newspapers for every scrap of information about what was happening on the new Eastern Front.

After lunch Peter turned to the arts pages of the *Sunday Times*, where Agate's headline caught his eye – 'A New Dramatist'. Wondering who was being lauded by the doyen of drama critics, he was astonished to discover that it was himself. Herbert Farjeon had had *House of Regrets* typed up at his own expense and had sent it to Agate for his opinion.

The critic's praise for the play exceeded that for the creation of

Madame Beethoven-Fink and ended: 'When peace permits the English theatre to return to the art of drama as opposed to the business of war entertainment, this play will be produced. Let not the ordinary playgoer be dismayed at the prospect before him. This tragi-comedy is funny to read and will be funnier to see. Yes, a new dramatist has arrived, and his play will be seen.'

His prophecy was right, except in its timing. It would be seen well before peace came but not until October 1942, by which time Peter was playing his part in a very different drama, wearing a costume he had to endure for four years – as a private in the British Army, initially with the 10th Battalion of the Royal Sussex Regiment.

Four

1942–1944
Private Ustinov, film-maker

Private Ustinov, service number 6411623, reported for duty at Canterbury on 16 January 1942. Sixty years later he still says vehemently, 'I hated the army more than anything I've ever hated in my life, and I was continually shouted at by people who had no natural gift for conversation.'

One company sergeant-major found it difficult to pronounce Peter's name, which usually came out as Utnov, and was even more flummoxed by his vocabulary. After the company had been transferred to new and bigger quarters, he asked him, 'Ow's the new billet, Utnov?'

'Oh, much better, sir, thank you, it's much less congested.'

'I know,' he snarled. 'More room too, i'n there?'

Demonstrating the new plastic grenade, the CSM barked at the men, 'I want you to look at this 'ighly careful. This grenade I got 'ere is 'ighly detrimental to henemy morals.'

But it was Peter who was demoralised by this alien world, and he wrote many despairing letters to his mother, whose heart ached for him. His father showed very little sympathy, after his own dashing career in the First World War. So Peter took comfort from the few kindred spirits he met in these first months of his service.

'When we had kit inspections in the army, we were supposed to have our socks in squares. I'm a round person, and even if my socks were in squares at one point, they gradually became like buns. The sergeant major, who was as mad as a hatter, came in and said, "What's all this fuckin' shower? Look at your socks, you wait till the officer sees that!" The officer came in and said, "Your picture's in *Tatler* this week." It was very difficult to explain to the sergeant major, because when the officer had gone out the sergeant major said, "What'd he say to you?"

' "He saw my picture in *Tatler*."

' "What the fuck's that?" '

The officer, who had been an ASM at the Open-Air Theatre in Regent's Park, found service life as unappealing as Peter and recognised that it must have been even worse for him as a private.

The Ustinov sense of initiative did little to win him favour in the conventional military mind. An example of this came in the exercise to test the preparedness of the Kent Home Guard for the defence of Maidstone. His regiment played the part of the German invasion force, and Peter devised a plan to infiltrate himself alone into the centre of the town. He broke off from the rest of the unit and started knocking on the doors of houses at five in the morning. The occupants came to the door in their nightwear, in some dudgeon.

'What is it? You know the time!?'

'Yes, it's a military manoeuvre.'

'Oh, you'd better come in then. What do you want to do?'

'I want to go out the back way.'

'Just through the house?'

'Yes, just through the house.'

'All right.'

He went into the garden, climbed over a hedge into someone else's back garden, and knocked on the back window.

'What is it? Why don't you go round to the front?'

'I want to go to the front, but could you let me through?'

In this manner he zigzagged across the street without being challenged until he reached the middle of Maidstone, where he saw the general commanding the Home Guard getting into his car. He pointed his unloaded rifle, pulled the trigger with a click and said, 'Bang. You're dead, sir.'

'Don't be so preposterous.'

He was a very angry general and the umpire, who had observed this, had an unfortunate stutter. Second Lieutenant Biddle only got out, 'I'm sorry, sir, you are ... d ... d ... d ...' when the general said, 'Don't you start,' and ordered the Home Guard to arrest this 'German prisoner'.

Peter maintained his role-play by answering questions only in German, so they locked him up in the armoury. He seized a machine-gun, rushed out and threw ink all over their documents. The drama was now beginning to get seriously out of hand, so the Home Guard sent for his colonel, a man whose posture resembled that of a tortoise, with his head coming out of his uniform at such an angle that it was possible to see the name of the tailor inside the jacket. He attempted to calm the atmosphere of outrage.

'Now, what seems to have gone on here?'

'Well, sir, you told us the purpose of this exercise was to prepare the Home Guard for a possible German attack.'

'Yes?'

'Well, I talked to them in German, and they were furious.'

'H'm, yes, I see more or less what's happened. Come with me and we'll get you home. I must say it's very rash for you to do what you did, but congratulations all the same. Ha, ha, ha . . .'

The absurd inability of the army to see how best to utilise the Ustinov talents was highlighted when his first play finally reached the stage of the Arts Theatre in October 1942. *House of Regrets*, directed by Alec Clunes, with a cast including Max Adrian, Noel Willman, John Ruddock, and David Bird, told the story of a group of Russian exiles in Kensington in 1939 and 1940, reliving their experiences of the earlier war and arguing about their response to this one.

Richard Attenborough had just left RADA and had appeared in the opening play of the Clunes regime, *Awake and Sing* by Clifford Odets. He was bowled over when he went to see this first play by a new writer, finding it 'bewilderingly beautiful, and wonderfully acted'. Afterwards Alec Clunes told him excitedly, 'I've discovered a genius, you must work with him.' Attenborough had to wait four years for a proper opportunity to do so, but he and his wife-to-be, Sheila Sim, quickly got to know Peter and his wife, enjoying a number of evenings together as a foursome.

House of Regrets impressed the critics as much as it did other actors. The *Daily Mail* praised 'the perfect acting of all concerned', under the banner headline 'Best Play of the War'; *The Times* thought it showed 'brilliant promise'; and although Ivor Brown expressed some reservations in the *Observer*, he concluded that 'it is lively and touching and encourages one to believe that Mr Ustinov will very soon write as brilliantly as he already acts.'

It was the evidence of his writing ability that rescued him from the drudgery of army life, which had so blighted his first months. Morale was low among his fellow soldiers after recent reverses, and it was decided that the medium of film should be used to correct this.

Peter was seconded to the Directorate of Army Psychiatry, where he had access to secret reports. He read with growing disbelief the observation that 'When men went to the cinema and saw the High Seas fleet on manoeuvres, and slowly the big guns turned towards the audience, it was noticed that many men after that slept uneasily, with their tin helmets over their private parts, because of a castration complex due to the High Seas Fleet.'

He was only too happy to get away from what he regarded as 'a very odd lot', to join a small group that many in the army regarded as even odder. It included Carol Reed, who had been called up as a captain but had no idea about army regulations. Peter accompanied him to Savile Row to collect his uniform. 'He came out into the street and was immediately saluted by a sergeant major from the Black Watch. Carol took off his hat and said, "Good morning." The sergeant major stopped dead, as though he was hot on the trail of a German infiltrator. I hurried Carol out of there, and he said, "Why was that man looking at me like that?"

' "Because you don't take your hat off, you salute."

' "Oh, I see." '

The third key member of the group was Major Eric Ambler, the writer, who had done his time in basic training like Peter. The first film they were supposed to make was about beachmasters and commandos, so they were sent up to Troon on the Scottish west coast. Peter travelled separately, with a stopover at a barracks in Glasgow, 'in a storeroom full of mattresses piled on each other so that I had to sleep very near the ceiling. I felt like the Hans

Christian Andersen princess with the pea. I stayed in Troon with a strange old American who was living out his retirement there. He tried to teach me golf, which I learnt to hate immediately.'

This was not Peter's only strange encounter at Troon. The commanding officer was Colonel Jack Churchill, who was almost albino, with red eyes and white eyelashes. Carol Reed knew him from pre-war film work whenever archery was needed. He would be told, 'We just want you to fire the arrow so that it impales the wimple without hurting the woman.'

'Oh, I see, yes, that's easy enough. You ready?'

Phfft. A twenty-five-guinea fee, and he went home.

Now the situation was reversed. He was a colonel and Carol was only a captain, and this operation was on a much bigger scale. Asked about the average casualties on a commando raid, Churchill replied, 'Well, the last raid we did was on Lillehammer in Norway, and you've got to realise first of all that your casualties come from your supporting fire, because you're so exposed to that kind of thing. The casualties on that raid were about 70 per cent, but I don't think you should frighten people, let's say 60 per cent.'

Carol Reed went as white as a sheet. It turned out that this film project was aborted by the disaster of the Dieppe raid, with enormous Canadian losses, and it was realised that no training film could keep pace with developments.

The group was threatened with dispersal, but none of them wanted to go back to their units, least of all Peter. He came up with the bright idea of making a film for new recruits, to humanise the army and make it seem less terrifying. The Army Council approved it, so they were posted to the Army Kinematograph Service in Wembley Park. The forty-minute film they made there, entitled *The New Lot*, was written by Eric Ambler and Peter, directed by Carol Reed, and it starred Robert Donat. The cast also included Stanley Holloway, Raymond Huntley, James Hanley, and William Hartnell.

Some of the older generals hated it, spluttering furiously, 'You can't call those men soldiers, they do nothing but grumble. Real soldiers never grumble,' proving just how out of touch with reality they were. But the high-ranking officers in the Adjutant General's office and the War Office Public Relations Directorate were keen that the general public should see it.

So it was decided to make a feature-length version called *The Way Ahead*, dealing with the relationships between officers and the other ranks. David Niven, who had rejoined the Rifle Brigade, agreed to star in the new picture. As he was both an established film star and a former regular officer, his credentials were impeccable.

Peter was now sent off to an officer selection board but found it impossible to take either the selectors or their curious games seriously. The board concluded, 'On no account is this man to be put in charge of others.'

This was potentially a problem for Peter, working closely on a film with officer colleagues, and the only solution was to make him David Niven's batman. They worked in a room at the Ritz Hotel, and to make life easier for Private Ustinov, he was given a pass conceived by Colonel Niven, which stated, 'This man may go anywhere, and do anything at his discretion in the cause of his duty.' It proved invaluable whenever he was stopped by suspicious Military Policemen, though their incredulous reaction was often expressed in obscenities.

The film unit received a succession of colonels as technical advisers, most of whom had very little useful advice to offer. One of them arrived with an attaché case, which looked to be bulging with secret documents. He sat down and said, 'Now what exactly do you want to know?'

'Well, there are manoeuvres going on, and David Niven is marching his platoon along a causeway, behind a hedge. He suddenly hears rifle-fire. What would he do normally?'

'Let me get this clear in my mind. He's marching along ... a hedge, did you say?'

'Yes, a hedge.'

'Yes, marching along a hedge with his platoon ... and suddenly he hears ... What was it?'

'Rifle-fire.'

'Yes ... Oh drat! So long since I've done this stuff.'

The private tried to help the colonel with this knotty technical problem. 'Would he halt them?'

'That's it! That's exactly what he would do. He'd halt them.'

Then he opened his attaché case, which was full to the brim with pipe tobacco, filled his pipe and lit it. 'Next question?'

Peter had acted in *The New Lot*, but he played a different role in *The Way Ahead*. He was very upset about that, but Carol Reed thought he would be better as the owner of an Italian restaurant in North Africa. To get to that location, the unit was put on a troopship taking a long route out into the Atlantic and then back up to North Africa. They shot there for a month, where it was more convenient to turn Peter temporarily back into a civilian so that he could deal with the high-ranking military advisers on equal terms.

The Way Ahead opened on D-Day and was generally regarded as a great success. Dilys Powell vindicated Carol Reed's decision to recast Peter by ending her review in the *Sunday Times*: '*The Way Ahead*, in fact, is to be admired and recommended for its direction, its writing and its playing. I should not leave it without pointing to a sketch by Ustinov as a village café proprietor: a ravishing study in sullen lethargy and "*je m'en foutisme*" turning at last to fight.'

Peter's demobilisation was only temporary – as soon as he returned to England, he found himself back in uniform again. To add insult to injury, the first thing he had to do was to march nineteen miles to be shown the film that he had made originally to encourage new recruits when they arrived. This was even more unendurable than his first call-up. 'My return to the army was one of the bitterest moments of my life really, because having done all this, been congratulated by generals, to have to go back again as a private, marching around and cleaning potatoes, and not sure of my future, was absolutely terrible.'

To add to his depression, his second full-length play, *Blow Your Own Trumpet*, was, in Peter's own words, 'an unqualified disaster'. It was directed by Michael Redgrave for the Old Vic Company, with sets by Feliks Topolski, and was acted by a cast including Noel Willman, Esmé Percy, and Michael Warre. Redgrave asked the author to rewrite the love scene between the two young people, which he produced on the backs of envelopes; the director was nonplussed to discover that not a word had been changed. (Later directors would share the same discovery after similar requests.)

Peter admits now, 'I was rather influenced by Saroyan. I thought it was a new way of doing things. That's the only time I've ever acknowledged an influence. It was a very strange play.' At the time the critics savaged it almost unanimously.

The dramatist's first champion, James Agate, tried to let him down gently, but the sting was in the tail: 'Mr Ustinov possesses every quality of the first-class playwright except one. He cannot think of a story. Power of characterisation, life-like dialogue, wit, dramatic sense, though as yet there is no drama to exercise it on, fun, with a nice glozing of philosophy – all these, yes. Alas, they are not enough.'

It ran in August 1943 for just thirteen performances. Redgrave was stung by the dismissive notices and wrote in his memoirs, 'With all its faults it had ambition, and I felt it deserved better treatment from its reviewers.'

Peter had never been one to give up easily, and he next tried a dramatic form that was even more ambitious. *The Banbury Nose* progresses backwards in time from 1943 to 1884, following the military fortunes of the Hume-Banbury family through four generations.

Thus Roger Livesey began the play as a crusty embittered old general, shedding his years lightly as he changed back in stages to a youthful idealist who wished to break the family mould. Others in the cast were Hugh Burden, Michael Shepley, Lyn Evans, Eric Messiter, Richard Wordsworth, Ursula Jeans, and Isolde Denham. At least this gave the Ustinovs a chance to see something of each other. Opportunities had been few and far between after Peter was called up. When he did get home on leave to join Isolde in their flat in Kensington Close, he was called in by the manager of the building, who said, 'We see that two people occupied the room last night.'

'Yes, there's nothing wrong, is there?'

'No, but it's rented by only one person.'

Eventually Peter said, 'Well, it's my wife and me.'

'Oh, I see. Well, it's wartime, and that will be all right, so long as you don't tell anyone it's your wife.'

After all the opprobrium heaped on *Blow Your Own Trumpet*, critical opinion now swung decisively back in favour of the playwright and his players. In the *Observer*, J.C. Trewin said: 'This flutter through the Army Lists offers that happy experience in the theatre – an evening of good writing with acting to match.'

The Times added: 'It has, moreover, the great advantage of putting Mr Ustinov's *forte* in the first movement of this family symphony. That *forte* is the creation of grotesque old age, dancing pathetically on a razor edge of pride and disillusion.'

Under the headline 'Right Music, Wrong Words', James Agate began his long column in the *Sunday Times* by quarrelling with the author's view of the military but ended it with: 'One word more. This play may be full of sedition, false doctrine, heresy and schism. That doesn't matter. I find it entrancing to listen to for the reason that Mr Ustinov is probably the greatest master of stage-craft now writing in this country. He has as much wit as Mr Coward. He has a far greater sense of the theatre than Mr Priestley deigns to have nowadays. His stream of mind is perpetual, and I am not worried that the stream is running the wrong way. He writes magnificent parts for actors, and if I had the space I could write a whole column about the performance of the players.'

The audience enthusiasm matched that of the critics; this was the first Ustinov play to notch up over a hundred performances. The army response was less encouraging – the author was put on a charge for taking his first night curtain call in uniform, wearing suede shoes.

His disenchantment with the army was reaching breaking-point. After *The Way Ahead*, he was allowed to direct his first film – a ten-minute training exercise entitled *Tanks – best use of smoke, No. 4*, which he shot in Richmond Park, trying to avoid the deer. He and the directors of *Tanks – best use of smoke Nos. 1, 2, 3, and 5* gathered together in a viewing room to meet the general who was coming to see if the films were acceptable. 'The lights went down. The general sat there with a non-committal expression – I never saw him with any other expression on his face – and he watched the five films. Afterwards, we all rather sheepishly got up to be congratulated, and the general walked right past us, opened the door of the projection booth, went up to the projectionist and said, "Damn good show." '

The frustration affected Peter's health. He was taken off to a military hospital with gall-bladder trouble, diagnosed as of nervous origin, and was ordered to have a complete rest. That might have been more effective had his hospital wing not overlooked the playground of a lunatic asylum.

He was then sent to a personnel selection officer, 'to find me employment compatible with my inclinations'. Once more, there was a total failure to understand the Ustinov situation, centring largely on a fruitless argument about the scale of his freelance earnings over and above his private's pay. At the end of this the officer gave his judgment: 'You are clearly psychologically unsuited to film writing, therefore I am sending you as a clerk-storeman to the Royal Army Ordnance depot in Donnington Park, where your duties will be to grade underwear in sizes ...' He never finished the sentence.

It provoked one of the few recorded occasions when Peter totally lost his temper. In his boiling anger at this example of crass stupidity, he picked up the child's board-game with round holes and square pegs so beloved of army psychiatrists and hurled it out of the window. He was immediately arrested and taken to see the senior resident psychiatrist, a colonel, 'a lady of sombre colour with "Bermuda" written on her arm'.

She questioned him about the violence of his response to the personnel selection officer's decision, and seemed to take his point that he could hardly be psychologically unfit for film writing when he had written the script for *The Way Ahead*, which had just gone on general release to extraordinary praise from critics and public.

She told him not to worry; she would shortly have him transferred from the Film Unit to the Theatrical Unit, for entertaining the troops. This transfer was carried out to some revealing and appropriate dialogue.

The sergeant major at the Army Kinematograph Service helped to load him with all his kit, saying malevolently, 'You wait till the sergeant major in charge sees this, you'll get a bollocking.'

After all his previous experiences, Peter feared he might be right. But when he arrived at his destination in Grosvenor Square, he was greeted with, 'Oh my dear, let me help you get all that shit off your back. It must be awful having to carry that stuff all the way from Wembley Park, you must hate it.'

The sergeant major in charge turned out to be the celebrated wigmaker, Stanley Hall, of Wig Creations. They never met again, but after Stanley died Peter was touched to receive a long letter from his boyfriend, who must have been about eighty by then, telling him how Stanley had often talked about Peter and had always held him in high esteem, and he wanted Peter to know that he had gone.

Sending Private Ustinov back to the world of theatre did not end his problems, but now they were theatrical rather than army problems, and he could cope with those, even when they reached Ustinovian dimensions.

Five

1944–1946
From *The Rivals* to
School for Secrets

The Garrison Theatre at Salisbury was the first assignment given to Peter by his new commanders – to direct and play in *The Rivals* by Sheridan. Edith Evans had decided to abandon the West End and do her bit for the war effort by touring for the troops. She played Mrs Malaprop for the first time, and Peter was Sir Anthony Absolute. Casting all the men's parts was difficult in wartime and some of it depended on chance encounters.

When James Cairncross was invalided out of the army in 1944, he went to London with his sister for a holiday and to catch up with the plays there; those theatres left standing after the Blitz had now reopened for business. On the corner of Shaftesbury Avenue and Wardour Street he bumped into Isolde Ustinov, who was on her way to Wyndham's Theatre for *The Banbury Nose*.

'Oh my goodness,' she said, 'Peter's looking everywhere for you. He wants you to come to Salisbury and play Faulkland in *The Rivals*.'

James leapt at the opportunity, although in fact he ended up playing the more agreeable part of Bob Acres. For him, 'It was an extraordinarily happy time. The war was still on, but one was quit of all the miseries. We toured it round various camps and always came back in the bus and then would have supper in the Bluebird Café.'

Theoretically the play was co-directed by the two co-stars although, as James commented, 'Edith couldn't direct really, but she kept giving you confidence that you could do it. I was stuck with a long speech one day and said, "I can't do this." She replied,

"Oh yes, you can, dear," and on we went. She and Peter got on wonderfully well together. He was a great company manager and was terribly sympathetic to the actors. He mildly resented being criticised as a director. A knowledgeable friend of mine thought it wasn't well directed and when I passed this on to Peter he seemed astonished that such a criticism should have been made.'

This was not the moment to apply the critical standards of the metropolis. The Garrison Theatre had improvised and inadequate stages, and the audience had to endure very hard seats. In an attempt to forestall criticism of the latter and to create a sympathetic atmosphere, Peter wrote a Prologue, to be spoken by Edith Evans:

> Good evening, warriors, gentlemen sombrely attired,
> By discipline bound, by warlike thoughts inspired.
> Good evening, Amazons, ladies dressed to kill,
> We have come to purge your thoughts of CB and of swill.
> Forget, forget the barrack square,
> Forget the blanco brush,
> Bask in the comfort of your chair,
> And hush.
> Pour souls of 1944,
> Poor victims of this everlasting War,
> Smile on us the dead, though very much alive,
> The carefree ghosts of 1775.

As a director, Peter was initially overjoyed when he was given the unanticipated support of a small orchestra, drawn from eight former members of the Berlin Philharmonic, under their leader, now Lance Corporal Professor Doktor Reinhard Strietzel, and seven former members of the Vienna Philharmonic under their leader, Private Professor Doktor Rudolf Stiasny. They had all been drafted into the Pioneer Corps, but although they were united against Hitler, the two orchestras hated each other. The lance corporal at one point pulled his army rank on his musical peer, who was only a private, and threatened to put him under close arrest.

The rift between Berlin and Vienna was healed when the leading actress chose to remind everyone that this was not an opera with dialogue, but a play with accompanying music. Now they were united against 'zis woman'. Peter observed with some alarm that the musicians whiled away what were for them boring spoken scenes between their playing, by conducting a chess match between the two capital cities.

'I hoped to God Edith wouldn't notice this. She was wonderful on the first night and got great applause. On the second night in mid-speech she stopped dead. She saw the chessboard, and because she was an actress of great experience she turned to me and said, "What did you say?"

'I invented some Sheridan. "Madam, though the humours of Bath be but a diversion to our contumely, I will not presume on your generosity to the extent of belittling those very qualities which, while they look to us but scant justice before the evil tongues of the town, nevertheless becalm the odious and bring success to fools."

'She, not unnaturally, said, "What!?"

'We gradually pushed each other off the stage, and she exclaimed, "It's a Gilbertian situation. I can't have them playing chess."

'So I went to Dr Strietzel afterwards and began by saying, "It was better tonight."

' "You noticed, you are a real musician. You noticed the Boccherini was good for the first time. These people from Vienna, they have such a soft touch."

' "Yes, that was better, but there's one thing I complain about."

' "Yes please, ve are open to criticisms."

' "Is it really necessary to play chess on a miniature board?"

' "It disturbs you?"

' "Yes."

' "No, that's not true. You it doesn't disturb, because you are a real actor. It disturbs zis woman."

' "She is a very famous actress and a very good person."

' "Ve don't see zis, and it's only a very little board."

' "It makes it worse because you have to reach further."

' "All right. If you say ve can't play chess, ve don't play chess."

47

'He walked out and I dreaded the future. I was right, because at the next performance Edith didn't get any laughs at all. She couldn't concentrate, she was all over the place. When I went on the stage I saw exactly what had happened. They had abandoned the chess, but had now arranged themselves in a long line facing us and lit from underneath. They looked like the dock at Nuremberg. Their eyes followed Edith wherever she went. Afterwards I went up to Dr Strietzel and said, "Look, this won't do."

' "So, tell me if I'm wrong, no? First it was the chessboard, ve shouldn't play chess. Why? The woman doesn't like it. Now, ve can't even watch her, you think it gives us pleasure to watch her? Ve who have seen Paula Wessely at her greatest!!"

'I said, "No, that doesn't enter into it. It's very, very unpleasant this, I felt you watching us all the time."

' "You ve weren't watching, ve know you. Ve were watching her!"

'I made them promise to stop. The next night she didn't get any laughs at all, though I couldn't see why not. There were a lot of generals in, but I didn't think they could be as dim as all that. So when I was off stage I nipped round to the back of the auditorium, and the musicians had turned themselves with their backs to the stage, still lit from underneath, but now just staring at the audience. I can only tell you they went back to their chess, and Edith never mentioned it again; because the one thing she couldn't bear was someone astride her lines of communication with the public.'

This was Peter's first insight into the markedly different temperament of actors and musicians, but he also crossed swords at this time with a theatre practitioner of an older generation. In a lecture to the British Drama League Conference, he took issue with Lewis Casson's assertion the previous day: 'Every line of dialogue has only one possible intonation.'

Casson wrote to Peter denying that he had said any such thing, but ended his long letter of amplification:

Working with sensitive actors with trained voices, if the producer and actor agree on the mood and situation the actor's intonation will automatically satisfy the producer. If they differ the producer can elaborately explain the thought and emotion and eventually the actor will express it. But with such actors the quickest method often is to suggest the intonation (if, as is by no means certain, he is competent to do it). The actor will at once pick up from it the thought and emotion desired and will automatically create for himself an intonation approximately the same. He must of course make it his own or it will not really live.

But nevertheless when working not with sensitive, competent artists but with the common or garden actor of commerce with no vocal imagination whatever and a set of about five monotonous intonations of his own, the producer can often get better results in the time by hammering the musical intonation into his head than by leaving the matter to his own limited skill and resources.

It was three months before Peter managed to reply, when he courteously rebutted this prescriptive approach:

Speaking as an actor, I consistently refuse to take intonations, because I flatter myself I know what I am talking about, and the intonations one is given are nearly always the least imaginative ones possible. Even if this is a stratagem of desperation, performed at the last dress rehearsal, I am dead against it.

I am sure that it pays high dividends to encourage imagination in the inexperienced by friendliness and interest, rather than to hammer musical phrases into their undeveloped minds.

Laurence Olivier, John Gielgud, Donald Wolfit, and Alec Guinness, all have completely different conceptions of Hamlet, and yet all their conceptions are justifiable, even if one does not agree with any of them. That is really the only point I wish to make.

Many actors who have been directed by Peter Ustinov in the years since he expressed those views have cause to be grateful for the performances he managed to draw from them by his light and flexible touch.

The Rivals turned out to be his only production for the Garrison Theatre. There was talk of him touring in a farce for the troops in the Far East, but that prospect disappeared when SHAEF, the Allied Supreme Headquarters, required his services on an official film about the war in the West. He joined Carol Reed in the British contingent, with Garson Kanin and some other Americans, and Claude Dauphin from France. Much of the news film footage was shot in the front line, and Peter's task was to select the most dramatic scenes for use in the edited version. A large amount of that viewing was boring, but some of it was astonishing, as when the captured Goering was seen fraternising with American officers seeking his autograph, to the fury of Eisenhower when he saw it; some was harrowing, like the British troops entering Belsen and literally throwing up with shock and horror at what they saw.

So Peter was relieved to come across one sequence that appealed to him immensely. When Reichs-Marschal Milch formally surrendered, he saluted smartly by bringing his baton up to his cap and then handed it to the much younger British general. The latter weighed it in his hand for a moment, then smacked it down on the German's head, knocking him headlong – a piece of pure slapstick, which Peter thought was irresistibly comic, though the military censors refused to pass such a breach of the Geneva Convention.

His vocal skills were also called upon for this film. He and Richard Attenborough between them created what the latter described with a chuckle as 'most of the voices of the common soldiers'. The footage brought back was all mute, so the fakery was necessary, but it seems to have been accepted by the audiences of the time.

Then, out of the blue, came Peter's biggest break of the war. Through Carol Reed he had got to know Filippo del Giudice, who was the moving spirit behind Laurence Olivier's stirring film of *Henry V*. The Air Ministry now wanted their own patriotic movie about the invention of radar. Del Giudice considered that, at the age of twenty-four, Ustinov had gained quite enough experience to write and direct a film on his own, but this meant that he had to be attached to the RAF while he was awaiting demobilisation.

The senior Air Ministry official, Sir Robert Renwick, was a great one for cutting through red tape and liked to fix things rapidly over the telephone. Things moved faster than Peter expected after his first call.

'You've to go to Malvern and see the secret establishment, and as it's rather a formal occasion, I should wear your uniform.'

'But, sir . . .'

'Yes, yes, why don't you wear the uniform, I think it's a good idea.'

'But I can't help feeling –'

'The car will be there to fetch you at nine o'clock in the morning.'

A little after 9 a.m., Peter was waiting with his kitbag and rifle, when a Humber staff car drew up. The RAF sergeant-driver called him over and asked, 'You any idea where Mr Ustinov lives?'

'I've been waiting for some time.'

Peter climbed in the back of the car and the journey to Malvern was completed in silence. His orders were to report to the Officers' Mess, where he told a courteous squadron leader that he was booked in.

'No, no, I'm afraid not, sonny, no, I'm afraid that's not on. Now look here, there's a camp towards the Welsh border. If you can hog a lift . . .'

'No, I'm sorry to insist, but I was told to report here, it was an instruction.'

'Now, look here, I don't want to get unpleasant . . .'

When the officer eventually looked in the books, he saw that the reservation had been made in a suite for visiting air marshals, to everyone's utter astonishment, not least that of Private Ustinov. 'As if that was not bad enough, I had to go on a tour of inspection, in company with Sir Charles Portal, Chief of the Air Staff, and Air Vice-Marshal Sir Victor Tait, Director-General of Signals. I wasn't introduced to the other two before the inspection was over. So they couldn't understand what this private soldier was doing, following them about, and I didn't know what to say to the group captains. When Bob Renwick joined us all for tea he thought it was a huge joke and said, "Why didn't you tell me you were only a private?" I stayed in my uniform, because I'd nothing else to put on. It was a paradoxical situation, very typical of the time.'

Paradoxical situations seemed to keep confronting Peter at this time. When he arrived at the Garrick Club near the end of the war, wearing his private's uniform, he was a bit amazed that they let him in, even though he was a member. 'There were two old men fast asleep under the glass cupola, having military dreams; one had a leg that suddenly departed on its own, running over No Man's Land. Suddenly the V2s began and I thought what do I do; do I wake these two up, or would it be better for us all to perish in a perfumed dream? While I was pondering this, the old sergeant-commissionaire began shutting the big wrought-iron gates leading into the street. I went up to him, feeling rather shy, since he was a sergeant, and said, "Sergeant, what are you doing?"

'He looked at me and said, "I'm closing the gates, sir, against any hysterical women seeking to take refuge in the club."

'That's another great English tradition.'

At Malvern, Peter learnt that great scientists could be just as competitive as any prima donna. One professor would say to Peter something like, 'Have you heard of the galvanic screw?'

'No, I don't know about that.'

'Well, you'll hear about it quite often when you get here. It was actually invented by a dear little man in the other building called Thomas Jones. I gave him a few elementary pointers and eventually refined the whole idea when he'd finished it. Have you seen Professor Tomkins yet?'

'No, not yet.'

'Ha, ha. Oh, he's a delightful man, but he will lay claim to having invented the galvanic screw. Of course, I wish it were true for his sake, but it's just not true. It's the little fellow in the other building I helped initially, I don't think he would have got on to it unless he'd had my help.'

Peter next went to Professor Tomkins, who said, 'Now I presume that I'm the first person you're talking to?'

'No, I've already seen Professor Idris Evans.'

'Oh yes, he's a very nice fellow, isn't he? We knew each other at Bangor University. Did he tell you about the galvanic screw?'

The climax of this research trip was dinner with the Principal, who also claimed responsibility for the galvanic screw.

Water was the only accompanying beverage, and that was none too fresh. After the meal the guest offered his host a cigar.

'Would you care for this?'

'What's that?'

'It's a Havana cigar.'

'Oh no, it's far too grand for me, ha, ha, ha. Are you really offering it to me?'

'Yes, yes, do, because they are rather too strong for me, and my father brought it from Lisbon.'

'Well ... oh, well, thank you very much.'

He lit the cigar and puffed away.

'Oh my God, it's been a long time ...'

Then Peter's host thought that he must reciprocate such generosity. After some cogitation, inspiration struck.

'I know what.' Opening a drawer, he said, 'Have a piece of barley sugar.'

It had been there a long time and was all stuck together, looking like Medusa's head, so Peter failed to break a piece off. At last the Principal got carried away and cried, 'Oh never mind, take two bits.'

The script of *School for Secrets* was completed while the writer was technically still in the army, and he was not formally discharged from its clutches until after he started shooting the film on the studio floor. Other key participants faced similar problems with their army status.

Corporal Michael Anderson had been first assistant director to Carol Reed on *In Which We Serve* and had got to know Peter well. After their group was disbanded he was awaiting a posting to Burma with the Royal Corps of Signals, when he bumped into George Brown, an old producer friend. Brown was helping to set up *School for Secrets*, and he commented that it was a shame that Michael was not free, as he would be the ideal first assistant on the new film.

Then he said, 'Look here, why don't I talk to Peter, and if he agrees, we'll try and get you out.' He then took down all Michael Anderson's army particulars. The latter thought this was just a pipe dream and forgot all about it. Six weeks later he was summoned by his commanding officer and told he was being discharged for an important film assignment. 'The deed had been done, and Peter's magic wand had been waved in a way that was to change my life for ever.'

Their paths were to cross fruitfully on a number of occasions over the ensuing years, and Peter soon came to rely on him, saying, 'Mickey joined me as a first assistant, but from the beginning he was much more than that – a mentor, a collaborator, and a friend.'

Even at the end of the war, things were not easy for film-makers. As Michael Anderson pointed out, 'Supplies, transportation and organisation for a film in those early years were hard to come by and for me, certainly, my time was cut out to ensure that George and Peter were protected from those outside hardships as well as I could manage.'

There was one particular crisis of supply and transportation, involving the star of the film, Ralph Richardson, where Michael Anderson needed to move very fast to keep the third day of shooting on schedule.

At the time, the actor was playing Falstaff with the Old Vic Company at the New Theatre. Peter remembers him arriving full of beans, 'bellowing his delight at being alive, but whistling like a kettle on certain sibilants, a sound that he evidently attributed to someone other than himself, since he kept looking around him to find its origin'. His director guessed that he had left home without his rather complicated dental bridgework. He sent his assistant off to telephone the Richardson home, but his attempts to delay the shooting only seemed to infuriate his star.

'Why can't we shoot?'

'The camera is broken.'

This was a mistake. Richardson immediately advanced on the cameraman, Jack Hildyard. 'I hear the camera is broken.'

'No.'

If the cameraman was unaware of the real problem, the sound

recordist was in no doubt at all. When Peter hastily pleaded inexperience and said the real fault was with the sound-mixing machine, the recordist backed him up with some technical jargon that seemed to satisfy the star. At this point Michael Anderson returned to say that there was an urgent telephone call from his home, and Richardson grumpily went off to take it. When he came back a couple of minutes later he looked unwell, holding his hand to his brow. Peter went up to him anxiously.

'It's nothing, just a migraine. I have some powders on prescription for them, and like a fool I left them at home. They're bringing them out straight away. I'll go and lie down until they arrive.'

He disappeared into his dressing room. Twenty minutes later a Bentley arrived at the studio gates, to deliver a small packet for Mr Ralph Richardson.

Shortly afterwards the star reappeared, complete with dentures, saying that he felt much better and adding, as if to prove that all was now well, '*Mens sana in corpore sano.*' The sibilance had completely disappeared.

That personal drama has never been forgotten by the former first assistant. 'What a day. Until much later I firmly believed that no one had known about it, except of course Peter, the director; and what a skilled and talented director Peter was proving to be.'

He had learnt many of the necessary technical skills of film direction at the army's expense, but the other requirement, that of drawing sensitive performance out of the actors, seems to have been instinctive from the beginning. Peter later worked under some of the real martinets in the directing fraternity, which only confirmed him in his belief that the best performances are never achieved when the actors are nervous or unhappy.

Richard Attenborough shares this view, so he had a whale of a time on this film: 'The set was in hysterics for most of the shooting. Peter was a whirlwind of energy and impersonated everybody, especially Ralphie, of course. He did him so well that on the phone you really couldn't tell which was the real Ralph and which was Peter. As an actor himself, he was wonderful at directing us, because he had such an insight into how actors work. It was a joyous experience, and I'm only sorry that we never managed to work together again.' The film was a great success when it was released in 1946.

Peter was at last back in charge of his own destiny, but the years in uniform had left their indelible mark. They provided him with a rich source of material, both comic and serious, for his subsequent plays, films, and novels, and many of his funniest performances have been of military or political leaders; so it is with great glee that he says, 'Oh, I've had my revenge gradually over the years.'

That revenge has been wonderfully entertaining for audiences, but the more he talked to me about that period in his life, the more convinced I became that it engendered a deep distrust of the military mind, shaping his whole approach to people and to life in general.

Six

1946–1949
From *Crime and Punishment*
to *Love in Albania*

The coming of peace brought the hope that a proper family life could at last be established. The first of the Ustinov children arrived on 25 July 1945 and was named Tamara. Her godparents were Roger Livesey and his wife Ursula Jeans. Tamara regrets that she never met them. There was no christening, because neither of her parents was religious.

Peter and Isolde had been apart for much of the war and had had little chance to develop a close marital understanding. Their temperamental incompatibility quickly became apparent when they were living together all the time. He was anxious to make up for lost time in his career, as writer, actor and director; she wanted a steady, undramatic life, without stress.

The break finally came when Isolde announced that she wanted to marry someone else, a journalist named Derek Dempster. Tamara was just four years old, and Peter's greatest concern was about the effect it would have on his daughter. He was granted technical custody, but because she was so young she went to live with her mother and new stepfather. She joined her father for holidays, often when he was filming abroad, and says that, for some while, 'I wasn't really conscious that he was famous, just that he was very jolly.'

The success of *School for Secrets* established Peter's reputation as an exciting new film director, but he was just as keen to pick up the other threads of his career. His first appearance on the post-war stage was as the Chief of Police in Rodney Ackland's adaptation of Dostoevsky's epic novel, *Crime and Punishment*.

The original plan was for Robert Helpmann to play Raskolnikoff, but there was some difficulty in finding a director. Olivier was too busy, Redgrave was undecided, Guthrie was in America, and several other directors turned it down. After John Gielgud finally agreed to direct, Helpmann had to withdraw through illness. Binkie Beaumont, the head of H.M. Tennent Ltd, then asked Gielgud to switch to playing the leading role, and Anthony Quayle was brought in to direct. Gielgud was worried that at forty-two he was rather too old to play a Russian student in his twenties. Ustinov was equally concerned by the opposite challenge of playing Petrovitch, a man of sixty; much more difficult, as he now discovered, than the wonderful ancients he had created in revue.

He was reunited with Edith Evans, playing the youthful Katerina, and Peter observed that she had not lost her knack of disconcerting the company. 'Edith suddenly noticed during rehearsal that there was somebody in the auditorium who shouldn't be there and exclaimed, "Are we all of the family?"'

The pre-London tour opened in Manchester, where their joint forgetfulness caused momentary embarrassment to both the older and the younger actor. It took Peter longer than Gielgud to remove his complicated character make-up, and as he exited from the stage door he spotted a small pink and white suitcase that had been left behind. He took it to the Midland Hotel, where he joined several members of the cast, listening to stories by the comedian Max Bacon. At 3 a.m. he suddenly remembered the suitcase and thought he should deliver it to its owner. He knocked quietly at Gielgud's door and heard the ringing command, 'Come in!'

He entered to find the actor stark naked on his bed, and Gielgud declaimed emotionally, 'My pyjamas are in that bag.'

Such absent-mindedness was in sharp contrast to his on-stage intensity. With a cast of forty constantly flowing in and out, the wings were rather crowded, and the actors did their best to be unobtrusive. But that only disturbed Gielgud's concentration the more. As the curtain fell on Act One at the opening night in London, he cried out, 'If there are going to have to be all these people in the wings, they *must look at me*!'

Peter cherished the whole experience, even if he had his own reservations about the central performance. His assistant was played by Peter Jones, who said to Peter that it did not make sense his bringing the Chief to the scene; since Gielgud's Raskolnikoff was so obviously guilty, the police chief would be expected to arrest him straight away and take him to the station. Peter had to admit that Gielgud did look terribly guilty right from the beginning.

Despite this, the critical response was mostly favourable. *The Times* hailed it as 'a palpable success . . . and among the other good performances Mr Peter Ustinov's Chief of Police is admirably observed'. James Agate went further in the *Sunday Times*, concluding: 'I cannot imagine a better reduction to stage terms of a masterpiece conceived away from the theatre.' However, his praise of two actors he frequently admired was, as so often, a little two-edged: 'In the present play Mr Gielgud makes his limitations work for instead of against him. The result is the best thing after Hamlet he has ever given us . . . To Mr Ustinov goes the credit of giving identity and character to the Chief of Police. This is an admirable brick made out of straw which continually promises and never fulfils.'

The sourest note was struck by Ivor Brown in the *Observer*, who saw no tension in the story, because there was no mystery about the murder by Raskolnikoff, and he asserted that 'Gielgud without poetry is surely something of a wasted voice and squandered glory.' That regretful note for the star was then sharpened into something much more dismissive for the others: 'Dame Edith Evans's Katerina is very like Dame Edith Evans. Mr Peter Ustinov, as an elderly police official, gives a performance which is very ingeniously a performance. But the kind of knock-you-down veracity which Charles Laughton was putting into just this kind of part on the London stage twenty years ago is missing.'

Attempting to demolish one actor's performance by comparing it unfavourably with what another might have done is rarely helpful, even if the comparison is apt, but any similarity between Ustinov and Laughton could only really be seen in their physical shape. Their acting styles were so different that they would prove to be brilliant foils to each other, when they played together on screen much later in *Spartacus*.

Peter's real itch was to write more plays. During his last year in the army he finished *The Tragedy of Good Intentions*, about the First Crusade, relying heavily on the *Cambridge Medieval History.* This was completely new territory, but, he says, 'Everything was a departure for me, I tried everything.' The Old Vic Company put it on at the Liverpool Playhouse in 1945, and audiences there liked it, but it never travelled further afield.

For his next play, Peter thought for once he would heed his critics and write a realistic play in a realistic setting. *The Indifferent Shepherd* told the story of an idealistic but ineffectual vicar with an embittered wife, and her brother, who is also a priest, an unpleasant individual but practical and decisive. A pregnant servant-girl gets homilies but no help from the former, and sensible advice from the latter, which prevents her committing suicide in despair.

It was strongly cast, with Francis Lister and Andrew Cruickshank as the contrasting clergymen and, most notably, Gladys Cooper as the shrewish wife. She returned to the London stage after nine years away in America to play this part and received a huge ovation on the first night. Her magnetism helped fill the Criterion Theatre for a good run, so the author forgave her for being very shaky on her lines.

Ivor Brown registered in the *Observer* this 'calamitous crawl while lines were being groped for', but approved the author's intentions: 'If the play is not throughout tidy or persuasive as to all its happenings it has the stamp of reflection, and has the courage to be seriously concerned with high matters as well as low ones.'

The other reviews were mixed, and Peter drew his own conclusions: 'It was as though the critics resented the fact that I had, in some measure, heeded their advice. This was encouraging.'

For the second film he directed, *Vice Versa*, Peter backed his own judgement and was unconcerned when it was considered to be ahead of its time. His screenplay was based on the novel by F. Anstey, in which a Victorian father tells his son to stop blubbering because he is going back to his harsh boarding school, as for the father they were the happiest days of his life. The boy has a magic stone from India, which enables him to switch their bodies, and it is the father who now finds himself back at school.

The comic possibilities depended on the clever casting, with Roger Livesey as the father and the fourteen-year-old Anthony Newley as the boy with the father's mind. For the terrifying headmaster Peter chose an unknown actor who had worked with his father as a journalist, James Robertson Justice, and for the head's daughter Petula Clark. She was only thirteen, but a very experienced child star, with several films behind her.

Petula had never met anyone like her new director. 'He didn't look English, he was flamboyant, but in a very boyish way. He was just hysterically funny, and that was the most important thing for me; he didn't frighten me like Michael Powell, who terrified me. This was such a joy to be with somebody who was such fun. There was a piano on the set for anybody who fancied playing, so it was really like a huge party.'

The film is suffused with a subversive sense of humour, right from the opening credits when one of the slides is put in the wrong way up, and a finger comes in and pulls it out. The title sequence was created like an echo of the silent movies, enhanced by the music, composed by Antony Hopkins. 'Peter said he wanted something like a French fire brigade, and I wrote an absolutely lunatic piece for two trumpets, piano and drums, which actually got quite loud applause at the première in the Leicester Square Odeon.' This was the start of a long relationship between the two men on the musical front.

One of the director's favourite scenes involves Robert Eddison, as the romantically inclined sports master. He is sitting on the grass reading a book, while the boys are fooling around instead of playing football; when the headmaster's mortarboard is spotted travelling along above a hedge, the boys pretend to resume the game but without the ball. The headmaster watches for a while before comprehension dawns and he thunders, 'Where is the ball?'

James Robertson Justice was a larger-than-life character off-set as well as on and provided Peter with one of his favourite encounters.

'It was in Rome in the bar of the Excelsior Hotel in the Via Veneto, which was always slightly Fellini-ish, and an extremely beautiful German girl was sitting there in the Happy Hour. She suddenly came up to me and said, "Well, I guess I win my bet."

' "Your bet? I'm sorry, I don't know what you mean."

' "Oohh, that's what I swore would happen, and you promised me it wouldn't."

' "Look, I really don't know what you're talking about."

' "That night which I shall never forget, in bed. You said to me it was one of the most important nights of your life, and you said you had to go back to your wife and family, which I understand. After all, I'm only a prostitute, but you said you'd never forget me, and I said, oh yes you will. Like all men you will forget me. Well, I win my bet, don't I?"

' "No you don't, because I don't remember any of this."

' "Well, then, let me tell you something. You are not a very honourable man, Mr James Robertson Justice."

'I had a beard then too, of course. I told James I'd met someone who evidently knew him very well and I had been told that I was not a very honourable man, and he said, "Oh Christ! Well, thank you anyway." '

Petula Clark was a bit scared of this big, booming figure playing her screen father, but it was her real father who caused a few scheduling problems about her call-times and hours of work. He was keen that her schooling should not suffer, but it was his on-set role that strained Peter's patience. 'He was always there, giving her notes when I tried to do so. He was an awful nuisance; he was in the same league as Mr Dokic and Mr Capriati at Wimbledon.' But Peter brushed aside any attempted interference. Petula's memory of the experience now is that 'it always seemed to me as if we were improvising. I'm sure we weren't, but it seemed to be so free and easy. Laurence Olivier was making *Hamlet* at the same time at Pinewood, and he was very strict, he had signs up everywhere on the sound studio doors – No Visitors, Keep Out. Peter had signs put up – Visitors Welcome.'

This is the only film that the two of them have made together, but in more recent years they have become close friends and have often shared a stage on behalf of UNICEF, with her singing and him compèring.

Michael Anderson was impressed by the rapport that Peter created between the different generations on *Vice Versa*. 'Petula was totally professional and delightful to work with; we all adored her and when the film finished she was the one who cried and thanked everyone. I think the young Newley was equally moved but managed to keep a stoic and rather memorable straight face that everyone could see straight through. As for the older members of the cast getting along with the younger ones, you would have thought that they were the kids, and the youngsters the mature and knowing members of their craft, which indeed they were.'

Vice Versa made friendships and reputations, but not much money at the box office. Peter's next film, *Private Angelo*, was to do all three. When his screenplay was accepted, Peter told Michael Anderson that he had been asked not only to direct and produce the film, but to star in it himself. Conscious of the load of responsibility he would be carrying, he said to Michael, 'I'd like you to do it with me.'

Thinking this meant first assistant director again, Michael agreed immediately, but he was overwhelmed when Peter added, 'I mean I'd like you to direct it with me. You will be the man behind the camera.'

Casting was not quite so easy. Peter wanted Joan Greenwood, but she was committed to filming *Whisky Galore* in the Hebrides. The producer of that film, Monja Danischewsky, was suddenly bombarded on the Isle of Barra by a series of telegrams and postcards, requesting Joan's release. They were addressed to 'Comrade Danischewsky …', 'Hero of the Soviet Republic Danischewsky …', finally in desperation opening with 'Dear Commissar, in the name of our Leader, I beg you …' But in this case the appeals to Russian solidarity were in vain, and Maria Denis finally played the part. Peter was more successful in gaining the services of the distinguished Shakespearean actor Godfrey Tearle.

The source for *Private Angelo* was Eric Linklater's book about an Italian wartime private seeking the gift of courage. As it was shot on location in Italy so soon after the actual events (the film was released in 1949), there were some tricky technical problems to solve. The only German tanks available to them had been stolen by an ex-Luftwaffe officer and hidden away when the Germans fled Italy; the thief negotiated a price for their hire and joined the unit as technical adviser.

Technical advice is usually offered quietly and dispassionately, but not here. The Italian and German advisers got into a technical argument over the merits of a German versus an Italian hand grenade. They were on the brink of pulling the pins while the grenades were on their heads when Michael Anderson stepped in to confiscate them just in time.

Peter was conscious that he was treading on thin ice politically. 'It's a delicate subject, in the same sense that I've always said that Russian roulette is played with one live bullet, Japanese roulette is played with five live bullets, and Italian roulette is played with no live bullets. They consider that their lack of militarism is detrimental to their reputation. I don't think the film was shown in Italy at all.'

He was now able to indulge his love of fast cars, which he used to satisfy another craving, frequently driving from Rome to Siena for the Italian ice cream he loved, especially after the rigours of post-war rationing. His co-director often went with him. 'On one occasion, sitting in the seat of a huge Lagonda, we met a slow-moving funeral cortège in a country village. As we slowed and passed, with the imposing figure of Peter in a greatcoat from the film's wardrobe imperiously perched on high, there were whispers of "It must be Mussolini" ... We laughed and drove on.'

But he remembers *Private Angelo* for more than just the laughs they shared. 'The film was hugely successful and was described as the *Shoulder Arms* of 1949, and Peter, with his huge generosity, gave me the following credit:

"Written, produced and directed by Peter Ustinov with Michael Anderson."

'He had launched my career.'

That career took Michael to Hollywood, where his future credits included *Around the World in Eighty Days* (following Peter's suggestion of him to the film's producer, Mike Todd) and *Logan's*

Run, where he was reunited with Ustinov the actor.

Peter's epic movies were yet to come, and his next venture was to adapt for the stage Ingmar Bergman's script for Alf Sjoberg's film *Frenzy*.

Bergman was not yet directing his own films but was mostly writing for the theatre in Sweden. Peter, who met him there, admired his work, which, he says, was 'in a style very much ahead of us. He already had a play with a homosexual in it, whom he explored much as they would today.'

The film of *Frenzy* had created a stir in Britain, and also in America under the title of *Torment*. A sadistic schoolmaster bullies the boys in his Latin class, his drunken mistress is touched by the love of the youngest pupil, and when she dies the professor kills himself.

Few of the London critics took to the sordid subject, reserving their praise for the acting. The mistress and the boy were played by Joan Greenwood and Denholm Elliott, both of whom got good notices in the *Daily Mail*. 'But Peter Ustinov's study of the ogre in rimless glasses, blustering and blubbering, fearsome and cringing in turn as he slithers to the social depths, is the evening's crowning performance – a model of the macabre that gives distinction to a not entirely distinguished play.'

The *Evening Standard* thought him 'hauntingly good as the Professor. Not even Laurence Olivier has a keener sense of character. In fact, Mr Ustinov ought to play Macbeth to end all Macbeths. He would terrify the midnight hags.'

An intriguing prospect and more positive than the sound of Ivor Brown beating his now familiar drum in the *Observer*: 'It is plain that this actor can be the Charles Laughton of his generation if he wants to be; but his talents are wide and I hope he will not forget the pleasures of comedy.'

We may not have had his Macbeth, and we have indeed enjoyed many more of his trips to the well of comedy, but Peter had no intention of abandoning all the other theatrical forms he was eager to explore. His name was now up in lights in the West End in three different capacities – as author of *The Indifferent Shepherd*, as director of *Vice Versa*, and as actor as well as author for *Frenzy*.

He carried dual responsibilities in both his next two stage ventures. The first was his play *The Man in the Raincoat*, which he also directed himself. The story was of a judge, haunted by the fear of sending an innocent man to the scaffold, who is stalked by a man in a raincoat. He turns out to be the brother of a man convicted by this judge but is himself the real murderer and he now wants to confess his guilt. This news brings on a fatal heart attack in the judge.

The action of the play is continuous, but the author was forced to break it with an interval. His irritation at this division is apparent in his Note to the printed script: 'When this play is acted before a civilised audience, who do not demand liquid refreshment, or is played in a civilised theatre, which does not insist upon dispensing this non-dramatic diversion, it is permissible to drive from beginning to end without an interval.'

The judge and his wife were played by George Coulouris and Mary Ellis, and the animosity between the characters was only exceeded by that between the actors playing them. The subject was one dear to the author's heart and one he would return to, but its impact at the 1949 Edinburgh Festival was insufficient to justify a London transfer. It was, however, a great success in Oslo under the title of *Mannen i Regnfrakken*, the first of many subsequent Ustinov plays to enjoy a long run in another language.

Peter was already busy at the Bath Festival, wearing his two hats as actor and director, in *Love in Albania*, written by Eric Linklater who had provided the source material for the rewarding *Private Angelo*. Here Peter played Sergeant Dohda, an Albanian-born GI searching Europe for his long-lost partisan daughter. The young English couple were played by Robin Bailey and Brenda Bruce, the stuttering poet was Peter Jones, and Molly Urquhart was the Scottish maid.

Peter has always enjoyed playing Americans, with their idiomatic speech, ever since he first heard it during the war. He once passed an American lieutenant looking in a window in Bond Street, when the sergeant waiting for him suddenly said impatiently, 'Let's don't hang around, shall we, Lootenant?'

The play was a great success, transferring to the Lyric Ham-

mersmith and then to the West End at the St James's. The rave
reviews were more for the performances than the play. Peter Jones
and Robin Bailey appeared regularly with Ustinov over the coming
years, and the three of them all shared a weakness for corpsing
helplessly on stage. One night during this run they succumbed
more uncontrollably than usual, to the rage of the stage manager.
When he appeared upside-down in the fireplace, snarling 'Pull
yourselves together!' their mirth knew no bounds.

Peter drew an interesting distinction at the time between acting
in his own and other authors' plays. 'Whenever possible I like to
produce my own plays, but I never enjoy appearing in them, for
the simple reason that a character created by my author-self presents no problem to my actor-self. I know all the answers about
the role, which cannot possibly hold the same interest for me as
the creation of another writer – a character I meet as a stranger
and then come to know so intimately that actor and part are
indistinguishable. On that account I enjoy playing my present
part of Sergeant Dohda far better than any I could have written
myself.'

He enjoyed it much more than his next film part too, in Herbert
Wilcox's reverent biopic about the travails of the British agent
Odette in Occupied France, starring Wilcox's wife Anna Neagle,
with Trevor Howard and Marius Goring. The former private had
one scene in officer's uniform as Lieutenant Alex Rabinovic, code-
named 'Arnaud', but for most of the film he looked and sounded
authentically French, with his beret and impeccably accented
English.

It was not a rewarding experience for Peter. 'Anna was hope-
lessly unconvincing, and Herbert kept any bad notices or criticisms
away from her. He was a man of such profound silliness and
ignorance.'

During the shooting, the real Odette was awarded the Légion
d'Honneur, and Wilcox cancelled filming for the day to take the
cast to the ceremony. He wore morning-dress, and Anna Neagle
dressed entirely in black; they behaved as if it were the imitation
rather than the original who was being honoured. Trevor Howard
was irritated by all this, but Peter was just amused to observe that

while Anna was weeping with emotion, Odette caught his eye and winked at him.

Much better films than *Odette* now awaited the Ustinov touch. By the end of the 1940s his name was a major draw in the country of his birth, and he was about to step on to the international stage as a Hollywood actor, though he was almost tripped up a couple of times before he made his entrance.

Seven

1950–1953
Quo Vadis and
The Love of Four Colonels

When Metro-Goldwyn-Mayer decided to remake *Quo Vadis* the pre-production process spread over several years. John Huston was slated to direct, and one of the actors he invited to play Nero in 1947 was Robert Morley, who declined the part. Two years later, when Huston was still engaged in casting, he asked Peter to screen-test for the Emperor. (This was the first and only time that he has screen-tested for a part.)

Peter feared he was going over the top, screaming and shouting, but Huston was very encouraging and kept whispering, 'Just a little madder, come on, you can do it.'

'I'm as mad as a hatter already.'

'Oh, you can do a bit more, come on, a bit madder.'

His test was given approval in Hollywood, but then everything ground to a halt, and shooting was postponed for a year. John Huston lost patience after his two years of work and went off to work on something more definite. A new team took over, with Sam Zimbalist as producer and Mervyn Leroy as director, neither of whom Peter had met.

They sent him a telegram saying, 'We like your test, but we're fearful you may be a little too young for the part.'

Peter wired back, 'If you delay for another year, I'll be too old for the role.'

This prompted the reply, 'Historical Research Has Proved You Correct Stop The Part Is Yours.'

Peter guessed that they were influenced by the memory of Charles Laughton in *The Sign of the Cross*, who looked much older than thirty-one, the age at which Nero died.

The film was made in Rome in the blisteringly hot summer of 1950. Peter was anxious to find out how the new director saw his role when they first met on the day before shooting began.

'Nero? Son of a bitch,' Leroy said.

Peter indicated agreement.

'You know what he did to his mother? Son of a bitch.'

The two men established a good working relationship, but Peter could not resist sending up the American's fierce anti-Communist views. He persuaded one of the bulkier extras to masquerade as the Russian air attaché in Rome and introduced him to Leroy, who was too horrified to say anything except, 'How do you like the sets?'

Peter opened his mouth to admit the joke but was forestalled by the extra, who began to enjoy his new role. 'At home, we have beegar.'

'What do you think of the costumes?'

'At home they would be more colourful and richer.'

The director took Peter to one side. 'What did you say this guy was?'

'The Russian air attaché in Rome.'

'What's he doing on the set?'

'I invited him. He's a friend of mine.'

'Peter . . . you're playing with fire.'

'Isn't that what I'm supposed to do in this film?'

The producer's views were at the other end of the political spectrum. Sam Zimbalist had started out as an actor with the very left-wing Group Theater in New York before going into the movie business. When he first arrived on the set some weeks into the shooting, Peter was introduced to him.

'How do you do, Mr Zimbalist. Are you by any chance related to –'

'No, I'm not related to the violinist. What's your racial origin, Mr Ustinov?'

'Well . . . I had one grandmother who was born in Odessa.'

'Hasn't everybody?'

MGM had gone to enormous lengths to re-create the authentic

look of the period, and Peter came to believe that no nation could make Roman epics as well as the Americans. He was not quite so happy with the script but discovered that changing it was difficult to achieve. He worried about one particular line, which he feared would get a laugh in the wrong place.

'I was playing my lyre while an Italian girl was cutting my toenails. (The actress was subsequently named as co-respondent in the Barbara Stanwyck/Robert Taylor divorce, which I always found extraordinary because she wasn't much to look at.) She was supposed to nick my toe just as I reached a searingly high note on the lyre, at which I kicked her across the marble floor so she started to bleed, and I had to say "Take her away before she leaks to death." When I ventured to say that it was a very unpleasant line, the director told me I just had a dirty mind. But in order to change it they had to cable head office and change the shooting schedule.'

Nero's singing was taken even more seriously. Peter was sent off to the Rome Opera House for three singing lessons, where his arrival caused some tension. He had grown his hair long for the part, and as *Samson and Delilah* had been hissed the night before, he was assumed at first to be the replacement Samson from Paris.

The music professor, unaccustomed to the ways of the film world and especially to the style of film music, said, 'It's ridiculous, they send you here for three lessons, I take with Tito Gobbi six year to teach him. That means we have to do two years every lesson. It's ridiculous, I wouldn't accept, but they pay me, and I've got children, and grandchildren, and *la mamma*...'

Peter sympathised, 'That's why we all do everything.'

'The first lesson – always breathe with the forehead.'

The willing pupil puckered his brow to indicate a pulse, and the teacher seemed very impressed. At the second lesson he challenged him: 'Now you are forgetting the first lesson, I'm sure. You breathe with...?'

'The forehead.'

'Bravo! My God, what a talent. Now, the second lesson is always think with the stomach.'

This was more difficult to convey but seemed to be acceptable. Before the third lesson, Peter was interrogated again.

'Now we will see what you 'ave forgotten. You will breathe with . . . ?'

'The forehead.'

'And think with . . . ?'

'The stomach.'

'If only you were my pupil for six year I could make of you . . . And finally, whatever the situation, whatever the drama, always remember to sing with the eye.'

The eye-rolling that accompanied his singing with the lyre in the film may not have been particularly tuneful, but it certainly conveyed Nero's deranged mentality.

The international cast included the American Robert Taylor as a Roman general, in love with a senator's daughter played by the English Deborah Kerr, and Finlay Currie as a very Scottish Saint Peter. The trickiest piece of casting was the fighting bull, which Buddy Baer had to kill in the arena to save Deborah Kerr's life. The one sent from Portugal broke out of its pen and invaded the Commissary during a meal-break, so for the actual filming a chloroformed cow was substituted. It proved difficult to conceal the evidence of its sex, and every time it was killed it ruined the take by an unmistakable moo. At one point the public address system used for marshalling the crowd of extras in the stands broke into life with the exasperated complaint, 'Mr Leroy can still see de udder.'

The film was a great success all over the world and brought Peter a recognition that was not always to his liking. He was in New York for the opening and climbed into a cab, but before he could state his destination the driver enquired, '*Quo vadis*, Mr Ustinov?'

Not long afterwards he went to Mexico City, 'and children in the street ran away from me in terror. I'd never had that effect before.'

The impression he created as Nero haunted him for some years after that. When he was in Hollywood later, he was told that Hedda Hopper, the notorious and malicious gossip columnist, did not want to meet him, and he was advised to have lunch alone in his room instead of the restaurant, because she would be there. He bridled, 'Why the hell not?'

'Well, we don't want to go into that, Peter.'

'But you must. What the hell are you talking about? You can't do that to me. In any case, I'm not going to have lunch here, I'm coming to the restaurant.'

'Oh no, please don't.'

'Now you've got to tell me, otherwise I will, and I probably will, anyway.'

'Well, she said you were so brilliant in *Quo Vadis*, you've gotta be gay.'

'Is that all?'

So he went into the restaurant, marched straight up to her and said, in a very deep voice, 'How are you, Miss Hopper? I've been hearing a lot about you.'

This excessively macho approach rather shook her, as she was not expecting it and was more used to putting the frighteners herself on nervous film actors, several of whose reputations she had destroyed through her column.

But the Italian response by contrast was one of enduring respect and affection. Nearly half a century later Peter was touched to receive a fax from the Italian Minister of Culture, to say that after many years of work they had just reconstituted Nero's villa quite near to the Colosseum. They were planning an opening ceremony on a certain date, 'and it would be unthinkable for this ceremony to take place without its original owner present'.

So Peter went and was taken in a wheelchair round its 200 rooms. Then there was a screening of *Quo Vadis* on a huge screen in the Piazza del Popolo. Appropriately, the projector caught fire just before the burning of Rome, and Peter shouted out, '*Non ancora*.' After the showing, he was asked to address the public, and with that huge milling crowd he felt it was just like old times, except that he was in a suit, not a toga. In his speech he entered into the spirit of the occasion:

'You must forgive me for my indifferent Italian, but I must remind you that my native tongue is Latin, and I wish to congratulate the Minister, and the Mayor of Rome, for the brilliant things they've done to my city since I burned it. Rome is the seat of modern initiatives, which might have pleased Nero or not, but they are worthy of our respect, and that is the scene of the first great meeting with non-government organisations and elected members of governments, in order to begin to vote in the World Criminal Court, which is a laudable initiative and approved of by the Italian Government.' This speech was given a huge ovation.

The five months Peter spent in Rome in 1950 making that film left a lasting impression on him and 'widened my horizons irrevocably'. But the intensity of that experience, and the atmosphere of Rome, had made it impossible for him to work on any other project at the same time.

When he returned to London he conceived the idea of a play about a great-power quartet of colonels administering a town in Occupied Germany, where a mysterious castle turns out to be the palace of Sleeping Beauty. It was his most ambitious play yet, with a large cast. At the time he was quoted as saying: 'I tried to write several big parts, because I remembered the days when I got sick of acting in plays containing only one or two big ones. The more important parts you have, the better it is for both players and audience, and the more "body" you have in your play.'

He took great care over the casting. He had just appeared in the film *Hotel Sahara* with Yvonne de Carlo and failed to understand why she was always billed as 'the most beautiful woman in the world'; he frequently found the big film stars' stand-ins more interesting, because there was more to discover.

So for his Sleeping Beauty he chose, not an established star, but a promising young actress who was not yet well known, Moira Lister. She was overwhelmed by the offer.

'I was filming at Pinewood, and as I went into the restaurant for lunch I passed Sean Connery, who told me I had the best legs in the business, so I was already a bit on air. Then Peter came over to my table, and of course I knew who he was, but I hadn't met him before. He said, "How would you like to be my love?"

'I thought, two in one day is a bit much, so I said, "Well, Peter, it's very kind of you, but I actually have someone in my life at the moment," because I had already met my future husband by then.

'He said, "No, no, no, no, I mean in *The Love of Four Colonels*, I want you to play Sleeping Beauty.'

'He sent me the script, and I was thrilled to bits, and I said I'd absolutely adore to do it.'

The very opening of the play was a bit nerve-racking for Colin Gordon and Alan Gifford, playing the British and American colonels, seated on stage as the curtain rose.

The author's stage-direction reads: *There follows the longest pause in theatrical history, towards the end of which the audience should be convinced that the actors have been the victims of some administrative disaster. The pause is terminated after the adequate time for embarrassment has elapsed.*

Desmond We seem to have run out of conversation.
Another long pause.
Wesley Yeah . . .

When the French and Russian colonels (Eugene Deckers and Theodore Bikel) joined them, the audience discovered that they were all disgruntled men with unfulfilled dreams. A wicked fairy (Peter Ustinov) arrived to tempt them, followed by a good fairy (Gwen Cherrell) to keep the balance. When the scene moves to the enchanted palace, each of the colonels attempts to woo Sleeping Beauty in his own national style, in witty pastiches of Shakespeare, Molière, Chekhov, and Hollywood movies. None of them succeeds, and when their wives appear, the four colonels have to decide their own future. The Russian and the Englishman return home with their spouses, but the two romantics, the American and Frenchman, stay to share Beauty's next long sleep, in the hope of winning her in the end.

The play poked fun at all four national stereotypes in a literate but very accessible style, and was directed by John Fernald. The incidental music was specially composed by Antony Hopkins. There was one initial structural problem. When the play opened in Birmingham it ran for four hours. It received a standing ovation from an entranced audience, but the London management insisted it had to be cut to the normal West End length of two and a half hours.

Moira Lister remembers Peter's furious response: ' "What do you mean, cut it down to two and a half hours? *Hamlet* runs for four hours, and this is funnier," which was a wonderful phrase, I thought. Anyway, they did persuade him, and my one regret was that I didn't stand by that waste-paper basket and pick out all those wonderful sheets of paper that were thrown out of the play, because they were gems that would never be used again.'

The Times hailed it as 'a highly theatrical and richly rewarding evening', the *Sunday Times* as 'an immensely enjoyable fantasy', and the *Daily Telegraph* as 'a beautifully judged mixture of fantasy and satire'. Cecil Wilson began his review in the *Daily Mail* by saying, 'One might imagine that Mr Ustinov had written this play as an excuse for appearing in a succession of lavish disguises, had he not allowed others to bask in his brilliance.' He ended it: 'And home go we, illuminated by the versatile sparkle of Miss Lister, who makes the best of her best chance to date, and the perky charm of Miss Cherrell – and for all his faults of over-writing, dazzled by the fiendish cleverness of Mr Ustinov.'

The play was the smash-hit of the 1951 season and ran for nearly two years at Wyndham's Theatre to sell-out capacity. At the end of that time Peter said, 'Oh well, I'm afraid we'll have to come off soon, standing room's getting very thin now.'

It also had a great international appeal, playing in fourteen different European countries, with particular success in Berlin, and in Paris where it ran for six years. It was directed in New York by Rex Harrison, starring himself and his wife Lilli Palmer, and although it failed to run there as long as in London, it won the Critics Award for the Best Foreign Play of 1953.

The author never saw that Broadway production, but he did manage quick weekend visits to several of the European versions, in Italy, Germany, Holland, and Denmark, which were all very different; he found it hard to believe that Berlin and Hamburg were towns in the same country, so utterly divergent were the reactions of the audiences.

At the end of his report on those trips he confessed, 'I can tell you that, having seen the passions of twenty-four colonels expressed in four languages, I know much more about both passion and about colonelcy than when I ambitiously put pen to paper in order to write about a mere quartet of the fascinating breed.'

One city that has never seen the play, to his continuing regret, is Moscow, but at the height of the Cold War it presumably touched too sensitive a chord, despite its international even-handedness.

Even in London it got the very occasional odd response. Peter was mystified one night when the house manager came backstage about fifteen minutes into the show, to tell him there were two Americans creating a terrible scene in the foyer, demanding their money back. 'They say this show is an absolute disgrace, they've never seen such a travesty of a show in their lives, and they're absolutely horrified.'

Peter shrugged. 'Well, what can we do? Give them their money back.' Then he looked at the tickets and saw to his great amusement that they were for Alec Guinness's *Hamlet*, at the New Theatre in the next street.

Even those who came to the right theatre did not always catch on fully to what was happening on stage. One woman accosted Moira Lister at a party, saying, 'I understand you're an actress?'

'Yes.'

'Are you giving anything at the moment?'

'Yes. I'm in *The Love of Four Colonels*.'

'Oh, I've seen that. Now what part do you play?'

'Well, I play Sleeping Beauty.'

'Oh, well, you don't have much to do just lying in bed all evening, do you?'

'Well, actually I do play the other four parts as well.'

'Oh, that's most intriguing. I kept saying to my husband, I wonder who all these pretty girls are that keep coming on.'

Moira commented, with a huge laugh, 'So she hadn't understood one word of the play from beginning to end.'

Towards the end of the long run Peter became so exhausted that he found himself in the same situation as that switched-off member of the audience. 'After a while I became a zombie. I used to speak lines such as "I am going now" and wonder what on earth they meant.'

This was most unlike him. His normal habit once a play had settled in was to busy himself with writing, drawing, and voracious reading, as he did in the early months of this run.

Moira Lister was initially disconcerted by all this energy. 'I used to go into his dressing room, and he'd be sitting there with a tome of Roman history, and I'd say, "Now come on, Peter, you're just showing off, you're not reading that whole book." He said, "Yes I am, open any page and ask me about it." So I used to open a page in the middle of the book and say, "All right, who was Habeas Corpus?' He would tell me almost exactly what was on that page. He was the only real genius that I think I've ever worked with, and I use the word genius advisedly, because his brain was so extraordinary. He could do so many things, and with his insight into people and characters, and politics and governments, it was an amazing experience working with him.'

When he finally left the cast, the production was transferred to the Winter Garden, a vast unwelcoming barn of a theatre, where it closed after only eight weeks. It had lost not just its star, but its whole magical atmosphere.

During the run at Wyndham's, *Quo Vadis* was released, and Peter Ustinov received his first Oscar nomination as Best Supporting Actor. He did not win the Academy Award this time, but there were other chances to come, and his international film career was launched. He had more plays in the pipeline, and the broadcasting media were now laying siege to his door.

His personal life was also about to undergo a major change.

Peter by Nadia. Sent to Tamara at school in 1957, and inscribed on the back:

This is a photograph of a portrait of your father, Peter Ustinov, at the age of eleven, which I painted at the time

With love from your

Granny Nadia Benois

Klop and his brother Peter were both German pilots
in the First World War. Peter was killed in 1917.

Director and designer of the film *Vice Versa* on the set.
A happy working relationship for mother and son.

Liselotte Beethoven-Fink. 'An empire in ruins'.

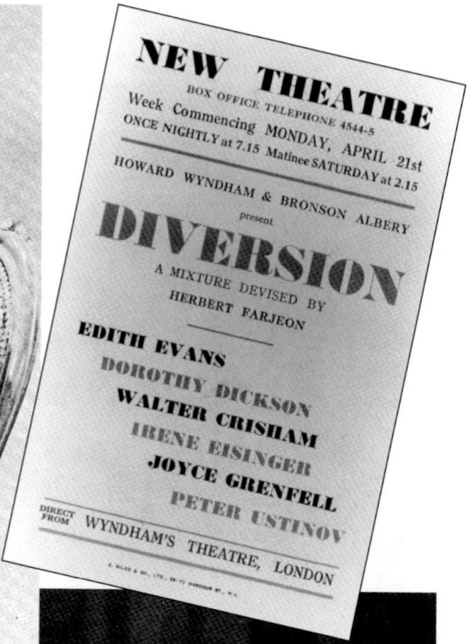

NEW THEATRE

BOX OFFICE TELEPHONE 4544-5

Week Commencing MONDAY, APRIL 21st
ONCE NIGHTLY at 7.15 Matinee SATURDAY at 2.15

HOWARD WYNDHAM & BRONSON ALBERY

present

DIVERSION

A MIXTURE DEVISED BY
HERBERT FARJEON

EDITH EVANS
DOROTHY DICKSON
WALTER CRISHAM
IRENE EISINGER
JOYCE GRENFELL
PETER USTINOV

DIRECT FROM WYNDHAM'S THEATRE, LONDON

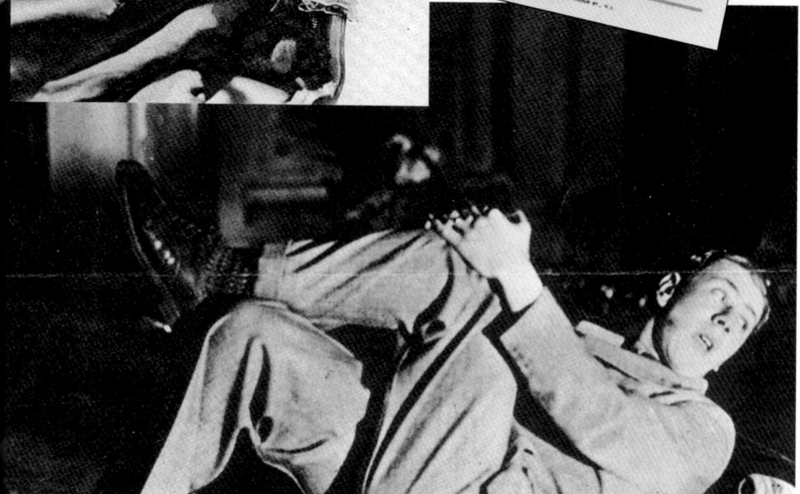

Producing *King Lear*. A modern parody in the same revue.

The aspiring author, 1941.

Opposite: With Isolde in Green Park,
the day after *House of Regrets* opened in 1942.

Sergeant Dohda in *Love in Albania*, 1949.

The Love of Four Colonels. The Russian fantasy,
with Peter Ustinov, Moira Lister and Theodore Bikel.

'I act for a living, I write because I must'.

Eight

1951–1953 (in parallel)
Battles with the critics
and *In All Directions*

The two-year run of *The Love of Four Colonels* left Peter with the days free, which he rapidly filled with a wide range of activity. He wrote a play whose subject and style were in sharp contrast to that comedy. *The Moment of Truth* was based on the Pétain/Laval relationship in Occupied France.

He originally wanted to call it *King Lear's Photographer*, and the Shakespearean analogy runs throughout the play. One of the thirteen names of the Marshal's daughter is Cordelia, and he carries on her body at the end. The photographer is brought in to get a picture of the octogenarian Marshal looking determined, an expression only achieved by telling him he can't have his usual plums today.

It was written out of 'a revulsion about the Pétain case, the fact that a nation could lift a man so high and then drop him so completely. I admit he was an old fool, but that was the whole point of the play. I was repelled by the whole ritual of a death sentence and the fact that Laval tried to poison himself, and they worked like beavers, pumping his stomach out, so as to be sure he was ready for execution the next day.'

Following the success of their collaboration on *The Love of Four Colonels* he entrusted the direction again to John Fernald. The play opened on 21 November 1951. The author managed to take his second curtain call of the night, rushing from Wyndham's to the Adelphi and being caught by a press photographer as he finished dressing in the taxi. Critical reaction this time was far from rapturous, the most caustic coming from T.C. Worsley in the *New Statesman*: 'It is apparently no use any longer for us to urge Mr Ustinov to concentrate his talent and try to produce one satisfying play instead of three or four near misses. If he won't stop to polish and shape, and above all to cut, that is because, we now must presume, he can't.'

J.C. Trewin struck a more thoughtful note in the *Illustrated London News*, saying that he found it a drama of quite unusual quality: 'Ustinov's *Lear* parallel can be hampering, and the play is apt to drift, especially its last scene, when the dotard is mad indeed. But the dramatist has written a piece that aims at both mind and heart, and it is acted with the excellence it needs: by Eric Portman as the living ghost; by Charles Goldner as the slippery, man-oeuvring realist, a subtly-detailed portrait; by Brian Wilde as Lear's photographer, Josephine Griffin as the Marshal's daughter, and the rest of the company of nine.'

The author was publicly philosophical at the time, saying, 'If I were sixty I suppose I'd be sad. But I am young and more concerned about tomorrow. I still think it's the best play I have written.'

Privately, he took comfort in some of the audience responses. 'At a matinée performance I sat behind Virginia McKenna, who was bathed in tears at the end, so I realised it had its effect on certain people who didn't read notices.'

The play ran for seven weeks, but it may well be that its lack of success was because it was put on at the wrong time in the wrong place. Four years later it was produced for BBC Television, with the author as the Marshal, Peter Cushing as the Prime Minister, Hugh Griffith as the photographer, and Jeanette Sterke as the daughter; it was performed live twice in the same week, in the days before videotape. Peter's faith in the play was now vindicated by the verdict in *The Times*: 'Last night's television performance of Mr Peter Ustinov's *The Moment of Truth* was so well acted that it was, perhaps, easier to get a just impression of the drama than when it failed at a theatre much too big for it years ago. Mr Rudolph Cartier's simple yet felicitous production, with Mr Ustinov himself as the octogenarian Marshal, brought out many happy subtleties that were lost on the large stage of the Adelphi Theatre.'

So as the war receded in time, it seemed that audiences could take a more balanced view of the theme. But not in the unnamed country where it is clearly set by the playwright. 'The French went mad. There was a whole section in *Paris Match*. I got a spate of terrifying letters, and it's still going on, you still can't talk about Pétain. My Laval figure says, "I've saved millions of lives, and I'll be executed for my pains." No, I have no ambition for it to be produced in France.'

In 1951 Peter joined battle against the critics on behalf of a fellow writer. For the Festival of Britain that year, Alec Clunes, Director of the Arts Theatre, decided to stage a second competition for new plays (the first had been in 1944). It was at the Arts that *House of Regrets* had made its debut, as had *The Lady's Not for Burning*. Both plays were much admired by Alec Clunes, so he invited Peter Ustinov and Christopher Fry to join him in the triumvirate of judges.

Nearly a thousand scripts were submitted, which were reduced to a shortlist of fifty, still far too many for busy judges to read. But Peter was not impressed with the final choice of five presented to him; so he asked to read some of the runners-up and was very struck by John Whiting's *Saint's Day*.

So was Christopher Fry. 'Peter and I were entirely agreed on our reactions to things, and we both went for the John Whiting play. Alec was uncertain and then had the rather brilliant idea of saying we'll put the first three choices on. The others were Enid Bagnold's *Poor Judas* and C.E. Webber's *Right Side Up*. The idea was to see how they played and what the press reaction was. The press were all fiercely against the Whiting, so we gave it the prize.'

That fierce savaging was considered so unfair and damaging by Peter that a few months later he went out of his way, in his lecture to the Royal Society of Arts on 'The Playwright', to defend the author by censuring his critics:

All wars, we are told, are fought with the weapons of the last. The pen, we are told, is mightier than the sword. The mighty critical pen, too often as intractable in its devotion to the immediate past as the unsheathed sword, launches its attacks guided by the mind and manner of two decades ago.

When they said Mr Whiting's play was obscure, they were right. When they suggested it was difficult, they were right. When they said it was disturbing, they were right. When they declared it was impossible, they were wrong. It was a deeply personal utterance, which held at least one spectator spellbound by its ability to bring him within uncomfortable distance of a vital and deliberate mind ... *Saint's Day* was, from a technical point of view, splendidly constructed and conceived as material for actors to give of their best. The little lights and brief shadows which played over the skin of the text were no accident; they did not fall into place as a result of some caprice. They were set there by a master hand, a hand immature in the matter of conception perhaps, but masterly in the matter of interpretation ... For a work so brilliant in texture to be demolished simply because the story provoked the mind to labour so late in the afternoon is a disgrace, and I must be forgiven if I cannot listen to the whinny of 'Where are the New Dramatists?' with much elation.

The further history of the play is interesting, for after its bad-tempered reception, many important people saw fit to write to various newspapers in order to register their positions in the argument. I may be wrong, but I do not see why Christopher Fry should be, or Alec Clunes, or John Gielgud, or Peter Brook, or Peggy Ashcroft, or Tyrone Guthrie, and once I find myself in such august company, I really do not see why all of us should be wrong together.

But however passionately felt or eloquently expressed, his strictures on the shortcomings of critics were not likely to be well received, and their pens were sharpened for his next two plays to appear in the West End.

Before that happened, he created what was seen as a revolutionary art form for the BBC, although it was one he had been developing since his teens. The initiative came from a pioneering radio producer named Pat Dixon, and two of his young scriptwriters, Frank Muir and Denis Norden, who had worked with

Bernard Braden on his innovative radio show *Breakfast with Braden*.

Denis Norden had first come across Peter at the Players' Theatre, where 'he used to put one of those heavy square green ashtrays on his head, and a cloak around him, and sit down and give an impression of Queen Victoria opening the first water-closet, which was for those days quite scabrous, but hilarious.'

He knew that the Ustinov creativity was at its most inspired when he was free-associating and not bound by a script. These were the days when the BBC was still nervous even about unscripted political discussions, and all its comedy absolutely had to have a script. Somehow Pat Dixon persuaded his superiors to make a very grudging exception in this case, and he took Muir, Norden, and Ustinov off to the Caprice for lunch to discuss it. This alone nearly caused apoplexy in BBC Administration. Pat Dixon was told that this was the most expensive bill for entertainment put on an expenses chit that had ever gone through BBC Accounts.

Denis Norden remembered the occasion for other reasons: 'Peter never used the same voice for more than ten minutes at a time; he became different people throughout the meal. Then we had to wait quite a long time for a taxi, and Peter became Dudley Grosvenor, the suburban spiv. "What is it with these people, you can't get any service?" When he got into his taxi he turned back and said in a Hollywood voice, "Well, you get your people to get in touch with my New York office, and I'll get my people to get back to you soonest." '

They decided that the way to give Peter the freest rein was not to tie him down to a specific setting but to send him on a series of journeys where he could have any kind of encounter on the way. They found the title for the series in a favourite quotation from Stephen Leacock: 'He jumped on his horse and galloped off madly in all directions.'

The co-star of *In All Directions* was Peter Jones who, Peter knew from their previous stage and film work together, could match him and follow him in his surrealistic flights of fancy.

He always insisted that Peter Jones's name should be equally prominent in all the billings and publicity. Their regular characters were the brothers Morris and Dudley Grosvenor, small-time criminals deeply into self-justification and always complaining about the rest of the world:

'You can't get the staff, why is it?'

'What is it they want, is it money?'

'Money they want?'

The justification for all their journeys was the search for a road called Copthorne Avenue, which prompted letters saying, 'You've spent four weeks now trying to find Copthorne Avenue, I've spent fourteen years trying to get out of it.'

They would discuss the general idea, then improvise the whole dialogue with no idea where it might end up. Peter Ustinov as Dudley began one riff:

'Oh, incidentally, Morrie, I've fixed the boy.'

'What did you do that for? We need the boy to do the schlepping.'

'I know that, but we are used-car dealers.'

'I know that.'

'Yes, I sent the boy out for some tea, for the back axle of that Alfa-Romeo, to make it sound smoother.'

'Yes?'

'Well, he came back with Earl Grey!'

They also originated a letter to the Editor, which has since been often used without attribution: 'Dear Sir, I have at home a round disc with a hole in the middle. Is this a record?'

Having tried out various improvisations, Muir and Norden would choose the best ones to record in the studio, but the two Peters would continue to build on their fantasies. Denis Norden has had a long and distinguished career in the world of broadcast comedy, and half a century later he still says of Ustinov, 'He would move towards the ending that we had indicated, but he would wing off in another direction; he was the most inventive person that I've ever had the experience of working with, and that includes Spike Milligan.'

The first series began its run in September 1952, quickly followed by a second in May 1953, and finally a third in 1955. By then both Peters felt that the idea had run its course, and they were getting too busy on other projects anyway to have time to continue with it.

The significance of *In All Directions* was not just that it succeeded in winning a large and appreciative audience but that it also paved the way for Pat Dixon to move on and create *The Goon Show* for radio.

Simultaneously with his breaking that new ground, Peter retrieved one of his earlier works for the stage. *High Balcony* was written in 1946 but was rejected by every management as too provocative at the time. It is set in a German legation in neutral 'Noland', and the action opens with news of the invasion of Poland in 1939 and ends with the German surrender of 1945. The Nazis and the non-Nazis in the story all have their lives ruined by the war, and it is easy to see why its bleak message was not considered commercial in 1946.

Directed in 1952 by André van Gyseghem, the cast included Milton Rosmer, Mark Dignam, Ursula Howells, Marne Maitland, and Donald Pleasence.

The play was only ever scheduled to run for three weeks at the Embassy Theatre in Swiss Cottage, and it is a mark of actors' appreciation of the juicy parts offered by the playwright that such a short engagement should attract a cast of this calibre. The play packed a considerable dramatic punch, but it was still ahead of its time in its sympathy for the German predicament.

For *The Times* 'their plight makes a very human, and very real, but not a very enjoyable play'. For the *Evening Standard* the setting 'cannot possibly typify Germany as a whole. This exposes the author to a charge of special pleading. But as a special plea his play, tightly constructed and acutely written, both moves and convinces.'

The *Observer*'s general welcome was qualified by a reservation about what it perceived as the author's message: 'that the German ruling caste, minus the nastier Nazis, were fine, human fellows and good Europeans? Believe it who may. Throughout there are plenty of challenging ideas; it is indeed a relief to have a dramatist excited by the larger world of politics and principles and sparing us the monotony of sex without stint.'

In the same year Peter directed a play written by his then secretary, Penny Pakenham-Walsh, entitled *A Fiddle at the Wedding*. She was very much under the influence of Jean Anouilh, so her style was over-derivative of his writing. The cast included a friend of hers, Denholm Elliott, but he was not yet well enough known to bring it success, and after a short tour it folded without ever coming in to London.

Despite all these other public activities during the two-year run of *The Love of Four Colonels*, Peter was beginning to feel a void at the heart of his private life since the divorce from Isolde. As he put it in his autobiography, 'You look around you at the growing edifice of your life and admit to yourself that it is beautiful, but beautiful to what purpose? What and who is it for? Solitude is a necessary ingredient in the act of creation, but loneliness is very different – not loneliness while alone, but loneliness in public places, in the midst of gaiety and joy.'

According to Moira Lister, he had a series of girlfriends 'and they were all ravishingly beautiful'. One of them was Elaine Dundy, who rejected Kenneth Tynan's first proposal of marriage by saying, 'I'm sorry, but I can't marry you, I've just met Peter Ustinov. I'm mad about him.' Tynan riposted, 'Oh, I shouldn't bother about him. He's recently divorced, but he's already been taken.'

But Peter's heart was not so easily engaged and certainly not by just one meeting with Miss Dundy. He admits it leapt once, on the tennis court where he first met Hélène du Lau d'Allemans, when there was an immediate mutual attraction. Had she stayed in England, he is convinced they would have married then, but she went back to Paris and then to Barcelona, and they lost touch for a while.

Some while later he spotted the picture of a very beautiful girl on the cover of one of the foreign magazines that he now bought regularly, and he added it to his regular purchase that day. Three days later she appeared in the flesh in his dressing room at Wyndham's in the company of his French agent, André Bernheim. She was Suzanne Cloutier, a young French-Canadian actress most famous for having played Desdemona to Orson Welles's Othello in his recent film. She saw her cover photograph on his dressing table, and Peter told her how he had acquired it. Much later he said ruefully, 'Such providential acts can sometimes rush one into an impression that destiny was at work.'

Destiny had to wait upon the workings of the law for a while. Suzanne was still legally married to someone else, a doctor she had wed to please her parents but whom she left immediately after the reception to become a model in New York and later an actress.

Meanwhile, Peter found her a small part in his next play, which he directed himself, *No Sign of the Dove*. She only had one word to say – 'Boccaccio' – though she was not to get the chance to say even that for very long. Nadia Benois designed the sets and costumes (which she had done for his first play, *House of Regrets*. She had also advised on costumes for his films *Vice Versa* and *Private Angelo*. Their professional relationship was as harmonious as their personal one.)

Act One takes place on the ground floor of a country house while the floods are rising; Act Two on the first-floor landing outside the bedrooms; and the final Act on the roof as the house faces imminent submersion.

Suzanne played Hope, a young girl accompanying an old man in his early hundreds, who constructs a two-seater ark to save them, but not his son and daughter, nor the other members of the pretentious literary house-party who are present for the weekend. Miles Malleson played the Captain Shotover–Noah figure, supported by Raymond Huntley, Beatrix Lehmann, David Kossoff, and one of Peter's favourite actors and a frequent colleague, Robin Bailey.

The play was well received on its five-week pre-London tour, so the company was ill-prepared for its first night reception at the Savoy Theatre. The booing from the gallery began, by the author's estimate, 'just forty-five seconds after the curtain rose', which would indicate it was a claque organised by someone who had taken a dislike to the play on seeing it at one of its provincial dates. Beatrix Lehmann's line, 'I forgive you all,' was answered from the gallery, 'That's more than we can do.' The curtain finally fell to more boos.

The next morning W.A. Darlington bemoaned this 'melancholy occasion' in the *Daily Telegraph*, calling it 'a poor broken-backed piece of satire, quite unworthy of its author's brilliant talents'.

Cecil Wilson sniffed in the *Daily Mail*, 'Booing is not a thing to be encouraged, but neither is this kind of play, and I must say Mr Ustinov asked for the gallery's cold douche.' the *Sunday Times* minced even fewer words: 'Clever Mr Ustinov has tried to re-write *Heartbreak House*, a bedroom farce, and parts of the Bible. He has resoundingly and crashingly failed.'

Whatever the critics' thoughts, Peter's conviction that the raucous gallery response was a put-up job was supported by the loud applause at the end of the second night's performance. The *Daily Express* headline on 4 December, 'Ustinov hears the jeers for his new play', was followed on 5 December by one saying, 'Now Ustinov is cheered on Night No. 2.' That later audience rose to face the author in his box as they applauded him. He responded by saying, 'Don't make me feel like President Lincoln.'

But the damage had been done, and the show closed after just eleven performances. Although Philip Hope-Wallace found the piece 'intractable', he expressed the hope in the *Manchester Guardian* that the author would not be unduly discouraged by the unfriendly reception, as 'the theatre could ill spare so talented a man.'

At this distance in time, Peter shrugs philosophically and says, 'It's not the first or the last time I've been booed.' However, it was unquestionably the worst occasion when it happened to him.

His initial reaction of numb disgust was followed by an upsurge of confidence, 'a kind of controlled rage with the outward aspect of insolent serenity'. If one medium looked for the moment less promising, there were several others clamouring for his services.

He had had four of his plays presented in London in the space of two years, only one of which was a great success, but that one had also triumphed in the USA and across Europe. The theatre would now have to wait three years for his next play, as most of his time for the next decade would be taken up with the film studios.

After the huge international success of *Quo Vadis*, MGM recalled him to its colours to play a more recent historical figure – the Prince Regent in *Beau Brummell*.

Nine

1954–1958
From *Beau Brummell* to
Romanoff and Juliet

For his second MGM film Peter had the same producer, Sam Zimbalist, but a different director, the German-born Curtis Bernhardt, who had a fondness for Americanisms such as 'Zis I want like a hole in ze head.'

The British cast of *Beau Brummell* included Stewart Granger in the title role; Elizabeth Taylor as the woman he loved, Lady Patricia; Paul Rogers as the Prime Minister, William Pitt; Peter Bull as Charles James Fox; plus Finlay Currie, James Hayter, Noel Willman, and James Donald. Robert Morley made a brief appearance as the mad King George III, who tried, all too realistically, to strangle his son and heir. When they shot that scene, Morley nearly choked him in earnest. Sheridan Morley says his father never knew his own strength, and Peter noted ruefully, 'Robert had huge hands, and unfortunately they're the only hands I could imagine that fitted round my neck, which is also on the large side. But he was really very frightening, and I had to be rescued.'

He has happier memories of working with Rosemary Harris. 'I really fell for her, she's a great actress. She played Mrs Fitzherbert, so I was supposed to look at her like that, and it was no strain on me at all.' It was her first time before the camera, and her delight at playing opposite Peter was so great it overflowed. In the middle of the big ballroom scene, with crowds of extras on set, the two of them got the giggles and couldn't stop. The director got so angry that he broke off the filming and sent them home in disgrace. She says now, with a slightly shamefaced laugh, 'It's hard to believe that that would have happened, that I would have had so little control then, but we just couldn't get through the scene together. Curtis Bernhardt was a bit of a martinet, and somehow that made it worse.'

The film marked the start of a long friendship, and I am sure that now she would have the self-control not to giggle when acting with Peter. However, I did notice that when I rang her up in New York in 2001 to ask if I could come and talk to her about working with him, her response on the phone was, 'Oh, Peter Ustinov . . .', followed by a long peal of reminiscent laughter. That sound also punctuated much of the morning that we then spent together talking about him.

Paul Rogers' reaction was much the same. This was his first meeting with Peter in the flesh, though he had played the old General in *House of Regrets* at the Colchester Repertory Company. He stood in for Peter at the screen-tests of three actresses for the part of Mrs Fitzherbert and was then offered the role of Pitt, a relatively small part in screen-time but an important one in the story. 'That's when the friendship began. Peter's company was an intoxicant, it was irresistible. In those days there was a gulf between the stars and directors and executives who sat at the high table in the canteen, and the rest – the featured players and so forth. Well, among the featured players in that lot were people like James Donald and Noel Willman, whom Peter had trained with at Michel Saint-Denis's school. So he joined us and we had a fabulous table. I laughed so much I had to go and lie down in my dressing room afterwards. Stewart Granger used to escape from the top table; he heard all this laughter and he couldn't bear it.'

The central relationship in the film between Beau Brummell and the Prince was as tricky as that between the actors playing them, because they were never tuned in to each other's wavelength. 'Stewart Granger got on my nerves tremendously with his macho character. He was very abrupt, and I pulled back a little each time as Prince Regent, because I was smaller than he was. He suddenly said, "Every time I come close to you, you back off. What's the matter? Have I got bad breath or something?"

'I said, "No, but your eyes are so close together, I have to select one or the other to look at."

'He was terribly physical. Later on I had a drink in the bar at his home in Hollywood, when he was still with Jean Simmons, and everything in it – chairs, table, the bar itself – was composed entirely of things he'd shot. So there were heads of rampant gnus and lions on the walls, and when you sat on one of those sofas you became covered with hair from the hide of some kind of bush-cow he'd shot. I thought it was a real slaughterhouse of a bar.'

Beau Brummell is quite frequently rerun on television and it stands up well, though Peter Ustinov steals the acting honours effortlessly from the titular star. But the film is perhaps remembered now mostly for the crass insensitivity of the film industry in choosing it for the Royal Command Performance of 1954. In the second year of her reign, the young Queen Elizabeth II was reported to be not best pleased at the sight of one of her forebears trying to throttle another.

From a personal point of view, the film is more memorable for the Ustinov family in the fact that during the shooting Peter and Suzanne Cloutier got married. He took her with him to the studio straight from the Chelsea Registry Office, and later that day there was an informal wedding reception at his home in the King's Road, for family, friends, and some of the MGM film company.

Shortly afterwards the newly-weds left for Los Angeles. Peter's first two films for Hollywood had been shot in Rome and London; now he was to work at the home base of the great Dream Factory itself. His director was Michael Curtiz, the Hungarian whose shaky knowledge of English provided David Niven with the title of his second volume of memoirs – *Bring on the Empty Horses*.

The Egyptian was supposed to star Marlon Brando, who cried off sick when he read the script, to be replaced by Edmund Purdom. Others in the large cast included Victor Mature, Jean Simmons, and Michael Wilding. The sets were massive and dwarfed the actors who appeared on them. Peter found it difficult to take any of it seriously, including the instructions of Michael Curtiz.

'The next shot, Ustinov, you vill come running down the hill and visper in the ear of Purdom.'

'What do you want me to whisper?'

'Son of a bitch, vot it matters, ven you are vispering in the ear, I'm not hearing anyvay.'

'All right, all right!'

But the film was being shot in the new wide-screen process, Cinemascope, and the letter-box format required some often artificial groupings to fill the screen. Peter came running down the hill and whispered in Purdom's ear.

'Cut! Cinemascope! Ven you visper in ear, Purdom must be four feet apart.'

The exasperated actor replied, 'In that case you will have to tell me what to whisper.'

To Peter the whole film was 'like playing *Aida* without the music; it was like the libretto for a ridiculous opera'. He never saw the finished film, 'since I found it so profoundly silly while I was making it'.

However, the experience did have one very beneficial result. When it finished, Michael Curtiz asked him to be in his next film, *We're No Angels*, from the Broadway play based on Albert Husson's *La Cuisine des Anges*. He played one of three convicts on work release, together with Aldo Ray and Humphrey Bogart. The latter knew the directorial shortcomings of Michael Curtiz and advised Peter, 'You gotta remember, he's got no sense of humour. So we'll just have to take things into our own hands without letting him know what we're doing.'

The three old lags did just that, and the comedy came off triumphantly. The *Herald Tribune* awarded the palm to the visitor: 'Ustinov is an urbane Britisher who can cajole any lock to open. He is also the most agile farceur in the cast, and it is a joy to see how casually – almost carelessly – he delivers his dry and witty comments.'

The script and the casting both appealed to Peter, but there was an additional personal reason why he was more than ready to stay on in Hollywood just then.

Suzanne was pregnant with their first child and unable to travel as she was about to give birth. They found a Canadian doctor who was happy to be paid in sterling as he was planning a holiday in Europe, which eased the Ustinov dollar allowance situation. Pavla was born on the afternoon of 2 June 1954.

That evening the happy father was invited to the home of the Bogarts, and he was greeted first by the man of the house, who was fixing martinis in the bar outside the living room. For once Peter's sense of humour was upstaged by that of his host. When Bogart heard the news he pulled a face and then explained that he was anticipating the noise all the women would make when they were told, mimicking an exaggerated 'Aaaoow...'

The two men went in and Bogart announced in ringing tones, 'Peter's just become the proud father of a baby girl. Both mother and child are doing well.' As the chorus of 'Aaaaooow ...' went up, Bogart threw his friend a conspiratorial look, and Peter realised his prediction had not been at all exaggerated.

A less agreeable response was the fear in the hearts of the Hollywood community caused by the wild accusations of Communist sympathies alleged by Senator Joe McCarthy. Peter, appalled by the way people's nerve crumbled in the face of these attacks, readily agreed to make a broadcast for the BBC about the hearings on the so-called subversion in the army. He recorded the fifteen-minute talk in a local radio station and pulled no punches in his description of the way the senator appeared to him:

It is as though he had cheated the physical restrictions placed on him by nature, and had trained the very shortcomings of his equipment into weapons. His own evident lack of wit makes him impervious to the wit of others; his own inability to listen makes him immune to argument; his own tortuous train of thought wears down the opposition; his crawling reflexes, his unnaturally slow and often muddled delivery force quicker minds to function at a disadvantage below their normal speeds. And yet, cumbersome as is the Senator in action, his changes of direction, like those of the charging rhinoceros, are often executed with alarming ease. A mind trained in all the arts of tactical expediency urges the ponderous machinery on its provocative way.

Whenever he is compelled to admit that he doesn't know, he does so with an inflection suggesting that it isn't worth knowing. Whenever he says he does know, he does so with an inflection suggesting that others don't – and won't. This then is the outward face of the man who has heard voices telling him to go and root out Communists – and this is the face of a man who recognises his potential enemy in everyone he meets. Like a water-diviner, he treads the desert with a home-made rod, and shouts his triumph with every flicker of the instrument, leaving hard-working professional men to scratch the soil for evidence.

A crowd of astonished Americans had gathered in the control room by the time he finished, as no one there was then brave enough to challenge the senator in public, until Joseph Welch's celebrated criticism at the televised Senate hearings began the fightback that broke McCarthy's malign influence. Someone at the station sold the news of the Ustinov broadcast to one of the American papers, which printed a garbled version, causing even more nervousness among the studio chiefs.

We're No Angels was both a critical and a commercial success, and restored Peter's faith in the Hollywood machine after the debacle of *The Egyptian*. The Ustinov family returned home to London briefly, before his presence was required in Paris by the great German director Max Ophuls. The maker of *La Ronde*, *Madame de . . .*, and several other classics was embarking on his first film in colour. Sadly *Lola Montès* would also be his final movie.

Many of his films were set in nineteenth-century Vienna or the second French Empire and dealt in the transitoriness of love, to the accompaniment of lyrical music; his style is instantly recognisable with its swooping camerawork. Virtually every shot is on the move. James Mason, who worked for him in *Caught* and *The Reckless Moment*, captured this compulsion in a telling little quatrain:

> A shot that does not call for tracks
> Is agony for poor dear Max,

Who, separated from his dolly,
Is wrapped in deepest melancholy.

Peter had his doubts about the movie itself but became devoted
to its director. 'Max was a very human character and an inveterate
giggler. I've never come across a kindred spirit among the directors, who are not really giggly people. Zinnemann for instance
was a sweet man but extremely solemn.'

Lola Montès is based on a circus performance in which the
famous courtesan looks back on her life and her love affairs with
Liszt, King Ludwig I of Bavaria, a student, and several other men.
Peter played the circus ringmaster, and it took him a little while
to see behind what appeared to be a professionalism bordering
on callousness. 'There was a moment where he had dwarfs and
Lilliputians suspended, going up and down with the music in
special harnesses. Of course dwarfs are massively built compared
with their size, whereas Lilliputians have very ordinary proportions
but are just tiny. The harness slipped on one of them, who was in
danger of falling or being strangled. Ophuls saw this and shouted
in German, "Let the dwarfs hang." I looked at him in horror. He
saw me out of the corner of his eye, turned to me and giggled,
then called, "Cut." So I caught him at his Prussian best.'

The film was shot in three different language versions – English,
French, and German – which made shooting a much longer and
more expensive operation than usual.

Peter quickly discovered that there was very little money in the
kitty when his pay-cheque bounced, and the circus scenes were
particularly pressurised, with 800 extras, lions, and other performing animals.

'I had to walk across the middle of all this livestock and then
climb a spiral staircase, singing a song composed by Georges Auric
and talking about Lola Montès until I reached the top of the
staircase. There was Lola, and I had to introduce her. I did the
German version first, because it was the most difficult. On the
way across the ring I felt a frog in my throat, and I thought this
is going to spoil the whole thing. I came across a German dwarf
and said, "Ein glass wasser."

' "Eh?"

' "Ein glass wasser, schnell!"'

'He ran off, and I was about to climb the staircase when he arrived with it. I drank the water, sang the song, got to the top and bellowed out some more stuff, introduced Lola Montès, put the glass down, and I was through. All the extras clapped, because it was a very long take, even by Ophuls standards, and I hadn't put a word wrong. I came down the staircase, went up to Ophuls's chair, and found him sulking. I said, "How was that?"

'No answer.

'I said, "For God's sake, you must tell me something."

'Silence.

'I said, "Once and for all, how was it?"

'He said, "I wish *I'd* had the idea of the glass of water." '

Lola was played by Martine Carol, whose beauty exceeded her acting ability, which worried others much more than it did the director. When they quietly cautioned, 'Martine Carol isn't really very good in this,' he countered, 'The worse she is the better, the more kitschy, that's the whole point of my film.'

Not that that was much comfort to her co-star, especially when it came to shooting the scenes in German, as she didn't speak a word of it. She had the script written up phonetically on a blackboard behind Peter's back, and he had to keep adjusting his position so that she could read it. They gave eye signals to each other to pick up their cues. The German version has never been shown, and the film was only released in the other languages when heavily cut. Ophuls fought against this mutilation, and he did not live to see his original conception restored, which is now regarded as a classic.

Peter is still a little puzzled by that acclaim, as he always thought of it as a rather formless film, even though he admired much of the technique. 'It was a disaster at the première, because the film broke a couple of times. I was sitting next to Max, and of course every time it broke he went into fits of giggles. The film is based on a mediocrity and shows how easily mediocrity succeeds in the world. I thought it was a rather risky film. Its reception at the beginning was appalling.'

Max Ophuls was an admirer of *The Love of Four Colonels* and bought the film rights, but when Peter saw his first treatment he bought it back again, and that film has never been made.

I wondered why he had never attempted to translate it to the screen himself or, indeed, any of the novels he wrote later, several of which would adapt well to film treatment. But he insisted, 'I can't write the screenplays myself. I find it impossible to digest the same meal twice. I had enough difficulty with *Romanoff and Juliet*.'

The difficulty was only with the film, not the original play. That was written in three acts, in what he likes to think of as his neo-classical period, with the use of asides to the audience, a technique he had also used in *The Love of Four Colonels*. Both plays were sparked by the idiocies and mutual suspicions of the Cold War. 'I was trying to furnish some kind of antidote, which would make people feel happier about the whole thing.'

He took the star-crossed lovers from *Romeo and Juliet* and translated them into a 1950s situation – set in the capital city of the smallest country in Europe – where the son of the Russian Ambassador and the daughter of the American Ambassador fall ecstatically in love. The American and Soviet Embassies face each other across the city square, so there are two balconies for the lovelorn pair. Juliet keeps her Shakespearean name, but Romeo has become Igor Romanoff.

They were played by Katy Vail and Michael David, and their respective fathers by John Phillips and Frederick Valk. Fending off the Superpowers' pressures to choose between their political systems as the non-aligned President, maintaining his own 'balance of feebleness', was the author himself.

The play went on a long pre-West End tour, opening in Manchester and concluding in Golders Green. The night it opened there, Suzanne gave birth to a son, who was given the same name as the young lover in the play – Igor. The proud father acted his part 'euphorically that night'.

The day before its first night at the Piccadilly Theatre, the playwright drew some interesting comparisons between different national attitudes to the theatre: 'The audience rarely allows us to forget that the roots of the English drama are in the fairground, and that its repute was for many centuries ill-repute. In Scandinavia and in Germany you will see audiences content to sit in a silence scarcely disturbed by breathing while Strindberg's low opinion of women is made perfectly clear – in France the public will be more than happy to indulge in love's wine-tasting with Marivaux, delighted as the elegant equations work out the tidy sum of human relations. These Continental theatregoers start the evening quietly, and only begin to fidget when things go wrong. Our own public tends to begin by fidgeting, and calms down if things go right.'

There was little, if any, fidgeting at the Piccadilly the following night. The play, the cast, and Denis Carey's production were all welcomed with open arms. W.A. Darlington expressed his gratitude in the *Daily Telegraph*: 'Mr Ustinov the dramatist has a world of fantasy in which he moves with superb ease, and in that world he has a way of appointing his other self, Mr Ustinov the actor, to act as a master of ceremonies . . . The quality of this production consists not in its story, nor even in its satire – which is not so biting that either Americans or Russians need feel offended – but in the richness of its theatrical invention.'

In the *Observer*, Kenneth Tynan similarly delighted in the double contribution: 'Mr Ustinov presides over our enlightenment with a sort of ruffled tact that combines the best features of Chorus, Pandarus and fleet-footed Mercury. It has been said of this elusive author that he writes not so much plays of ideas as ideas from plays. In *Romanoff and Juliet* the idea has come out happy and whole, a blithe Ruritania with echoes for all of us, a satirical touchstone against which to test the pretensions of both Eastern bloc and Western alliance.'

Anthony Cookman ended a long paean of praise in the *Tatler and Bystander*: 'The final act, so often in the theatre today a dragging anti-climax, is in this play what it should be, one long *coup de théâtre* which adroitly and satisfyingly dovetails political satire with romantic fantasy and enables Mr Edward Atienza to make a wonderfully comic figure of an almost completely fossilized archbishop.'

Peter wondered whether Darlington was right in his prediction that the satire would not give offence. When former US President Truman paid a visit to the Piccadilly a month after the play opened, he and his wife had a glass of champagne afterwards with Peter and Suzanne. The author said to him, 'I hope you don't think I'm a Communist, because I wrote an even-handed play?' Harry Truman's response was characteristically succinct: 'Jesus, Peter, if there weren't people like you, where would we be?'

The Russian response began good-naturedly but ended painfully. When the Minister-Counsellor at the Soviet Embassy in London, Mr Romanov, challenged Peter to a tennis match, he told Peter that he wanted his revenge for the use of his name in the play, indicating an admirable sense of humour. On the appointed day the heavens opened but the match had to go on. Great Britain defeated the Soviet Union, but Peter's exertions gave him a slipped disc. He had to come out of the play for a couple of weeks until he could move again, so Mr Romanov had his revenge after all.

The timing of the play was most unfortunate in Germany, where the rest of the Ustinov repertoire has been exceptionally well received. But this one coincided with the Russian invasion of Hungary, and as Peter wryly commented, 'They lost all their sense of humour about that sort of thing; they were too close.'

Reading the text of the play now, the part of the President is so clearly tailor-made for the Ustinov comic genius that I asked him if, like Noël Coward, he always wrote a part for himself. 'No, I don't, but I very often hear the door closing behind me, as someone says, "You're obviously going to play in this, aren't you?" I wrote parts that I thought I could play in any case, but it's no use writing for yourself, because I had much bigger ambitions that these things could be played abroad, and what are you going to do then?'

Not just abroad; he has frequently had two or more of his plays running simultaneously in England. He was on the pre-London tour of *Romanoff and Juliet* when his play *The Empty Chair* was presented at the Bristol Old Vic, so the company staged a special dress rehearsal for him on a Sunday. The action takes place at the height of the Terror in the French Revolution, in an ante-room of the Revolutionary Council. It opens with three cleaning ladies like a Greek Chorus, who have a superstition that whoever sits in the ornate gilt chair taken from Versailles will go to the guillotine. It had a strong cast, with Joseph O'Conor as Danton, Alan Dobie as Robespierre, Graham Crowden as Collot, Derek Godfrey as the spy Mouche, and the virtually unknown Peter O'Toole as Hébert.

For Edward Hardwicke, who played Camille Desmoulins, this was the first time that he met his hero. He had taken his father to see *The Love of Four Colonels*, which did not impress Sir Cedric as much as his son. He commented to Edward as they left the theatre, 'I would have preferred to see *The Love of Two Colonels*.' Edward was not about to confide that story to the author when he came down to Bristol.

'We were all in awe of him, because at that time he was the great comic actor, and this was quite a serious play. At the end, the room is deserted and the banner falls. The director, John Moody, was a rather shy man, and he went round whispering notes to the actors, so Peter couldn't hear what he was saying. Finally John turned to him and asked, 'What do you think, Mr Ustinov, about the production?'

'Peter said, "Fine, I'm just worried by the banner at the end."

' "Oh yes, what's the matter?"

' "Well, at the moment it looks like a direction indicator saying the set will now turn left." '

It is virtually impossible in any play about these events for the larger-than-life Danton not to tower over the other figures, and that is just as true of *The Empty Chair*. At his fall from power, Danton denounces Robespierre: 'The moment my head falls, you may begin to compose your own last words, because I am the actor who captures the public imagination, while you are but a creature of the wings, the prompter of the Revolution. When I am gone, you will be pushed onto the stage, but the lights will be too strong for you, and you will be stifled by the blanket of public boredom and disdain. You need me more than I need you.'

It was televised three years later by Southern Television, with

Joss Ackland as Danton, and Derek Godfrey this time as Robespierre. Only the American television audience has had the opportunity of seeing the author play Danton, opposite the Robespierre of George C. Scott.

Peter was so busy at this time that he was unable to visit the Oxford Playhouse première of an earlier play of his, *Paris Not So Gay*. In the 1950s and 1960s Frank Hauser presented an adventurous programme of work by major European playwrights, but in his seventeen years at the Playhouse the advance booking for this play was the greatest he ever experienced. 'It was a tribute to Peter Ustinov's drawing-power.'

Frank Hauser thought the play was a bit long, so he wrote to Peter, suggesting that he cut pages 4, 5, 6 and 7. When he received a reply saying, 'Yes, cut those and substitute knave, queen, king!' he decided that it would be best to go along with the author's original wishes after all.

Romanoff and Juliet ran for a year at the Piccadilly, before Peter was invited to take it to Broadway. The only other member of the British cast to accompany him was Edward Atienza. Peter was quite happy to have Americans in all the other parts but was furious when the New York unions refused to let him credit his French designer, Jean-Denis Malclès. They tried to insist that it had to be an American, but the author dug his heels in and flatly refused to credit anybody else. 'It's one of my phobias.'

The play was also supposedly re-directed for the American taste by George Kaufman, who had an impressive reputation in the American theatre but was unfortunately no longer up to the task, so once again it fell back on the author/star. The notices were only lukewarm, but the run lasted for a season on Broadway, before going on the road for a lengthy American tour. Between the two Peter gave a long interview to Henry Brandon in the *Sunday Times*, in which he reflected on the different responses each side of the Atlantic: 'For pretty obvious reasons the English audience has a greater sense of irony; at the same time the American audience has a greater sense of fantasy. At the end of my play I have a line in which I say to the young lovers, "You invented everything, including the country which is yours," which never fails to affect an American audience; whereas in England there was always a dead silence.'

Peter has always been fascinated by the quirks of national character, and he observed in the same conversation, 'I once said and it's not quite true, but I thought it was true enough – that in order to reach the truth the French subtract, the Germans add, and the English change the subject.'

The success of *Romanoff and Juliet* led to its being the only one of his plays so far to be filmed. He adapted the screenplay himself, directed it, and reprised his role as the President. The young lovers were played by Sandra Dee and John Gavin, whom he got for virtually nothing, because part of the deal with Universal Pictures was that he had to use their two contract stars.

This film only came about in 1961, after his success in the same studio's production of *Spartacus*, but that story deserves a chapter to itself.

Ten

1958–1960
From *Spartacus* to
The Sundowners

The year 1958 marked the entry of two new activities into the Ustinov lifestyle, both of which have brought him great pleasure and satisfaction.

Before taking *Romanoff and Juliet* on the road in the States, he took a holiday in the South of France, where he was invited to a cocktail party in Cannes, on board a yacht moored in the harbour. Within the hour he had bought it – a fifty-eight-foot ketch named *Christina*, which he soon found kept receiving messages intended for a somewhat larger vessel of the same name owned by Aristotle Onassis, the Greek shipping magnate.

He promptly renamed it *Nitchevo*, which is Russian for 'nothing'. In the years since then, the family have enjoyed many wonderful holidays on the boat. When the children were small they all used to sail on it together, including Tamara, and it was where she really got to know her half-siblings. Now that they are grown up, the *Nitchevo* is too small to accommodate them all together, so they take it in turns to have the boat through the summer. Peter has owned a succession of cars and several different homes, but has never parted with his first yacht.

It has always held a special place in the affections of his daughter Pavla: 'The *Nitchevo* was and still is the only "constant" familiar roof I have ever known, as we moved around so much. Going on the *Nitchevo* is the equivalent for me to going home. I believe Peter has kept it all these years because he realised that. I am very grateful to him for that. In his own way he compensated for the "normal" family structure that we didn't have. The *Nitchevo* symbolises our roots, and the Mediterranean by now is a member of our family.'

The second departure for him was a creative one. During his Broadway sojourn, Edward Weeks of the *Atlantic Monthly* was prompted by the theme of his play to ask for a playlet about the Russians and Americans on the Moon. Peter accepted the commission but forgot all about it in the excitement of buying the boat, until returning to New York. 'Suddenly to my horror I got a letter from Ted Weeks saying, "We expect your copy within five days, because we've kept a space for it." I thought, Oh my God. I locked myself up and wrote a short story, not about the Russians and Americans on the Moon, but about the Swiss on the Moon, who by some quirk of fate had got there before them. I sent it off and waited for the explosion, and instead received a commission for seven more short stories.'

He wrote the others in hotel rooms right across the States on tour. Two of them were set in the USA – in a nightclub and on a TV chat show; one at a disputatious Soviet Writers' Union meeting; one in a British Criminal Court where an inoffensive witness tries to tell the honest truth and ends up in an asylum; one at a disastrous bullfight in a small Spanish town; and one where four Axis generals, the only survivors of a retreat from the Red Army at the end of the war, argue before going to their deaths.

The story that gave its title to the later published collection *Add a Dash of Pity*, tells of the quest for the truth about who was to blame for a wartime disaster in the British Army and how the man wrongly blamed for it refuses to correct the record, out of pity for the general whose fault it really was. The colonel says to the young investigating historian: 'I can't allow you to stir up all those dormant sorrows in the hearts of the parents of these boys by making them realise that these deaths could have been avoided. I would rather take the blame. And d'you know why? Because I've shoulders broad enough to carry the burden; Crowdy hasn't. For me, it's a closed chapter; for him, it isn't. He'll spend the rest of his life trying to justify his action, fearful lest controversy should reopen.'

The tale is compelling and suspenseful, and had a remarkable impact on one particular reader. Peter received a letter from the American publishers Doubleday, 'who said they had found out that Admiral Nimitz was the only important war leader not to have written his autobiography. They approached him with a promise of a large advance, and he replied, "No. Ever since I read Ustinov's short story in the *Atlantic Monthly* I've decided not to write my memoirs, because it can lead to so much heartbreak and unhappiness." That was extraordinary. I suddenly felt a private again and irresponsible. I think he had real scruples about the position of a general or an admiral.'

These short stories whetted the appetite of publishers for more from his pen, and he had discovered a new outlet for his creative energies during the empty hours spent hanging around on film sets, waiting for the call of 'Action'.

He had so much time on his hands during the making of *Spartacus* that he managed to write a full-length novel. The filming went on for so long that his youngest child Andrea, who was born on 30 March 1959, had grown up enough before it finished to be able to answer a playmate's question about what her father did for a living, with a single word.

'*Spartacus*' was Andrea's reply.

Both the setting-up and the shooting of that film provide an object lesson in the problems of making epic Hollywood movies. Kirk Douglas bought the rights to Howard Fast's novel about the leader of the slave revolt against the might of the Roman Empire. The novelist's own screenplay was unusable, so Douglas secretly hired the blacklisted Dalton Trumbo, one of the Hollywood Ten, who had spent a year in jail for refusing to co-operate with the McCarthyite witch-hunt for Communists.

Nobody would back the film without several other bankable stars, so Douglas set out to woo Laurence Olivier, Charles Laughton, and Peter Ustinov. First of all, Olivier wanted to play Spartacus (which the actor-producer had earmarked for himself); then he wanted to direct it as well as play in it. When he agreed to play Coriolanus for Peter Hall in the 1959 Stratford-upon-Avon Theatre season, he wrote to withdraw as director. 'If, however, you can still see your way to improving the part of Crassus in relation to the other roles, then I should be more than happy to look at it again, as it is such a gallant enterprise and one I should be extremely proud to be part of. Could you be so kind as to let me see something just as soon as you possibly can?'

Laughton's reaction to the first draft was expressed to Douglas's face more succinctly: 'I glanced at the script. Really, a piece of shit.' It was the fee that swayed him into acceptance.

Then, as Kirk Douglas records in his memoir *The Ragman's Son*, 'We got word that Peter Ustinov had many comments and suggestions about the part, but was amenable to playing the role.'

The pitch to all three actors was nuanced differently for each about the importance of their role. However, by the time they all met for the first reading in Hollywood, the script had gone through several more drafts. Someone should really have filmed that bizarre scene. Kirk Douglas was dressed as a slave; Laurence Olivier and Peter Ustinov were in their everyday street clothes; Charles Laughton was in a towelling dressing gown, with his hair in curlers ready for his senatorial hairdo as Gracchus; and John Gavin, as the young Julius Caesar, was in full Roman uniform complete with helmet. Olivier had arrived a week before the others, so he had had more input into the latest version, which was absolutely different from the one they had accepted.

Even for someone like Peter, well used to actors' temperaments, the occasion was very highly charged. 'The person most affected was Charles Laughton, who was always waiting to be offended in any case. The reading began with a scene between Douglas and Olivier, which we'd never seen before. Kirk started very quietly, "Oh God, give me the strength of . . ." We all looked at each other. Then Larry put on some glasses and said, also very softly, "Oh Rome, how great you are, I will not hesitate . . ." I thought to myself, if the race is going to be run at that pace I'm not going to make a fool of myself by sprinting. So when my turn came I said, equally softly, "Ha, ha, oh you men, you don't know what . . ."

'The only one who had no sense of occasion or sensitivity at all was John Gavin, who said in stentorian tones, "Oh mighty Crassus, although my triremes will row to your greater glory..." '

The reading ploughed on until Charles Laughton stopped dead and said, 'I don't know what this new scene's about. Would anyone help me?'

A look was exchanged between Douglas and Olivier, who said, 'It's my idea, dear boy, in this scene I represent the future, John Gavin the present, and you, dear boy, the past.'

'Why do I represent the future?'

'No, dear boy, *you* represent the *past*, *I* represent the future, and John Gavin represents the present.'

After more of this interchange Olivier lost his nerve first. He took off his glasses and asked, 'Would it help you, dear boy, if I read it for you?'

Laughton reacted as if he had had his face slapped, then thought about it and said slowly, 'Yeeess.' The intensity of his listening was so tangible that Olivier never finished the speech, trailing off '... more or less like that.'

Laughton waited for a long pause to elapse, and then said, 'Yeess, I thought there might be a moment when I could understand what you're saying, but now I'm afraid I'm *totally* lost.'

That first reading was adjourned before the end, but the script struggles continued. Shooting began on 27 January 1959, with Anthony Mann as director, whom Universal had foisted on Douglas against his will. To the latter's surprise, the first week on the mine sequence, shot in Death Valley, went well. 'But when we got to the gladiator school, it all started to fall apart. It was clear that Tony Mann was not in control. He let Peter Ustinov direct his own scenes by taking every suggestion Peter made. The suggestions were good – for Peter, but not necessarily for the picture.'

Belatedly, the studio agreed with the producer's view of the director, who was fired after just two weeks' shooting. Douglas now asked for Stanley Kubrick, who had previously directed him in *Paths of Glory*. He was only thirty, and Universal were not keen, but to avoid shutting down the film they had to agree.

Ironically, Kubrick then proceeded to accept even more of the Ustinov creative input than his predecessor. When Laughton dug in his heels and refused to play his scenes as written, Peter was deputed to find out what the problem was. The upshot of that conversation was that Peter rewrote all their scenes together, which the two of them rehearsed at home, often late into the night. Kubrick then shot the scenes virtually unchanged, in half a day each because the two actors arrived on set so well-rehearsed and relaxed.

They have a naturalness together on the screen that is a joy to watch for connoisseurs of good film acting. Laughton loved his craft and delighted in saying, 'Acting is whoring!' However, he had a sharp sense of his own worth, coupled with a vulnerability that often surprised Peter.

The older man took to referring to the younger as the Crown Prince, with the clear implication of who was therefore the reigning King.

Universal Studios followed the Hollywood habit, much disliked by the actors, of making money by allowing in busloads of tourists to see how films were made. One day when the two men were sitting on the steps of Laughton's caravan, sipping his favourite drink called Bullshot – a Bloody Mary made with beef tea instead of tomato juice, only made palatable by a hefty slug of vodka – two ladies who were obviously sisters saw them and stopped. The elder one looked at Laughton and breathed, 'Oh ... the greatest.' He was always open to flattery and assumed a humble look.

'Thank you very much.'

'Oh, you are just so great, you are the greatest actor that has ever graced the boards or the silver screen.'

He was purring like a kitten, until she said, 'Your Big Daddy was just one of the finest things...'

When the fans finally left, Laughton was so childishly hurt that Peter expostulated, 'Charles, for God's sake, two women like that, and you're hurt?'

'How would you feel if they addressed that to you and made that mistake?'

Peter tried to console him. 'Listen, when such things happen, you've always got to think what could be worse.'

'What could be worse than that?'

'Worse than that, they could realise their mistake and come back.'

Which was precisely what they did.

'What are you going to think of me? I made that foolish mistake. Hell, Amy, why didn't you stop me?'

'I tried to stop you.'

'You did not. Anyway, I want you to know something, and this is from my heart. You're every bit as good as Burl Ives.'

By now the actor had recovered his poise and deflected their attention by turning to his friend and saying silkily, 'I bet you don't know who this is.'

His ploy worked. They struggled for recognition, until the elder one blurted, 'Oh, yeah, don't tell me, oh God, it's right on the tip of my tongue . . . Gosh . . . Oh, oh I know, Walter Hustonov.'

It was not just the scenes with Laughton that drew on the Ustinov writing talent. He had a scene with Olivier near the end of the film, where Crassus ordered him to attend the final battle and identify Spartacus. The aghast response of Batiatus is so quintessentially Ustinovian that it could not possibly have come from the pen of Dalton Trumbo: 'I'm a civilian. I'm even more of a civilian than most civilians.'

For Peter, the difference between playing opposite Laughton and Olivier was that the latter would often surprise Ustinov in rehearsal, but never in the take. This may suit other actors, but not Peter, who offered a criticism that reveals much about his own technique: 'I'm talking out of turn, but with conviction: the reason why an actor like Larry Olivier seems old-fashioned now is that he did exactly what he rehearsed. I think that actors ideally have to take themselves by surprise up to a point, and go one step further than rehearsing, and although they have rehearsed they must give the impression that what they're doing is actually happening for the first time. With improvisation that's inevitable.'

It is of course also true that not all actors could respond like Charles Laughton to his gift for improvisation on camera.

As the Olivier/Laughton feud simmered on, Peter constantly found himself in the middle, trying to keep the peace, as he had friendly relations with both parties. But the mistrust went too deep, even if the civilities were preserved. When Olivier heard that Laughton was also joining the Shakespeare Memorial Company in 1959, he came in and said, 'Charles, dear boy, I know you're going to do *King Lear* in Stratford, and I've made a little diagram of the areas in which you cannot be heard on the stage.'

'Oh, how kind you are, thank you very much, Larry, I shan't forget that in a hurry.'

The moment Olivier left the room, Laughton turned to Ustinov and hissed, 'I'm sure these are the only areas from which you *can* be heard!'

But it was the difference of opinion between Dalton Trumbo and Stanley Kubrick that caused the long overrun on the schedule. After the director produced his first rough assembly, the screen-writer wrote an eighty-page critique, which argued the need for a full-scale battle at the end and a consequent number of extra scenes. The battle itself was eventually shot in Spain and the rest in Hollywood. It was worth it in the end, as *Spartacus* was a great success in many countries, especially Russia. It received a number of Academy Award Nominations, but the only Oscar-winner for acting in it was Peter Ustinov as Best Supporting Actor. He received a telegram from Laurence Olivier, saying, 'Thank you for having supported me so well.' This became a running joke between them.

Later on they were both nominated for an Emmy Award, Olivier for *The Moon and Sixpence* and Ustinov for playing Socrates in *Barefoot in Athens*. The latter was working in New York at the time, but Olivier was in London, so he sent a telegram to the Academy of Television Arts and Sciences, apologising for his absence from the ceremony and stating that if he won, he would like Peter Ustinov to accept the award for him.

When Peter was announced as the winner, he began by saying, 'Unfortunately I've got nothing ready, because I didn't anticipate this, but I have a speech I prepared for Sir Laurence Olivier in case he won, which I will now give you.'

Stanley Kubrick's career went from strength to strength after *Spartacus,* but he and Peter never worked together again, despite having got on so well during the shooting of that film. After the director died nearly forty years later, Peter was amazed when Mrs Kubrick insisted that he should accept her husband's posthumous British Film Directors' Award on his behalf, because Kubrick had never made any attempt to contact him in the intervening period. Peter had watched his career with great interest, but he had not known that the director had also followed his very closely.

Mrs Kubrick now told him that her husband had never missed a Ustinov TV appearance; he would always collect the family round him and say, 'Now we're going to watch this.' Peter told her, 'Well, I never wanted to disturb him, because I'd read that he'd become a sort of recluse. I have great respect for that, and I certainly didn't want to be the noise from the next room that disturbed him. I'd much rather leave him alone and admire him from far away.'

She said, 'Yes, but he had exactly the same impression of you. He felt you didn't really want to be haunted by things from the past and that you were on your own way, and must be allowed to do that.'

So out of a sense of mutual respect they never got in touch with each other, which Peter now much regrets. 'Suzanne and his wife Christiane were both pregnant at the same time, and both booked into the Cedars of Lebanon Hospital. I couldn't remember who had won the race, until I took Andrea along to a ceremony, and she met Kubrick's daughter, and I had apparently won by four days. It was a very touching reunion, without Stanley unfortunately.'

The long *Spartacus* experience was important to him, not just for the Oscar, but for the time and incentive it gave him to write his first full-length novel, *The Loser*. It tells the story of Hans Winterschild, a convinced Nazi, who is decorated for bravery in action in Poland and is then posted to the Italian front. He falls in love with an Italian prostitute and takes part in a German reprisal against the partisans, massacring civilians in a small village.

The narrative is told both from the German and the Italian point of view, although the author's sympathies are clear: 'The story of San Rocco al Monte soon became known as an example of the Italian capacity for martyrdom in comprehensible and fundamental causes. It was only when the reason for death was tinged with doubt, only when the cessation of life seemed even in the minutest degree unnecessary, that the Italians preferred surrender, and the hazardous joys of survival. It would be unfair to their inherent bravery to say that they cling desperately to life; fairer to say that life clings desperately, and lovingly, to them.'

After the German surrender, Hans stays on in Italy under a false identity and bizarrely finds himself playing a German private in the American film, re-creating the atrocity at San Rocco al Monte. Here the tragi-comedy descends into black farce and confirms this writer's view that the filming sequence would be the high-spot of a most atmospheric movie based on the novel. There was talk of making one, which sadly came to nothing.

By the time *The Loser* was published in 1961, the author had been sufficiently frustrated by his first experience of 'digesting the same meal twice' with his film of *Romanoff and Juliet* to have no heart for attempting to film this first novel himself. In any case, he was already busy with other films and a new play, not to mention the strains of moving his place of residence to Switzerland.

He had enjoyed living in Ellen Terry's old house in the King's Road in Chelsea, though interestingly he was less impressed by her previous occupancy than that of Thomas Arne, who had composed 'Rule Britannia' whilst living there. But when they returned to England after *Spartacus* finished, Suzanne persuaded Peter to give up living in the land of his birth. There were pressing financial reasons for doing so, as the tax rates were punitive for authors as prolific as Noël Coward and Peter Ustinov.

They began their Swiss life in a rented chalet in Villars-sur-Ollon, but Peter found the high altitude made him drowsy. They tried a permanent suite in a Montreux hotel, which was even less agreeable. Finally, in desperation he bought a plot of land in the intriguingly named Les Diablerets and commissioned the building of a chalet there.

The tax incentive no longer exists, as international performers are taxed where they work, instead of where they live, but he says, 'Now that I'm there, I wouldn't leave it for anything. It's a wonderful part of the world, and the Swiss themselves are a very lovable and peculiar people. They suspect each other, and dislike each other, and write hostile things about each other in their newspapers, based on language and regional issues. As soon as anybody attacks them, they all become Swiss, which is very civilised; and as a counterbalance to the thin-lipped bankers, it's a nation that has produced more clowns than any other country in the world. All the great clowns – like Grock, Dmitri, and modern clowns too – are Swiss.'

But the first months of living there were difficult for him, as the marriage was beginning to show signs of strain. Suzanne had tried his patience by constantly finding fault with a stream of different nannies; when they took a furnished flat in Paris and he needed a secretary, he soon found that the turnover in secretaries was just as disconcerting and inconvenient. So it was with some relief that he took off to Australia to play an eccentric English remittance man in *The Sundowners*, directed by Fred Zinnemann.

He admired the director's talent and integrity, although he could be so demanding that there were moments during the strenuous shoot when Peter felt it was like doing a stint in the Foreign Legion. He had to do a lot of his scenes on horseback, and the Australian horses were a bit too wild for him. When the director said, 'Ride your horse into the fire,' Peter demurred.

'I'll never be able to handle it, the horse won't go into it.'

Zinnemann scoffed, 'It's funny, some actors don't have the same integrity as others. When I did *From Here to Eternity*, I asked Monty Clift to learn to play the bugle and he did.'

Peter retorted, 'This isn't *at all* the same thing. Ask me to play a bugle and I'll learn it if I can, but I don't think even Monty Clift could manage to ride a horse *into* a fire.'

So a double was brought in to do the stunt, but he also failed to make the horse go into the fire.

On another occasion the director lost his temper with Peter because he went through his part smoking a cigarette. Zinnemann tore it out of Peter's mouth and threw it away, so violently that he cut Peter's lip, saying, 'You can't work with that in your mouth.'

Peter, restraining his anger, said, 'No, *you* can't work with that in my mouth, and why don't you ask me to remove it, rather than tearing it out like that?'

The other two stars were Robert Mitchum as the sheep-shearer, with a very convincing Australian accent, and Deborah Kerr as his wife. She had loved working with Peter on *Quo Vadis* and enjoyed it even more in this film, for 'his enormous talent – as well as his unique brand of wit and his amazing sense of fun'.

The three of them got on well, and they all rose to the demands of the script. Peter was 'amazed how much strength I had then, because I had to carry Mitchum over my shoulder across a street, and he was a very big man, while being attacked by a dog who was trying to bite my ankles. That was the kind of technique that Fred Zinnemann took for granted.'

Because they were in the Outback for a long time, they were each given a little rented house to stay in. Peter's was owned by a German immigrant family called Schutt. He forgot its address, so he said to the taxi driver, 'I don't know where I live, but it's down that long street, towards the end of it.'

'You know the owner's name?'

'Yes, I think it belongs to a German family called Schutt.'

'Ah yes, the Shithouse, I know where that is.'

Peter was captivated by the beautiful film that Zinnemann created, 'a Western without gunfire, but with human problems unsugared and devoid of artificial colouring'.

In retrospect, his admiration for Zinnemann's integrity of purpose and refusal to compromise over the script was heightened by his own experience of the battle with the studio to bring *Billy Budd* unsugared to the screen.

Eleven

1961–1962
Billy Budd, Photo Finish,
and first steps in opera

Herman Melville's novel *Billy Budd, Foretopman* had been dramatised for the stage by two other American writers, Louis O. Coxe and Robert H. Chapman, and Peter based his screenplay on both texts. He also directed and produced the film, adding that he reluctantly played the part of Captain Vere as well, 'because I was the only actor I could get at the price'.

The budget for the whole film was less than $1 million, but he managed to assemble a remarkably impressive cast, which included Paul Rogers, John Neville, Cyril Luckham, David McCallum, Niall McGinnis, Lee Montague, and Ray McAnally. Peter originally cast that extraordinary actor Wilfrid Lawson as the Dansker; he had actually flown out to join the company in Spain when the insurance company got cold feet about his reputation for heavy drinking and refused to insure him in case he fell into the sea.

Shooting was about to begin, so Peter acted swiftly in the face of this crisis. He heard that Melvyn Douglas had retired and was taking a holiday in Spain; so he drove up from Alicante and found the old actor on the beach. His powers of persuasion worked, and Melvyn Douglas said, 'Well, just the one last fling.'

For the embodiment of evil as Claggart, he got the Hollywood star Robert Ryan, but by far the biggest problem was whom to cast in the title role as the spirit of innocence. He was determined that it should be an unknown actor, to make the greatest impact on the audience, and that search took quite a time. The American company, Allied Artists, which was financing the film, was exceedingly nervous about Peter's insistence and never really got used to the idea.

After screen-testing a number of young actors, he found Terence Stamp; the more nervous he became, the more he convinced the director that he was perfect for the part. The clincher was the improvisation that Peter asked him to do – to react silently while being harangued in the manner of Claggart. Peter stood behind the camera and accused him of all sorts of crimes he had not committed, while the emotions welled up in the young man. When the film ran out the director dropped his Claggart voice for his own and said, 'Thank you. That was ... tumultuous.'

The following day, in the Ustinov suite at the Connaught, Suzanne told him that Peter was determined to take him for the part. 'But you will have to be patient, it is not easy to convince the studio to take an unknown, especially an English. It may take time.'

It took so long that he had almost given up hope, when Peter rang to apologise for the delay and confirmed that he was to play Billy Budd. 'Then that adventure began. He took a gamble on me and' – unknowingly echoing Michael Anderson's gratitude – 'that movie changed my life for ever.'

It began by changing his appearance. The cameraman Robert Krasker suggested he had his hair dyed blond, as Peter was making the film in black and white for greater realism. Krasker had been the lighting cameraman on Peter's first major film, *One of Our Aircraft is Missing*, as well as on *Romanoff and Juliet*, and his string of credits included *The Third Man* with its masterly use of light and shadow.

Terence Stamp had never been abroad before, and the smallpox vaccination made him feel quite ill, so the Ustinovs took him into the spare room in their rented apartment in Alicante. He saw little of the other actors off the ship and nothing at all of Robert Ryan until they had their first meeting of the film. 'It wasn't until the movie came out that I realised he had done me this extraordinary favour, because he'd kept it like it was supposed to be. He didn't know whether I could act or not, and Robert Ryan gave me an extremely wide berth, so that when we did our big scene, which was done in long takes, it was just wonderful what Robert did, and I couldn't help but respond in the correct way. It would have been different if Robert Ryan had been chummy.'

HMS *Avenger* is sailing against Napoleon at the time of the Spithead mutiny and stops a merchant ship, *The Rights of Man*, to press-gang more crew. Billy Budd is the only sailor young and fit enough to be taken, and his innocent and sunny disposition soon wins the hearts of the tough naval crew, both officers and men; all except the dark and brooding master-at-arms, Mr Claggart.

The seeds of his jealous hatred of the new young recruit are planted at their very first meeting, and it is a crucial scene in the film. So Terence Stamp knew that this was his first big test. 'We came up to do the take, and it was absolutely right, there was a strange emotional upheaval, and then something sailed into the frame. The cameraman called out, "No, no, sorry, stop," and I couldn't do anything. This emotion was in place, and I moved away from the set-up and just burst into tears. Then I was really embarrassed and hiding in corners. Ustinov saw this and came over to me and said, "What is it?"

'I said, "I won't be able to do it again."

'He said, "You will be able to do it again. We're here until you're ready."

'There aren't many directors in the world that are tuned that finely. I've since worked with Wyler, and Fellini, and Soderbergh, but great dictators who have that level of sensitivity are rare. These days I work with many first-time directors who don't know anything about acting and the acting process, where the better you are the less visible it is.'

As writer and director, Peter was attuned not just to the needs of the actors, but to those of the audience too. 'Dramatically it's impossible to have somebody who is purely evil or purely good, and I thought when I wrote it, how can I make these symbols work? So I had that big scene on deck where they were tempted by each other's point of view. Eventually it's Claggart who breaks it off, saying, "What am I doing here, talking to you?" Funnily enough, when I analysed it later, it was very similar to the scene in *The Love of Four Colonels*, where the Good Fairy and the Wicked Fairy suddenly get together after all these years and are about to kiss, when the Wicked Fairy breaks off and says, "No, that will never do, it will torpedo the world if we do that." '

Terence Stamp's flatmate Michael Caine had stressed to him the importance of the big close-up shot, but Peter advised him not to go to see the rushes when they came back from processing in England: 'Because you've never made a movie, you couldn't help but just look at yourself, while I am looking at everything. So I'd rather you didn't do it, because it may interfere with what you're doing.'

Stamp took his director's advice, but when the rushes of his big scene arrived in Alicante he was downcast when nobody said anything to him about it. The next day he was not on call, and everyone else had left on the ship at 5.30 a.m. as usual. It was Suzanne who reassured him when she came across him alone and miserable in the restaurant. 'Listen, this is Peter Ustinov. Believe me, if he hasn't said anything, it's fine, because if it wasn't fine he would be doing something about it.'

Filming at sea brings additional logistical and technical problems. The vessel used was in the hands of a famous sailor called Alan Villiers who specialised in old sailing ships, but his Spanish orders were incomprehensible to both the English and Spanish crews, so the ship went all over the place. This infuriated Paul Rogers, who had served as a naval officer during the war and who once threatened, 'I'm not going to travel again on this ship, not under this captaincy.'

The film union chief, Jimmy Ridley, complained, 'The condition of the toilets on board is quite frankly not up to our standard.' A few days later he reluctantly threw down the union gauntlet.

'I'm sorry, Peter, the boys are going on strike.'

'Why? Not the toilets again?'

'Yes, it's the toilets. We've heard unofficially that two of the Spanish boys have gone sick with the crabs. So that's it, I'm afraid, I can't convince the boys any further. They're not going out until something is done.'

Luckily this exchange was overheard by the chief of the Spanish union, who erupted, 'What are you telling? You are deliberately poisoning the atmosphere between the two company working very well together. It's not true that two of our boys have gone sick with the crabs. What's true is that two have gone sick with gonorrhoea.'

This reassured Jimmy. 'Ah, I didn't know that. That's different, that's to do with the digestion, innit?'

The more intimate dialogue scenes were shot back at Shepperton on the main studio set, where the boat had been reconstructed on rockers, which made quite a noise in operation. Peter ran some test film, which revealed that it produced exactly the noise of a sailing ship in motion. It did, however, make it tricky getting the reverse angles right, 'and on one or two occasions we had to simulate it. Robert Ryan was wonderful, because he was addressing the crew, and they all swayed, following him. He was terribly good at accepting improvised disciplines of that sort, when I explained it.'

During his research for the film, Peter came across a sea-shanty of the time, 'They call me Hanging Johnny', which Antony Hopkins used in his music score. The two men were agreed that the film did not need great sweeps of background music. For the composer, 'The text was so good, that you could write music almost like doing an operatic score. You could write a piece of music, leave a hole for some dialogue, then pick it up, like having six bars of recitative. The Britten opera didn't impinge at all; I'd only heard the music once and didn't like it.'

Despite that musical divergence, Terence Stamp says, 'I often get stopped in the street by singers, who tell me that the film was definitive; the young baritones when they take on Billy Budd are advised to go and see the movie. He nailed the substance of it.'

But having nailed it, the real battle began, to preserve it unspoilt. Allied Artists were dismayed that Billy Budd was hanged after a court martial for accidentally killing Claggart and pressed for a happy ending, which they said would be more commercially successful. Peter tried irony. 'Yes, well, of course *The Greatest Story Ever Told* would be much better with a happy ending and no crucifixion!'

ABC in England suggested adding stock footage from other films about pirates, but Peter outwitted them with the unexpected help of the British film censor, John Trevelyan, who found out that Rank would distribute it, but only if ABC refused it and they did not have to fight for it. 'So the Censor gave it initially an X Certificate, and ABC dropped it like a hot brick. Then he said, "Cut out one whiplash and we'll make it Parental Guidance." So I cut out one whiplash, and it was immediately available for Rank. Trevelyan helped me a great deal.'

The first time Terence Stamp saw any of the film was at the première in the Odeon, Leicester Square. 'I was just astonished. When I realised the quality of the people I was up there with, those major actors, I thought it was a kind of masterpiece.'

He was not alone in that. In an article he wrote at the time, Peter said he had been more successful in fighting his way through to his own heart than ever before. One reaction that especially pleased him came at the Boston Film Festival, where he was told the husband of Herman Melville's only surviving daughter attended the screening. She was too old and sick to go herself, but Peter heard that she had been satisfied, from her husband's description of the film, that he had done justice to her father's work.

It was a critical success in Britain, where Dilys Powell perceptively noted in the *Sunday Times* the difficulty that Peter faced in casting the title role: 'An experienced young actor might not persuade; his familiarity to us might well defeat him. Mr Ustinov took the bold step of casting a boy unknown to the screen, Terence Stamp . . . and boldness was rewarded. Terence Stamp has everything the role asks: the candid look, the air of trust, gallantry, in short goodness. His performance is miraculous.'

This praise did not lead to the film breaking any box-office records in the UK, but it did better on both fronts in North America, largely because of the promotional tour that Peter made, accompanied by Terence Stamp. It got off to a bizarre start in Chicago. When a curvaceous blonde turned up, Peter asked, 'What's she doing here?'

'Peter, she's cheesecake in case we need it.'

121

Terence Stamp found the whole experience hysterical. 'These guys would meet us at the airport, and they would be the local reps of the film company; it didn't take us long to realise that they were all identical and interchangeable; so just for my benefit Peter would have conversations, calling them by the names of the last ones we'd met. I had the most fun time with him.'

Peter's tenacity in fighting for the movie he wanted to make resulted in what most critics also regard as his masterpiece, and its reputation has grown in the years since 1962. He is still approached by people who have been greatly affected by the film. Not long ago a woman in Canada said to him, 'There was a wonderful moment when Billy was about to be executed, and all the officers were going up the stairs, and you took a piece of lint off the clothing of one officer. That meant a great deal to me, at this solemn moment fixing something absolutely insignificant and stupid.'

Peter told her: 'I had terrible arguments with the film company, who wanted to cut that out. "What purpose is it serving, Peter? The lint-picking scene?"'

But it was the reaction of the American director of publicity that most irritated Peter. *Time*, the influential news magazine with the widest circulation across the USA, gave *Billy Budd* a rave review. Instead of being as thrilled as its director, this man said to him, 'Oh Jesus, don't say we got a good notice in *Time* magazine. That's the kiss of death.'

More recently, the Swiss Discothèque had a retrospective of all Peter's old films and began with *Billy Budd*, which the Swiss had never seen before. It was received with a minute's silence at the end, with nobody moving, and then suddenly a riot of applause that lasted for a long time – a standing ovation. Peter was very happy that the film had survived the years and was able to affect people. Then a man came up to him with a great amount of hair and a ring in his ear, a middle-aged man in blue jeans and a T-shirt, with filthy bare feet in sandals, saying, 'Peter, I want to shake your hand. I just want to thank you for having changed the course of my life. Because when I first saw the movie it resolved me to desert from the United States Armed Forces and go to spend the

Vietnam War in Canada. I just want to thank you for showing me the way and giving me a reason to change the whole course of my life. God bless you for that, Peter, I can never forget that.'

The cultural effect of the film in the United States is now assured, because many American universities use videotapes of the film as part of their literature courses. Melville's book is in the pantheon of American classics, and so too is the Ustinov film of it.

There were other more personal results of that film. For John Neville, 'a treasured memory for me was meeting Robert Ryan, a great American actor who always did one stage play a year. Our friendship led to him coming to Nottingham, where I invited him to play Othello, and Tyrone in *Long Day's Journey into Night*.'

Neville was the first Director of the new Nottingham Playhouse, and in 1964 he invited Peter Ustinov to join him as Associate Director. Their collaboration would bear theatrical fruit rewarding to both of them in years to come.

This was also the case for Paul Rogers. By the time *Billy Budd* was released he was sharing the stage of the Saville Theatre with Peter in his new play, *Photo Finish*. Having gone backwards in time with *The Banbury Nose*, this time Peter straddled the years by showing Sam, an eighty-year-old popular novelist now writing his memoirs, confronted by himself aged sixty, forty and twenty. The four ages of Sam were played, in descending order, by Peter Ustinov, Wensley Pithey, Robert Brown, and Edward Hardwicke. Paul Rogers played Sam's hypocritical father, Reginald Kinsale, and Diana Wynyard was Sam's wife Stella, moving from youthful gaiety to implacably hostile old age.

The physical resemblance of the four Sams was important if the audience were to accept this theatrical conjuring trick. The beard for all three older Sams helped, but there was a lot of advance measuring of profiles first and, in Paul Rogers' graphic phrase, 'The common denominator was the hooter.' (When Edward Albee tried the same theatrical trick in his play *Three Tall Women* three decades later, the suspension of disbelief was much harder because the physical resemblance between the three actresses who played the character in London was not so marked.)

Two other figures from the *Billy Budd* crew were involved in the play. Robert Brown (the forty-year-old Sam) had played an Able Seaman in the movie, and Don Ashton, who designed the film, was also responsible for the stage-set.

Since Sam Old was hardly ever off stage, Peter decided he needed a co-director out front, in the same way that he had asked Michael Anderson to be his eye behind the camera in *Private Angelo*. Peter Daubeny was presenting the play, and he introduced the author to a young man named Nicholas Garland, now the chief cartoonist for the *Daily Telegraph*, but then an aspiring director who had worked at the Cheltenham and Birmingham Repertory Companies and the Royal Court.

Paul Rogers and Diana Wynyard were cast by invitation, but there were auditions for the other roles. As Nicholas Garland had worked with Edward Hardwicke before, he suggested he came along to read for the part of Sam's son. Having already appeared in *The Empty Chair* at Bristol, Edward needed no encouragement to audition for another Ustinov play. 'I went to meet Peter and read, and he said, "Why doesn't he play Sam Young?" When Nick asked me, "Which part would you rather do?" I replied rather cheekily, "Well, can't I do both?" He said, "You're on."'

The conditions of Peter's tax exile limited him to just ninety days a year residence in England, so the play was rehearsed and premièred in Dublin. When the company arrived it was bitterly cold and snowing.

Edward Hardwicke cherishes two vivid memories of those early days. 'My first recollection of Peter was sitting in the rehearsal room, when he suddenly burst through the doors with a collection of the most beautiful woven Irish blankets, and he stood in the middle of the room, throwing them at Diana Wynyard and the other girls in the cast, as a gift to keep them warm. Diana had a tiny bit of a scene with me when we were both supposed to be about twenty; she was then in her fifties, and Peter thought she was wonderful doing this. He was sitting cross-legged at the end of the rehearsal room, and he said, "I'm going to make this scene bigger." I remember him sitting writing it, literally as long as it took him to write the words, he wrote this scene and just handed it to us.'

REV. DR. RHUBARBT BROWN, BISHOP PEADAR DOHENY REV. DR. WENSLEY PHEATHENY, REV. DR. NEACHOAILOÍN, GARLAOÍN, S.J., FATHER PEADAR O STEANNOIAGHA AND BISHOP PAOÍL RHUGHEAIRE S.J. & BAR ON THEIR WAY TO LOURDES BY AER LINGUS

The *Photo Finish* company en route to Dublin

He gave his young co-director his head and made him feel very confident, intervening quietly now and again with some suggestions if he thought he was directing against the text. 'We were rehearsing a scene Peter was in, and I was directing it up on stage, asking the actors to really underplay it, let the emotion come out of the situation, not through raised voices or any kind of melodrama. Peter got up out of the wheelchair, took me to one side and said, "Why are you so afraid of emotion?"

' "I'm not afraid of emotion."

'He said, "Just give them their heads, let them go a bit." '

Peter's natural tendency on stage is to let go a bit himself with his invention of comic business.

In the later stages of rehearsal it became clear on run-throughs that the play was too long. This worried their manager, who said in Dublin, 'Look, you've just got to take ten minutes off this.' So the co-directors sat down and worked quite late making the necessary cuts. They were rehearsing the new version the following morning when Peter Daubeny came in and asked, 'What are you rehearsing?'

Nicholas Garland replied, 'We're rehearsing these cuts we discussed yesterday.'

'You mean you did the cuts?'

'Yes, they're done, here they are.'

Daubeny was so angry he went white with rage. 'Why didn't you tell me you had done the cuts? All night I've been thinking we've got to have these cuts, all through breakfast, and I come in now and find you actually rehearsing them, and you didn't even think of telling me that you'd done them!'

'Peter, we worked until two o'clock in the morning doing this. We then had to go to get them photocopied and get some sleep. I got up to come and start rehearsing them. Surely the important thing is that they are done. OK?'

Now Nicholas Garland lost his temper, swore at a man he much admired, and stormed out of the auditorium to Ustinov's dressing-room in search of sympathy for what he saw as an unfair reprimand.

All the comfort he got was, 'Oh, Peter, he gets so upset, don't worry about it, forget it.'

Not only did the two Peters' friendship go back to drama school, but the author had been round this circuit before in disputes about the length of his plays and knew that it was probably not the end of the story on this one. Paul Rogers recalled that once they had opened, 'then the embellishments began, and the audience loved it. It was enormous fun but unfortunately the play began to stretch and stretch; after three weeks we'd put on twenty minutes! The stage management and front-of-house people were going out of their minds, because people were beginning to miss their last trains.'

One of the best scenes is between Sam at eighty and his father at sixty, when they talk about Sam's mother. Paul had a line, 'She was always smiling, it used to drive me mad!' It always got a big laugh. One night Peter waited for the laugh to die, then added, 'Yes, you'd have loved to see her smiling at your funeral.' The audience roared and clapped, and a surprised Paul Rogers came as near to corpsing as he ever did.

The off-stage relationship of these two actors was the reverse of their characters' hostility on stage. Their friendship and mutual admiration is very strong, and Paul Rogers has a treasured port-folio of mementoes from their time together in this play. Peter invented a fictional character for Paul and did a series of caricatures of him with real-life actors, two of which are reproduced overleaf. Further sketches from the Ustinov pen were presented to Nicholas Garland and later to Peter Daubeny. (He is as quick with this accomplishment as he is in writing a new page of dialogue; I was astonished by the speed at which he sketched a self-portrait for an admiring waiter who asked for his autograph one evening when we dined together.)

When *Photo Finish* opened, it was clear how much the critics regretted the long absence of Peter Ustinov from the London stage; from Harold Hobson in the *Sunday Times*: 'Paganini or Rastelli can hardly have been more dazzling in technical virtuosity than Mr Ustinov in this play. Mr Ustinov presents us with the utterly impossible, and completely convinces us that the impossible is real'; to W.A. Darlington in the *Daily Telegraph*: 'One of the chief assets in our theatre's treasury, though we see the glint of its gold too seldom, is Peter Ustinov's sure, light touch in his own kind of fantasy ... Like all author-actors, Mr Ustinov gives all his actors good chances, and himself plays the eighty-year-old Sam perfectly.'

Robert Muller echoed the last point in the *Daily Mail*: 'Apart from Mr Ustinov's own golden performance there is ripe playing by Paul Rogers as the father and by Diana Wynyard, highly effective as the terrifying wife.'

J.C. Trewin called it 'absorbing' and 'curiously affecting' in the *Illustrated London News* and judged it 'certainly a play of the year: it would be, I think, a play of any year, though Ustinov might prune a little better. He has long been luxuriant; and it would not harm *Photo Finish* if it were gently and judiciously trimmed.'

His recommendation was acted on after Peter left the cast when his ninety days were up, and Paul Rogers switched parts to play Sam Old. (His substitute as the father was Cyril Luckham, another of the *Billy Budd* cast.) 'When I took over,

JACK HAWKINS AS CHEOPS XII AND
E. MELLORS ROGERS AS THE HIGH PRIEST
PHNUT IN LAND OF THE PHARAOS

E MELLORS ROGERS
APPEARING WITH SIR JOHN AS THE
EIGHTH AGE OF MAN

Nick and I got together and said it could benefit from a snip or two here, and a snip or two there. When Peter came to see it he made no mention of the cuts and just told us I looked exactly like his Uncle Alexandre.'

When the play moved across the Atlantic, the only two actors to go with it were Paul Rogers and Peter; the rest of the new cast were American or Canadian, with Eileen Herlie as the wife. It opened in Boston, and they all thought it went well until the first notice came out in the *Boston Globe*, from the doyen of local critics. He slammed the play and complained about its excessive length.

The two British actors were both staying in the Ritz-Carlton, and Paul recalled what happened next.

'The telephone rang, and I picked it up gingerly. "Paul, are you busy?"

'Was I busy! "No," I said.

' "I wonder if you'd come up."

'So I went up to the top floor and was let into the apartment. It was like a wake, as if a death had occurred. I found a chair very near the door and just sat down. Nothing! It was the most intense atmosphere, I think, to which I've ever been exposed. After a considerable silence Peter said, "Paul ... what were the cuts that you and Nick made in London?"

'I got up, extremely gingerly, walked as silently as I possibly could across the carpet, and sat down beside him and the script. I turned the pages and said, "That ... and that ... and that ..."

'We went right through the script. Then Peter said, "Thank you, thank you very much."

'He took every single cut that Nick and I had worked out. Thank God the *Globe* was the first paper in, because the next was an absolute rave, or we might not have cut anything.'

The tightened production went down well in New York and, despite being hampered by a newspaper strike, did good business. Once again Peter relinquished his part to Paul Rogers before the end of the run. The play was equally successful in France with Bernard Blier as Sam Old, and Philippe Noiret as the father; it was even more so in Germany with Martin Held as Sam. More recently Peter was pleased to see it revived in St Petersburg and also in Switzerland.

Of the foreign productions, he was only involved in the French one, but he began to regret this on the morning of the dress rehearsal.

'We asked the actors to come in only after lunch, to give them a little rest, while we sat and arranged the lighting. I sat there with the stage manager and the director of the switchboard. The curtain rises on a dark stage, nothing lit, and they both wrote down – No. 1. First Cue: black stage.

'The old lady comes in, turns on all the lights, and begins a long monologue to her husband in the wheelchair. Cue No. 2. Then she exits and extinguishes all the lights again.

'The stage manager put down No. 3 and the lighting engineer put 1a. Then the argument started.

' "It's not logical to call it 3, when 3 is the same as 1, and you can't have 1 twice."

'The other one said, "It's not logical to have 1 after 2."

'We went on like this until lunch! We got nothing done at all. The actors began to arrive, and we hadn't got further than that first knot in the string.'

Lighting plots frequently take many hours of work to sort out, but few of them take so long to get past the third cue.

Photo Finish also marked the beginning of a quite different saga that ended by souring Peter's view of the French legal mind. As he celebrated his forty-first birthday during the pre-London tour, Suzanne wanted a special present. She tracked down a 1934 Hispano-Suiza in France and got a French motoring correspondent to drive it to Leeds, parking it outside the stage door with a huge ribbon on it. It was a great surprise and he was thrilled with it.

Since Edward Hardwicke shared Peter's passion for cars, Peter asked him to follow him back to London in his nippy Morgan sports car, in case the enormous vintage car broke down. It was twenty feet long and weighed three tons, one of the only two long-wheelbase versions in the world. The top of the radiator reached nearly to Edward's chin. 'It did nine miles to the gallon, and he went very fast, I had a job keeping up with him. When it backfired, it sounded as if he was breaking the sound barrier.'

Peter loved that car, but it was too big to keep shipping around with him, so he stored it in a lock-up garage near Nice. It was stolen in 1989, and he spent £120,000 on private detectives, tracking it down. The thieves had it resprayed and sold it to a French industrialist for £50,000. The French judge sent the robbers to jail but decided that the car could not be returned as the new owner had bought it in good faith. The legal saga only ended in 1999, when the French Court of Appeal ruled that the statute of limitations had now expired, so Peter could not have his car back.

After the verdict Peter observed bitterly, 'I wasn't optimistic about French law because Bonaparte changed it to justify his own thefts. And the French don't like anyone other than a Frenchman owning the best car they ever made. I was described in court as a thrice-married Hollywood star – me, a member of the Académie Française! Molière always made fun of French lawyers; now I know why.'

There have been other fast cars in his life and more than one personal drama connected to them, but none of them has occupied the place in his affections of that birthday present from his wife forty years ago.

For Peter 1962 was a year of extraordinary professional triumph, with the release of *Billy Budd* and the opening of *Photo Finish*. He was also invited by Sir Georg Solti to direct opera for the first time. It was a challenging prospect – three one-act operas for a triple bill in three different languages, with just five weeks' rehearsal, and on his own matinée days Peter could only rehearse in the mornings.

His greatest problems were with the three different designers. For Puccini's *Gianni Schicchi* the Italian Signior Clerici 'did it all on steps, with chests of drawers coming out of them, so it looked like a kind of mad, medieval house, and Joan Carlyle, who sang the famous aria, said, "I really can't kneel on all these steps, I'm pregnant."'

The French designer for Ravel's *L'Heure Espagnole* was Monsieur Jean-Pierre Ponnelle, 'who never came at all, but just sent a very rough sketch, because he was too busy working on *Kiss Me Kate* in Düsseldorf. I had to sit in Covent Garden all day Sunday, designing grandfather clocks big enough to get a man inside and transport him upstairs. I'd never had such a challenge in my life.'

The German designer for Schoenberg's *Erwartung* was Herr Schneider-Siemssen. Amy Shuard was a better singer than actress, so Peter had the set moving round her, with lots of slide projections. This designer delivered, 'but he asked for four thousand volts from the fire brigade for his projections. Unfortunately, he'd done all the slides on breakable glass, so they all cracked with far less than four thousand volts. I've never seen a grown man in tears to that extent. I told him, "Well, actually it looks much more abstract with the cracks." He said, "You're right." '

The press seemed to agree, saying that *Erwartung* was exactly the sort of work the Royal Opera House should be doing. Peter never managed to see any performances with an audience because of his stage commitments.

The year ended with a personal loss that affected him much more than he might have expected a few years earlier.

Twelve

1962–1966
From the loss of Klop
to *The Comedians*

The relationship between father and son was often strained in the early years because of Peter's resentment of the way Klop treated Nadia. It was not just his extramarital affairs but also the peremptory way he treated his wife's work that aroused Peter's ire. 'She did a wonderful free improvisation in a Japanese style, which I thought was marvellous, and when I got home from drama school it was no longer there. She had destroyed it because he said, "I think it is not worthy of you." I was furious, it was one of the best things she ever did. I treated him as though he were an enemy very often, because he was so quarrelsome and so absurd.'

Klop found it difficult to hold down a job. When Peter formed his own company for tax reasons in the 1950s, he made his father a director. But Klop never really understood what was going on and would relay messages from Peter's agents, Linnit and Dunfee, as 'You've had a phone call from Dunnit and Fifi.'

Klop worked for MI5 during the war and was listed in the Gestapo Black Book of enemies to be liquidated when they occupied Britain. When Peter read their description of Klop – 'Dangerous element, journalist, works for the British, goes under the name of Middleton-Pendleton' – he thought it was like something created by P.G. Wodehouse.

For a while after the war his parents had separate homes in London and the Cotswolds, but when Peter was away filming *Spartacus* in Hollywood, they moved into his house in Chelsea to look after it. In 1957 he and Nadia decided, to Peter's astonishment, to move permanently to the Cotswolds, and they found a house at Eastleach. They had no car and no telephone, until Klop began having heart problems, when Peter begged them to have a telephone installed so they could keep in closer touch. He arranged a car to drive them over to Paris to see the children and another later all the way to their home in Montreux. He and Suzanne visited them at Eastleach when they could. In those last few years the tensions between father and son seemed gradually to drop away.

In September 1962 Peter came out of the cast of *Photo Finish* and planned to go to America in December to prepare for the Broadway production. It was clear to him and his mother that Klop's heart condition was now very serious, so he gave her his itinerary for the period that he would be in the South of France.

His father had once confided to him during a wartime air raid, 'I won't live to be seventy.'

'Why not?'

'Because I know that I won't be enjoying myself any more, I won't be able to do some of the things I did in the past and enjoyed, and I shall be on a downhill slope. I see no reason why I should go on living, I hate the idea of that.'

At the time Peter thought this attitude ridiculous, especially as they could both have been killed at any moment, but now he was concerned that his father's prediction might come true. His seventieth birthday was due on 2 December.

Klop was so weak by November that he took to his bed. On the 29th, he asked Nadia, 'Weren't you expecting Peter today?'

'No, but would you like to see him?'

'Well, as a matter of fact, I would like to see him.'

'He will be going away for six months and it would be nice to see him before he goes.'

'Yes.'

'Would you like me to ring him up?'

'But I don't want to inconvenience him.'

'All right, I'll try, and I'm sure he will do his best to come.'

She called Peter in Paris, who rang half an hour later to say he was catching the four o'clock plane from Paris; he picked up a hire-car at the airport and was on the doorstep at Eastleach by

7.30 p.m. When Peter went into the bedroom, Klop whispered, 'We must have champagne.' He had only a tiny sip himself and then just held his son's hand in silence. He was now visibly failing. The next day, 'my father woke out of his coma for a moment, looked at me and said in French, "Oh hello, I recognise you from my dreams." That was the last thing he ever said to me. He died about five or six hours before his seventieth birthday, like a Roman; he didn't have to cut his veins and sit in a bath, he just willed himself not to go on living, in some mysterious way.'

Peter stayed with his mother until the cremation on 4 December. The funeral surprised him. 'All sorts of moustached gentlemen that I had never met turned up, old colleagues from MI5, and they all spoke highly of him.' The one part of his life about which Klop had been most reticent was his wartime heroism against the Nazis, the true extent of which has only come out in the last few years.

After the funeral Peter had to return to France before sailing to America a couple of days later. Following his recent successes on stage and screen, he was now in great demand for both. Peter Hall tried to woo him into going to Stratford-upon-Avon to play Falstaff in both parts of *Henry IV*; not only did he admire him as an actor, but he was also convinced that Ustinov had been influential in recommending him for his first job as a director – at the Arts Theatre in succession to John Fernald.

The Hall offer was gently declined in a letter from New York: 'I really think I am too bound up in the fortunes of Nottingham to betray that new threat to the artistic conscience of the nation.' But that was only part of the reason for his refusal.

Sheridan Morley has lamented 'one of the theatre's great lost Falstaffs', but that eagerness to see him in the part is not shared by the actor himself. 'Falstaff always seems to me like what are known as great English eccentrics, but I don't much care for great English eccentrics. Falstaff is a man who is moving at times but deeply annoying at others.'

He was also now offered the chance to create on film one of the great French eccentrics – Inspector Clouseau. He was not very keen on the script anyway, but then they changed his proposed leading lady from Ava Gardner to Capucine. 'I knew Capucine and I had no great faith in her acting abilities, so I said no, and they sued me. The case went on for ever. They didn't win, but then Peter Sellers got the role, and immediately afterwards I was offered the one he'd abandoned.'

This was in *Topkapi*, directed by Jules Dassin and co-starring his wife Melina Mercouri. Peter is a little wary of husband-and-wife teams and was not convinced that she was correctly cast in this film. 'It was very hard to imagine that I was deeply in love with that woman and would do anything for her. I don't think she was an actress at all in some ways; she knew what she was doing but saw herself as a kind of Marlene Dietrich in that film.'

He couldn't help teasing her. When they were in Istanbul she said, 'Really it's tragic that there are only nine million of us and thirty million of the Turks.'

'Yes, you're quite right, the world would be a much more restful place if there were twenty-one million Turks and none of you.'

She immediately rose to the bait and ran at him with her nails bared, as if she would scratch his eyes out.

His relations were better with his male co-stars, Robert Morley and Akim Tamiroff, both of whom had acted with him before. The latter played the Russian Ambassador in the film of *Romanoff and Juliet* and had at one time been a member of the Moscow Art Theatre. Peter found him fun to work with, 'but he was uncontrollable, mad as a hatter. He never stopped acting. When you said "Action" it didn't mean anything, except that he just continued talking. He was very over the top.' But he lit up the screen, and the Tamiroff/Ustinov scenes have the magnetism of the Laughton/Ustinov ones in *Spartacus*, with the same result – Peter won his second Oscar for Best Supporting Actor.

Topkapi was what film critics like to call 'a heist movie', and the story involved the theft of jewels from the famous Topkapi Palace Museum, but its interest lies in the comic relationships of the characters. These were more successfully realised than in his next film for Twentieth Century-Fox, *John Goldfarb, Please Come Home*.

He accepted this for the opportunity to appear with Shirley

MacLaine, with whom he dearly wanted to work. But he was unhappy with the film itself and began to feel that screen comedy as he knew it was beginning to lose its way. The film was released in 1964, the year that he began his association with the new Nottingham Playhouse under John Neville's leadership.

Neville pioneered the repertoire system, with several plays alternating through the week, which was then only practised by companies the size of the RSC and the National Theatre. He opened with *Coriolanus*, *The Importance of Being Earnest*, and the world première of a new Ustinov play, *The Life in My Hands*. John Neville was very conscious that this was an ambitious way to launch a new playhouse in the provinces and was enormously grateful for the presence and support of his new Associate Director. 'Peter was a huge international star and of course his name helped, also his talent and his generosity. Peter, typically generously, took NO royalties!'

The play portrays the case of a young man who rapes a fifteen-year-old mental defective, who subsequently dies. The issue of capital punishment is debated through the characters of a journalist, the minister with the power to grant a reprieve, and the minister's own son; the roles were played respectively by George Selway, Leo McKern, and Ian McKellen. The play received a mixed reception, but the performances were applauded, with Harold Hobson writing in the *Sunday Times*: 'Ian McKellen turns on a spirited flow of fervent declamation.'

The author warmed to this actor too, commenting after watching him in rehearsal, 'I found him putting inflections into speeches which I, as the playwright, had not even thought of. It was an illuminating experience.'

Peter had written the play because he always felt strongly about the arbitrary nature of the death sentence, and he spent quite a lot of time and money trying to influence people over the Bentley case. He sent a four-page telegram to the Home Secretary, Sir David Maxwell-Fyfe, arguing the impossibility of Bentley's guilt and denouncing the ignominy of the death sentence. 'I never got an acknowledgment. That really got under my skin. I was furious and resentful, which surprised me about myself.'

The play has had no further life in Britain but has been frequently revived in Germany, where there is no death penalty. Its subsequent abolition has taken the steam out of this issue in the UK, but *The Life in My Hands* retains its place in the affections of the author.

The challenge facing all the serious Ustinov plays is that of audience expectation – they want his comic genius so much that they feel disappointed when he deploys the other weapons in his dramatic armoury. But he has never left audiences wanting for long, and he used his improvisational skills to great effect on BBC Television in a programme entitled *Ustinov Ad Lib*, with two musician-collaborators, Antony Hopkins and Dudley Moore.

In the tradition of his radio series *In All Directions*, Peter created everything on the day in the studio – the songs, the interviews conducted by Bernard Keeffe, and the cartoons he swiftly sketched between the items. Antony Hopkins, who was attuned to his wavelength from their previous film work together, improvised different scores in the style of composers of different nationalities, as well as singing other parts from the piano. In American accents they sang a song from an 'unknown Menotti opera', with Hopkins as the daughter and Ustinov as the mother; a Debussy song in French; another supposedly from *Canute* by Purcell, as two counter-tenors; and the best was a mock-Schubert piece, 'The Maiden and the Halibut', sung in German. Peter's inspiration for it was the great lieder-singer, Dietrich Fischer-Dieskau, and he introduced it in a heavy German accent, saying, 'Zis is a recently discovered song with words by Eischendorff, and it's a girl who is walking in ze countryside, and it's green and it's springtime, and she is suddenly seeing in ze water, in ze estuary, a halibut, and she says, "Oh, it reminds me I am hungry, and I would like to eat ze halibut," and ze halibut answers, "Don't do that, because if you eat me, you will feel ill."'

'And she eats ze halibut and feels ill.'

In the interviews between the music, Peter assumed various roles: a Soviet music professor, describing playing on collective farms to animals and tractors; a German composer of electronic music: 'Music to be memorable must be disagreeable'; and an avant-garde American composer: 'There are four suites making this triptych' (which got an audible laugh from the camera crew). His own favourite was the old and very deaf Sir Banbury Cross, speaking in a high-pitched, cut-glass English accent: 'I've written two books – *The Elgar I Knew* and *The Elgar who Knew Me* – and I think *The Elgar who Knew Me* was the more successful of the two since I fancy he knew me rather better than I knew him.'

The television audience was also treated to one of his party pieces, where he mimed a cello solo to a vocal accompaniment so authentically that if you closed your eyes you were convinced the sound was coming from a real instrument instead of his mouth.

The second half of the programme had Dudley Moore at the piano, which was less successful because he tried to compete for laughs instead of following Peter's lead as Hopkins had done. It needed the right partner to pull off such a freewheeling trick, as Peter found again much later. 'For my eightieth birthday celebration I did the same thing, but with Barenboim. He was cautious and competent, but nothing like Hopkins. He said, "I can't improvise, I've got to have a score."

'I said, "The whole point is not to have one, let yourself go." '

The chemistry between performers is crucial to success on concert platform, stage or screen, and the lack of it caused Peter a number of problems on his next film.

MGM had owned the rights to *Lady L* for a long time and originally planned it as a vehicle for Gina Lollobrigida, but it never got off the ground. When Carlo Ponti came on board as producer, with his wife Sophia Loren as the star, Peter was invited to write the script, direct, and co-produce. In addition, he ended up playing a Bavarian prince in the film.

As this was the time of very long films with an intermission, *Lady L* was intended to follow that pattern. But after shooting had begun, one such film opened and was a huge flop, so Peter was suddenly instructed to shorten it and drop the intermission, to his great irritation. 'I'd written it to a certain length. It had a brothel scene in it too, and MGM sent me a directive, saying that they hoped it would be the kind of brothel to which the whole family could go.'

But his greatest concern was the incompatibility between his stars, Sophia Loren and Paul Newman. She thought her co-star was vulgar and uncouth and could not stand being near him. Peter regards Newman as a wonderful actor when playing Americans, but here he was a French revolutionary. In addition, the film needed a magnetism that was totally lacking in the central relationship.

So Peter took them both aside and said, 'Look, the chemistry between you isn't working and doesn't give the impression you're in love. You're fine when you're bickering, but very unconvincing when you're making it up.'

They both promised to try harder, and Peter made a separate appeal to Sophia privately. 'Be a little more tolerant towards him, and see whether we can't make this work. There may be sides of Paul that you don't know yet and which are very attractive.'

She tried her best to suppress her antipathy, and by way of small talk the next morning when they arrived on the set, she asked, 'Paul, how do you stick your moustache on every morning?' He replied laconically, 'Sperm.' So, as Peter told me with a rueful laugh, 'We were back to square one!'

He found it a great comfort having his old friend David Niven in the cast, 'who very much filled the niche he was expected to fill. On those occasions one didn't feel that he was born to act, but he had a wonderful sense of humour, and that made him a good companion.'

Sophia Loren responded well to his direction, 'especially when she was playing an old lady, because she had absolutely no knowledge of how to do that', unlike Peter, who was convincingly assuming the mannerisms of old age in his teens.

For the ball scene, shot at Castle Howard, most of the smart set of Yorkshire were hired as extras. They looked exactly right, but unlike professional extras they were not quite sure what was going on. One county lady approached the director during a break in filming and asked him if the pictures he had been taking would come out. Peter laid his reputation on the line. 'Madame,' he replied, 'if they don't I shall be looking for another job.'

He had high hopes of the film when he viewed the final cut in the projection room, 'but somehow with a big audience the story was so diffused that it didn't create the kind of enthusiasm that I'd hoped it might'.

Lady L was conceived on a large scale, but the intimate scenes actually work much better when it is reshown on television, much too late for the money men of the big studios. Peter has only directed twice since for the cinema; one movie was a failure and the second a disaster. His much longer list of film credits is as an actor for other directors, and his next major appearance, in *The Comedians*, deserved a greater success than it achieved.

Based on Graham Greene's novel, set in Haiti under the brutal dictatorship of 'Papa Doc' Duvalier, it attracted a cast including Alec Guinness, Lillian Gish, Richard Burton, and Elizabeth Taylor as the wife of an Ambassador, who was played by Peter. It was directed by Peter Glenville, a close friend of both Alec Guinness and Graham Greene. The novelist also forged a friendship with Ustinov when he came out to watch his story being filmed in West Africa. For political reasons Dahomey stood in for Haiti; curiously, at exactly the same time and for the same reasons, a film about West Africa had to be shot in Cuba.

Papa Doc was so incensed by Greene's accurate portrait of his savage regime that there were rumours he had sent a voodoo priest across the Atlantic, to cast spells against the unit and disrupt the filming; the mysterious death of one of the crew, and the illness of several others, caused uneasiness all round.

Elizabeth Taylor was too unwell to appear on several occasions, so on one free day Peter drove alone to visit a famous village on stilts. As a small boy he had developed a fear of 'Darkest Africa' as portrayed in the movies, when the leaves would part to show the menacing faces of natives with bones through their noses, as the drums beat in the background. These fears came back to him as he heard the distant sound of drums. He arrived at the village to witness a ceremony centred round an albino black, 'and if you've ever seen one of those they're quite frightening, but highly thought of by the locals, as mascots'.

He took some photographs and left, feeling it was vaguely touristy and ridiculous; 'and I lost all my fear of Africa.' When he got back, Graham Greene introduced him to a man with a big moustache.

'Peter, I don't think Liz is better, so we won't be able to shoot tomorrow. This is Colonel Witherspoon, well known in these parts as the great white hunter, and he's very kindly offered to take us to the famous village on stilts, if you're not doing anything.'

'That's where I was today.'

The colonel said, 'Alone? You're a rash man, aren't you?'

This only confirmed Peter's new conviction that he really could not be frightened of Africa any more, but he was assailed by a few moments of doubt. 'When there were mob scenes outside the embassy they were so realistic that one was nervous about when they were going to stop. People were told to make a demonstration, and they really did. It was a bit like starting the Drumcree March during the marching season.'

Peter became good friends with the Burtons, but he felt they lacked chemistry on the screen together because they knew each other too well. 'I'm not suggesting that Newman and Loren were better, but at least there was a kind of mystery there, even if it turned sour. It had no chance with these two. I thought he was a marvellous character, he was a really gifted man; he could have been a good writer. As an actor he had one failing: he could never do anything without it being important. He could never do anything trivial. When they made a very unfortunate remake of *Brief Encounter* with him and Sophia Loren, I was on the set watching it being shot. Burton was on a railway station and he went up to the buffet and said to the girl, "Can I have a cup of tea, please?" You thought, oh my God, he's coming in from the cold; what is the coded message he just handed to the girl? Because it was so cutting. All he wanted was a cup of tea, but you'd never have known it.'

Burton gave one of several powerful performances in *The Comedians*, and the realism was chilling to watch. When one of the Tontons Macoutes casually slit the throat of a black doctor in close-up, I was not the only one in the cinema to jump in my seat as the blood spurted. At a time when films were beginning to portray black people as heroes, suddenly here they were the villains, so violent that it was hard for the audiences to take, and the critics mostly failed to warm to it either.

Alec Guinness did not enjoy the stresses of the location work and could hardly wait to get on the plane home, but in his memoir *Blessings in Disguise* he pays eloquent tribute to his co-star: '*The Comedians* was not a particularly successful film but it contained one beautiful performance, unfortunately not properly appreciated by the critics, and that was given by Peter Ustinov. It was a serious, wise and sensitive portrayal of a sad diplomat, full of feeling and superbly well judged.'

The recipient of this praise was duly grateful. 'None of the professional critics said that; they said things like "rather a matt finish to Ustinov this time". I was always accused of slightly overdoing things, or being rather florid in my method, and there I was attacked for not doing enough.'

Peter Glenville's chief assistant, Judith Buckland, had long experience of film actors and film acting; she still savours one particular moment, which caught at her throat: 'The piece of acting that I shall always treasure, and which will always bring tears to my eyes, was a shot from behind as the Ambassador (Peter) took his wife out to the plane as they left Haiti in disgrace. All you saw was a large expanse of immobile back, with his hands clasped behind him. There was a moment when he gave a slight twist to his fingers. It was magic. You knew instantly the heartbreak he was experiencing. I'm in tears as I remember it now. One of the finest pieces of acting I saw in all the years I worked in the film industry.'

She shed different tears at another departure – the actor's own at the end of his part of the African filming, when she took him out to the airport. 'If anyone had told me that I would be weeping with laughter at 5.45 a.m. at Cotonou airport, I would not have believed them. But Peter doing his imitation of the President of Dahomey, a monstrous-sized man with a huge stomach, dancing with Elizabeth Taylor, was sheer heaven.'

Everyone who works with him seems to have been given their own special performance at some stage – a mark of appreciation that all of them remember vividly.

The Comedians was a well-made film, but the Graham Greene view of the world it reflected was, as so often in his work, ultimately a despairing vision of life. The Ustinov philosophy is a more optimistic one, and his next burst of creativity brought delight and laughter through some very different settings.

Thirteen

1966–1969
From *Frontiers of the Sea* to *Viva Max*

In the second half of the 1960s, Peter kept changing hats, one of them a mitre, as he wrote two new plays and starred in one of them, published another volume of short stories, directed opera for a second time, and acted in two very funny film comedies.

The nine stories in *The Frontiers of the Sea* had as wide a variety of geographical settings as those in *Add a Dash of Pity*, ranging across seven European countries, Australia, and the USA. They are, by turns, witty, moving, and thought-provoking. His brief pen-portraits bring his characters instantly to life, like the engaged English couple whose subsequent marriage is ruined by 'The Gift of a Dog': 'Their accents were identical; the clipped one of the English upper classes, with its irritating distortions of the rough majesty of Chaucer's and Shakespeare's tongue, its whimsical shortcuts, its triggered vowels, and its sudden baroque overshoot, investing a single sound with a rainbow of colours where, grammatically and aesthetically, there is room for only one.'

Peter was trying to place the two new plays at the same time. One of the first people to read them was John Gielgud, who told me how he got involved: 'I was in Hollywood, and Ustinov, whom I hadn't seen for years, was in the next bungalow in the hotel. He came and gave me two plays of his to read – one was *Halfway Up the Tree*, and the other was *The Unknown Soldier and His Wife* – I was very impressed with them, and I immediately thought that *Halfway Up the Tree* would be a wonderful vehicle for Ralph Richardson. So I rang him up in England and said, "You must read this play, it's so amusing and I'm sure you'd be splendid in it." He read it but didn't like it and said, "I won't play it because I have to be a dirty old tramp in the second act and take all my clothes off in the third act." I said, "That's a great pity," and so I gave Binkie Beaumont the script.' (Tennent's had long presented most Gielgud productions.)

Nothing happened for nearly a year, until Beaumont rang Gielgud and said, 'I've thought of somebody to play *Halfway Up the Tree* – Robert Morley, we'll get him.' Morley had always regretted turning down Gielgud's invitation to play Tattle in Congreve's *Love for Love* during the war, and later also Falstaff, so he felt he could not refuse this third chance to work with Gielgud. After he had read the script he told his son and biographer, Sheridan Morley, 'I think I can do this, as long as I'm allowed to change it,' which was in any case what he usually did to other authors' scripts.

When he started to do just that, Gielgud was horrified. 'We had the reading with Ustinov there, and Morley insulted Ustinov so much that I thought he would probably throw the play in his face. He said, 'This isn't any good, this is no good, children don't talk like this.' Then Ustinov went away to direct the play himself in America, and it was also being played in France and in Germany; everybody thought it was a winner. But ours, I might say with some pride, was the only production that was a great success; and while we were rehearsing it, Morley kept on chucking bits out, and writing new bits and putting things in. Ustinov was sending us new lines every day that he'd written in, and Morley used to tear them up and throw them in the bin. I got more and more alarmed about what Ustinov would say when he saw it. When it came to the dress rehearsal, Ustinov walked in, saw the play, hadn't a word of criticism, passed the entire thing, and I was so touched. Of course it was a great success, but it was extraordinary, because both of them being writers, and both of them terrific prima donnas, I thought surely the fur is going to begin to fly, and I shall have to hold the ropes, but it all came out all right.'

The cast included Ambrosine Phillpotts as the General's wife, Pinkie Johnstone as the pregnant daughter, and Mark Dignam as the Vicar. Jonathan Cecil, who played the naive scoutmaster, has never forgotten the interchange when Peter came down to Oxford to see a performance, the week before the play opened in London.

'The audience were absolutely hysterical with laughter, and we all lined up on stage after the curtain had come down. The formidable Binkie Beaumont, Sir John, and Peter appeared on the stage, and we all thought, What will Peter say?

'He said, "Well done, congratulations" to all of us.

'Robert said, "My goodness, by this stage usually my writers aren't speaking to me."

'Peter said, "You mean you've stopped talking to yourself?" Just like that.'

Peter has often joked about that occasion since, saying that he sat in the audience, letting out the occasional whoop of delight when he heard a line he recognised, but his main reaction was a fatalistic one. 'You couldn't do anything about it, he was like an enormous truant schoolboy. At certain things he was very effective, but he was a stuntman rather than an actor; everything he did was always very similar.'

The author's resignation was shared by his director. John Gielgud told Sheridan Morley, 'Trying to direct your father in a play was like trying to change the sequence on traffic lights.'

In *Halfway Up the Tree* General Sir Mallalieu Buttress returns to his Hampshire home after four years' service in Malaya to find his children have become hippies. To everyone's astonishment, instead of beating them he joins them, returning in the second act garbed as a Red Indian tramp and provoking outrage at his regimental dinner by arriving dressed in a kaftan. In the third act he decides to live up one of the trees in his garden with a young Malayan girl.

The critical reaction was mixed and in some cases directly contradictory. In *The Times*, Irving Wardle sighed that 'Mr Morley is under-exercised in this lethargic production'; J.C. Trewin's view in the *Illustrated London News* was that 'Gielgud's direction is always spirited'; while the *Sunday Times* critic felt that it was 'directed at vertiginous speed'. W.A. Darlington confessed in the *Daily Telegraph* to 'a strong prejudice in favour of any play that Peter Ustinov writes and another equally strong in favour of any play in which Robert Morley acts ... Nor was my confidence unjustified. With the help of John Gielgud as director, and an attractive company in support, they provided me with an evening in the theatre such as I have not enjoyed for months and months.'

His enjoyment was shared by audiences for months and months too, as the play settled into a run of over a year, much the longest consecutive run anywhere. Anthony Quayle gave quite a different performance as the General in New York, where its short run was not helped by another newspaper strike. Unfortunately, the play was not a great success in France or Germany.

But when Sheridan Morley challenged the author to admit that however displeased he was about the changes made to his play in London, they had given it a life not experienced elsewhere, Peter pointed out to him that it had run in the repertoire of the Mossoviet Theatre in Moscow for over ten years, alternating with other plays. Those separate performances added up to the equivalent of a two-year run. In Russia the play was retitled *Halfway Up the Mountain*.

The reason that it ran so long there was that not only was it popular with the Russian audience, but it was also the favourite play of the old actor playing the General, and it only came out of the repertoire when he died. Not long before that, Peter saw the production for the last time and was mystified to see that all the furniture had been rearranged. When the General entered, he immediately understood. The actor was now crippled with arthritis and needed the support of the furniture to help him get across the room. When Peter went round to his dressing room afterwards, the old Russian burst into tears.

'Oh God, I wish you hadn't come today.'

'Why not? It was wonderful, it's matured. I think it's better than when I first saw it.'

'No, no, no, no, no.'

'What's the matter? Why are you so upset?'

'You noticed. Why pretend you didn't notice? You know our language well enough.'

'I swear to you I didn't notice. What is it?'

'I changed a line.'

Peter kept to himself the memories of Robert Morley's inability to say the same line twice.

'What did you change it to?'

'You see that I'm struggling with arthritis?'

'Yes, I see that, but it has only enriched your performance.' This was a small lie, but uttered out of kindness.

'Well, I said I had been wounded by a partisan, I tried to explain my infirmity that way.'

'Well, that seems to me absolutely logical. I think that's a terribly good idea.'

'Ooohh,' and he shook with sobs again.

Peter was touched by this extraordinary fidelity to the integrity of the text, and it heightened his respect for the traditions of the Russian theatre; 'Sometimes a play was cut by a censor in Russia, but never by an actor.'

The second play to reach the stage in 1967 was *The Unknown Soldier and His Wife*, which was first directed by John Dexter at the Lincoln Center in New York, with a strong cast led by Brian Bedford, Howard Da Silva, and Christopher Walken. You needed to be strong to cope with John Dexter, as many other actors have discovered. Peter found him 'an autocratic director but very interesting. When I did the play in England, and he came to see it, I had the Romans marching and counter-marching, shouting, "Sinister Dexter, Sinister Dexter." He came round afterwards and said, "Bastard!"'

This was at Chichester where, in addition to being the author and director, Peter also played the Archbishop. He described the play as 'Two Acts of War separated by a Truce and Refreshments'. It opens with a group of soldiers assembled for the burial of the Unknown Soldier at a televised ceremony. They throw off their gas-capes to be revealed in Roman uniforms, and subsequent time-switches move the action to the Crusades, the Puritans, the French Revolution, and the First World War. The same characters reappear throughout – the General, the Sergeant, the Enemy Leader, the Rebel, the Archbishop, the Inventor, and the eponymous couple.

The latter two were played at Chichester by Simon Ward and

Prunella Scales; in the play the wife is constantly pregnant throughout the ages, and in rehearsal the actress discovered she was actually expecting her second son. The whole experience was a very happy time for her.

'Peter came back for supper one night, having very kindly given me a lift home. We lived in an Elizabethan cottage. I said, "Can I get you something to eat?" and went into the kitchen. When I came back, Peter was standing in the middle of the room, with his head wedged up under the lampshade, saying, "I wish to apply for the Turkish rights." '

The thrust stage at Chichester was admirably suited to the battlefields and processions of the play, and Peter enjoyed playing there so much that he made a point of coming back with a very different play of his in 1996. He also grew very appreciative of the cuisine offered by a very good French restaurant just up the road from the theatre, called Comme Ça.

He still cherishes a conversation he overheard there one day, when he popped in for an early lunch before rehearsal. He was sitting quietly alone in a corner, when suddenly two elderly Englishmen came in, wearing blazers with gold buttons and military-looking badges on their breast pockets, accompanied by their wives. They failed to notice him sitting there and, thinking that they were alone, behaved as though the place was theirs, speaking in extremely loud voices. One of them said, 'Yes, we have a new maître d'' in our local restaurant, French of course. Well, I suppose he's all right, but he has this frightful habit of kissing the women's hands.' One of the wives said, 'Oh, how awful!'

Peter finished his meal quickly and called the waiter. 'M'sieur ... l'addition, s'il vous plaît?'

'Oui, M'sieur.'

Then they had quite a long conversation in French, which attracted the attention of the other party.

'I say, that's Ustinov, isn't it? Well, why's he speaking French?'

It took Peter right back to his army days and the kind of incomprehension that he suffered at the hands of some sections of the military establishment.

The Unknown Soldier and His Wife did very good business at

Chichester but did not transfer for a London season until 1973. Some of the original cast came back to it then, but Prunella Scales, to her sadness, was unable to join them. Her place was taken by Tamara Ustinov, which was the first time she had worked with her father.

He never influenced her choice of career, and she says that her acting impetus came more from the drama department at Farlington School for Girls, which also produced the actresses Susan Fleetwood and Angela Thorne. 'He was not pushing, he always lets people get on with their own lives. But once I got started he was very encouraging, and has always been very helpful.'

He pulled no strings for her in this play, and she had to audition a couple of times before getting the part. She rapidly discovered, like Rosemary Harris before her, 'He's a terrible giggler when you act with him. But it's super working with him, because he makes such a good atmosphere – very relaxed and very good fun; everybody responds to him, it's terrific. When you see him working with crews, they all get on so well with him.'

He particularly needed close technical rapport at the New London Theatre, for which this was the opening production. It was built on the site of the old Winter Garden Theatre, as one of those multi-purpose auditoria that can be adapted into a stadium for tennis matches or chess championships, with plenty of lounges and bars for patrons. The stage revolve took in all the front seats on one side, which could revolve too when necessary. This may have seemed a good idea to the architects but, Peter discovered to his dismay, 'When the troops started stamping on the stage, for the people in the front seats it became almost unbearable to sit there, because they vibrated so underneath them. There was a great tingle like an electric shock, and the whole thing wobbled. I had to get on stage in an archbishop's cope and mitre, and I had to pass through something like sixteen fire-doors, and that's not easy with a train.'

The critics crossed their fingers about the future of this new theatre, with Irving Wardle commenting in *The Times*, 'Musicals (and films) apart, it is hard to imagine what kind of commercial show is going to be suitable for this setting: the average one-set four-character play would be lost in it. But for the meantime the management have found an answer in Peter Ustinov's strip cartoon history of mankind at war, which comes over with a good deal more conviction and panache than it did at Chichester five years ago.'

He particularly appreciated the author/director's third contribution as actor: 'With that melting profile, and his projection of benevolent intelligence and low cunning, the performance is constantly in motion and marvellously funny; especially in its hair-trigger secondary responses – bruising his fist after giving a general an ill-considered punch on the armour, or shooting a rapid smirk at Jove in the midst of a blasphemous conversation.'

J.C. Trewin in *The Lady* expressed his appreciation at seeing it again after Chichester: 'It is a much more complex play than it appears to be at first viewing; something, again, that is in the accepted Ustinov manner.' He too admired the comic acting: 'Ustinov's own protean expertise – no one can glide through the periods with more relish, more selective art in his emphasis – and such performances as Mark Kingston's everlasting Sergeant and Tony Jay's Inventor, ready with anything from the stirrup onwards.'

The humour was there to reinforce the serious point of the play, and at the end the action comes full circle to the burial of the Unknown Soldier, with the men back in their gas-capes, for the final confrontation:

Rebel You see, this is the real revolution at last. The one man who has never changed, the one constant factor throughout history, has woken up.
Inventor Woken up? What are you talking about? A man has refused to die, that's all. What is surprising about it?
Rebel We've all changed our opinions, endlessly flexible, endlessly adapting ourselves to the moment. The Archbishop has pecked at all the religions in turn, the General accepted whatever world he was born into without question, I opposed whoever was in power with burning conviction. This soldier was the only constant factor from the beginning of time. Constant in his goodness, constant in his

stupidity, constant in his obedience. Now, he has taken the initiative. He is in charge. We are awaiting his decision, awaiting his orders.

Inventor I am not awaiting his orders! The next time you will all be Unknown Soldiers, I've seen to that! This man is incapable of decision! It is I who can destroy the world!

Rebel He can prevent you.

Inventor I can order him to press the button!

Rebel He can refuse.

Inventor I am a genius! I harness the power of the earth and sky!

Rebel He is a simple man. He harnesses the imagination.

Peter considers this play to be the most ambitious of his works for the theatre and acknowledges that it is a difficult play too, but even in the rather forbidding space of the New London, he succeeded in harnessing the audience's imagination with great theatrical skill.

There was just one night when he met the cold world of a real war intruding to break the dramatic spell. 'Towards the end I saw the police in the wings, and suddenly the small orchestra wasn't playing any more. I thought, What the hell's happened? It changed the whole end of the play – no more cues, nothing, just the police standing there patiently, looking at their watches. I finished the final remarks and left the stage, and I was immediately bundled out. I thought we were all being arrested. The theatre is built over a car park on three or four levels, and there was believed to be an IRA bomb in a car. The Bomb Squad was there, so we were all shepherded into the street, and pushed away in case there was a blast. We stood there for half an hour, I dressed as an Archbishop, and then it was a false alarm.'

This was the first time that Peter had returned to the stage after an interval of several years to appear again in one of his own plays, and he was encouraged to find that he could bring something new to the production the second time. It is also true that he has often pioneered theatrical conventions well ahead of their time; audiences have come to accept them more easily when they cease to be new.

In 1968 he was given a second chance to direct in the opera

house; the invitation again came via Sir Georg Solti, but this time it was for Rolf Liebermann, the Director of Hamburg Opera. The work was *The Magic Flute*, by Peter's favourite composer. 'Mozart I would put first, because he has the most profound superficiality in the world. The surface of his operas is always calm, and the calm on the surface enables you to see the complication of the stones at the bottom. I love the idea of being able to write as he composed.'

In his first experience at Covent Garden he had rapidly distinguished between singers whose voices were not quite what they once were but who had acquired considerable acting skills, and those who had glorious voices but 'who can't act for toffee'. On the Continent, where he has now directed several operas, he encountered two more categories. He was dismayed by the first: old retired singers, who had acquired professorships but could neither sing nor act, and who were terribly aggressive towards him when he tried to direct them.

'Professor, would you mind moving away from . . .'

'Why should I move? I am here. You asked me to be here, and I stay here.'

'Well, I just want the other people to be visible when they come through the door.'

'Then change the door!'

But he has been greatly impressed by the very young singers, often from countries without a great operatic tradition, who have wonderful voices and can act brilliantly.

He still found the rehearsal period difficult. 'If you're in the theatre, you get very depressed towards the end when you still only have a piano to rehearse with. Everybody is singing away, and you think this is all very well, but this is really embarrassing the way she is doing it, and then suddenly Mozart comes to the rescue, and everything becomes magical, and all these other things become less important, because they know how to do *that*.'

He called on his old designer friend from *Romanoff and Juliet*, Jean-Denis Malclès, to create the sets for *The Magic Flute* and insisted on continuous action with no delays for scene-changes. His other innovation was to restore the original text, jettisoning the accretions of earlier directors and singers, which had become traditional. This provoked howls of outrage from the less knowledgeable, who accused him of tampering with the composer's intentions. After this production moved to the Maggio Musicale in Florence, he was pleased to read William Weaver's recognition in the *Herald Tribune* of what he had really done: 'When it was new, some time ago, this Peter Ustinov staging of *The Magic Flute* came in for some criticism. It's hard now to see why; it is surely respectful of the text and faithful to the music, and yet inventive.'

His respect for the text in the opera house or theatre did not always extend to the world of film. The original screenplay for *Hot Millions* was set in New York, but after the American producer Mildred Freed Alberg offered the script to Peter, the story was relocated in England, and he rewrote it. He was to star in the film and had director approval. While he was in the States directing the Broadway production of *Halfway Up the Tree*, he was introduced to Eric Till, who had read the American version of the screenplay and thought he had talked himself out of a job, because he had said it would need a total rewrite to work in an English setting.

That was exactly what Peter had in mind, so he had unwittingly said the right thing. They also discovered over dinner that they shared a great mutual admiration for the Canadian pianist, Glenn Gould. When Eric Till was invited to direct the film, he agreed instantly, 'but what I didn't know at that time was that I was about to embark on one of the most rewarding and memorable experiences of my life. *Hot Millions* is a little film, but full of warmth, and humour, and comic invention, and a good deal of that comes from the extraordinary rapport between Peter and Maggie Smith.'

These two actors had never worked together before, and they only met for the first time just before shooting started, at a meeting in the Savoy Hotel also attended by the director and the producer. Because of Maggie Smith's prior commitment to a BBC project, they lost her services for a couple of weeks after their first week's shooting. This proved to be a heaven-sent gap.

Only two days into the filming, Peter went to Eric Till and said,

'We have to do some rewriting. This lady is incredibly talented and we can't just leave the script the way it is. We have to do something about it.'

So while she was away, Peter substantially rewrote her scenes, giving her the thrust and the comic power in them, often at his own expense. He also listened to her advice on casting. She commented about one actor, 'You can't have him, it's like acting with a cupboard.' Peter soon discovered that her judgment was shrewd, and he quickly recast the part.

Their director encouraged them to play off each other, by setting up surprises that he knew they would use to the advantage of the film. The plot centres around an embezzler, played by Peter, who gets emotionally involved with a scatty girl who knows nothing about business but learns how to outwit them all financially. Just before the camera turned over one day, Eric Till whispered in Maggie's ear that maybe she should just lengthen the scene by asking Peter, 'What are assets?'

They played the scene, but instead of calling 'Cut' at the end, Eric Till waited. 'Maggie said, in that extraordinary voice of hers, "What are assets?" Without a pause Peter said, "Female donkeys." Of course it brought the studio into howls of laughter, and that kind of thing happened time and time again.'

On one occasion the two of them were improvising so brilliantly that Eric Till actually stopped shooting for the day, and carried on rehearsing so that he did not cut off their invention by shooting the scene too soon. 'As the director, I wanted my part in this film to be invisible, and to have the wherewithal to let these extraordinary performers do their thing. I was just there to hold on to the shape and the structure.'

The others in the cast included Peter Jones as the prison governor in the opening scene where the Ustinov character is let out of prison; Robert Morley as the businessman whose identity he assumes; Karl Malden, Bob Newhart, and Cesar Romero – a formidable comic team.

The film was well received on both sides of the Atlantic and did good, if not spectacular, business. It won Maggie Smith the Variety Club Award for Film Actress of the Year. She and Peter would work together again, and she remained one of his very favourite actresses, among a distinguished gallery that includes Deborah Kerr, Rosemary Harris, Diana Wynyard, and Susan Sarandon.

During the filming of *Hot Millions* he took a firm decision about the women in his life on the personal front. His marriage to Suzanne had been struggling for some while, and now they separated for good. Hélène du Lau d'Allemans had re-entered his life, and they had become inseparable. She joined him on location in Mexico for *Viva Max*, and they determined to marry when the divorce came through.

That took longer than expected and hardly fitted the Swiss description of an 'amicable divorce'. The settlement finally cost Peter half a million dollars, and he was given three years to complete the payments. He is still reluctant to talk about it, as much because of the emotional pain it caused, as the financial cost. He had to remortgage his house in Switzerland and sell off a lake and property he had bought in Canada.

But, he says, 'My chief ambition was to save the children from any kind of complex, and I think in that we probably succeeded, although not entirely. I was given custody, but I'm very glad they still see their mother. The last thing I wanted was to estrange them from her, because that would have been quite unjust. She made my life a misery, but there was no reason why the children should suffer because of that.'

At the time Pavla was fourteen, Igor twelve, and Andrea only nine. Their father took the decision to send them to Swiss boarding schools, since he was away from home so much. Indeed, he now had to work even harder to pay off the divorce settlement, and he accepted a number of film offers that in less straitened circumstances he might have turned down.

That was not the case in *Viva Max*, the fictional story of a blundering Mexican general who reoccupies the Alamo with fewer than a hundred soldiers, carrying rifles but no ammunition. They are surrounded by the San Antonio Police Department, the National Guard, the US Army, and a bizarre bunch of anti-Chinese Communist vigilantes. Peter's perfect Mexican accent was matched by his projection of the general's uncertainty as to whether his men would follow him, to great comic effect. The only drawback was that he had to overcome his deep aversion to being on horseback.

He says, 'I hate riding. My late uncle on my mother's side was the commanding general of the Cossack Savage Division, but not one of those genes has galloped in my direction. The trouble about being on a horse is that you can't see its face, you have to go by the ears. It was a stallion, so when we were out in the country, it would usually be sexually stimulated by all sorts of smells that entered its huge nostrils, and suddenly a fifth leg would develop. I would be sitting on this horse with all my dignity, with this terrible thing trailing on the ground. I couldn't see it, but everybody was roaring with laughter. I was very embarrassed, and suddenly, in answer to some primeval urge, it would take off with me on its back and gallop. I never felt more ridiculous in my life than at moments in this film, because I couldn't control this horse at all.'

That did not stop him from giving another accomplished comic performance for his last portrayal of the 1960s. It was the cinema that now claimed the lion's share of his time and restored the Ustinov finances throughout the next decade.

This particular chapter should not be closed without a brief digression on the significance of its number. Reading all the Ustinov plays in sequence, I came to the conclusion that he must be very intrigued by the number thirteen. Cordelia has thirteen names in *The Moment of Truth*; there are thirteen candles on Poldi's cake in *High Balcony*, and the Baron says, 'It's always been a kind of lucky number for her.'

When I asked Peter about this numerical recurrence he insisted it was not a conscious act. 'That's sheer coincidence. I've always resented the fact that it's an unlucky number, and I'm always surprised in Moscow to go up in the lift and find a thirteenth floor, because hardly anybody else has it. This has always irritated me slightly, so I suppose thirteen has been engraved in my mind as something that I don't find particularly dangerous. Although I must say my uncle in the First World War was killed on Friday the

The Prince Regent in *Beau Brummell*, 1954, with Rosemary Harris. 'I really fell for her, she's a great actress. She played Mrs Fitzherbert, so I was supposed to look at her like that.'

Wedding day with Suzanne, 15 February, 1954.

The Russian Embassy, left, with Michael David above, Peter Ustinov, Marianne Deeming and Frederick Valk below.

The American Embassy, right, with William Greene and Katy Vail, above, John Phillips and Jacqueline Lacey below.

The General. 'Mr Ustinov presides over our enlightenment with a sort of ruffled tact that combines the best features of Chorus, Pandarus and fleet-footed Mercury.'

PICCADILLY THEATRE
PICCADILLY CIRCUS, W.I.
GERrard 4506-7

LINNIT & DUNFEE LTD present

PETER USTINOV
FREDERICK VALK
JOHN PHILLIPS
and introduce
MICHAEL DAVID   KATY VAIL
as Romanoff   as Juliet
in
Peter Ustinov's
ROMANOFF
AND JULIET
a comedy
with
DELPHI LAWRENCE   DAVID LODGE
DAVID HURST   MARIANNE DEEMING
JOSEPHINE BARRINGTON   JOE GIBBONS
WILLIAM GREENE   EDWARD ATIENZA
directed by
DENIS CAREY
decor by JEAN DENIS MALCLES

Practising his penny whistle in *The Sundowners*, 1960. 'A Western without gunfire, but with human problems unsugared and devoid of artificial colouring'.

Billy Budd. Robert Ryan, Terence Stamp and Peter Ustinov. Terence Stamp: 'He took a gamble on me, and that movie changed my life for ever'.

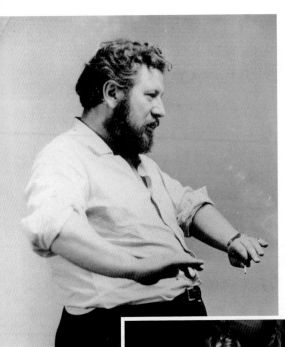

Directing *Photo Finish*, 1962. 'Mr Ustinov presents us with the utterly impossible, and completely convinces us that the impossible is real.'

Directing opera for the first time, Royal Opera House, 1962. With Amy Shuard, Joan Carlyle and Georg Solti.

Photo Finish. En route to Dublin for rehearsals, with Diana Wynyard and Paul Rogers.

Sam Old, with Diana Wynyard. 'Apart from Mr Ustinov's own golden performance there is ripe playing by Paul Rogers as the father and by Diana Wynyard, highly effective as the terrifying wife.'

The treasured Hispano-Suiza car, a birthday gift from Suzanne in 1962, later stolen and the subject of an abortive lawsuit for its return.

Topkapi, 1963, with Akim Tamiroff.
'He was uncontrollable, mad as a hatter'.

Meeting the cast of *Halfway Up The Tree* – Pinkie Johnstone, Michael Johnson and Robert Morley. 'Morley insulted Ustinov so much that I thought he would probably throw the play in his face'.

The Archbishop in *The Unknown Soldier and his Wife*, 1968. 'The performance is constantly in motion and marvellously funny'.

Rehearsing *The Unknown Soldier and his Wife* at Chichester.

thirteenth. I'm named after him, and maybe that's an influence that I can't control.'

The history of the stage abounds with superstitions, taboos, and theatrical ghosts, and it is typical of Peter Ustinov's non-conformity that he should, however unconsciously, champion the cause of many people's unluckiest number.

Fourteen

1970–1975
From *Hammersmith is Out* to *Logan's Run*

The 1970s began for Peter with a curious movie in which he was reunited with the Burtons, four years after *The Comedians*. Richard played Hammersmith, a deranged murderer incarcerated in a mental institution, who makes a Faustian bargain with one of the male nurses to help him escape. Paul Newman was offered the latter part but declined it, and Beau Bridges was cast instead, with Elizabeth Taylor as his girlfriend.

Peter was asked to direct, and the problems began with the financier of the film, who had made his fortune out of mobile homes. 'He was an uncouth American self-made millionaire, who therefore knew the secrets of all financial success,' Peter told me with heavy sarcasm. 'It was really a comment on the fragility of the American Dream, but since it didn't come from me, but from some other mind, I changed quite a bit of it. But evidently I was blamed for having ruined what was there. It was really unfocussed and belonged to a very unfocussed period, when they were doing all sorts of films that were supposed to be entertaining, but weren't. We'd lost the knack of comedy suddenly.'

Richard Burton found the script 'very wild and formless' but confided to his diary, 'It should be wildly funny and fun to do, especially with somebody as congenial as Ustinov and as brilliant, and might be a commercial success to boot.'

Hammersmith is Out was shot in Mexico, and may have been fun to do, but on screen it turned out to be neither funny nor successful. However, to the director's surprise, it won the Silver Bear at the Berlin Film Festival, 'but maybe,' as he said with a laugh, 'because they got the reels the wrong way round'.

Burton and Ustinov could not be less alike in temperament, and perhaps because of that they became very good friends. When they finished shooting, Peter was presented by the Burtons with a painting by a local artist, which Richard passed off as nothing special; it was in fact painted by the most famous living Mexican artist, Rufino Tamayo, and was highly priced, which Peter only discovered after they had gone.

That was not the end of the Welsh actor's generosity. When he threw a huge and extravagant fortieth birthday party for Elizabeth Taylor in Budapest in 1972, his pangs of conscience led him to pledge the equivalent of its cost to a good cause. A little later Peter received a cheque through the post, made payable to UNICEF, for the sum of $45,000. Peter had become a Goodwill Ambassador for that organisation in 1968, and in future years he would devote an increasing amount of his time to travelling on its behalf.

Another of the honorary duties he took on at this time was as Rector of Dundee University. In Scottish universities the holder of this post is elected by the students. Prior to Peter's election, it was often held by media or show-business figures and was not taken seriously. That was not the Ustinov approach.

When a small group of militant students refused to pay for their lodgings, as a gesture in aid of the campaign for higher grants, the new Rector refused to support their illegal action. He received a telegram demanding his resignation, on a motion carried by 40 votes to 6. He promptly demanded a new vote of confidence by secret ballot of the full student body and he campaigned through the press and on television; this time he was supported by 2000 votes to 46. He was re-elected for a second three-year term as Rector in 1971.

That slightly assuaged the frustration he felt about his next film, which should have been released then but never was. This was *Big Truck and Poor Clare*. Peter considered it quite an amusing film, but he only discovered after it was completed that it had been made as a tax loss, and there was never any intention of distributing it. 'I played an Israeli truck-driver. I've never driven a truck in my life. It had seventeen speeds forwards and twelve backwards – a huge Mercedes truck. Sometimes it had a platform built out, so they could photograph me at the wheel, which made the truck twice as wide and made my judgments very difficult on a thin two-lane highway.'

Peter's Israeli truck-driver picks up a Catholic nun, played by Francesca Annis. Peter had to learn an Israeli accent, which he did with his usual aplomb. He had lines like: 'Why shouldn't I carry a nun? If she was Israeli she wouldn't be a nun, but she is not Israeli, it's what I'm telling.'

Although the company were all paid for their efforts, the film was never submitted for a certificate. Peter was furious: 'I really blame him for wasting my time. I can't think of his name either, because when there are unpleasant things, you tend to forget people.'

It is understandable that he should have erased the memory, but the production credits read like one of those portmanteau groups that might be put together if you were looking for a sharp tax wheeze – 'Produced by Paul Maslansky for Kastner–Ladd–Kanter in association with Pashanel–Topol–Gottesman'. Actors like to be paid, but above all they want their work to be seen, which does not always happen in the strange world of film.

More satisfyingly, that year he also published his second full-length novel, *Krumnagel*. The chief of police in a small Midwest town, Bartram T. Krumnagel, is presented with round-the-world travel tickets for himself and his wife. In England he gets into an argument in a pub, and in an instinctive reaction he shoots a drunken Scotsman who reaches in his pocket for a handkerchief. The incident escalates into an Anglo-American diplomatic embarrassment, as Krumnagel is jailed for seven years. He escapes and returns to America.

Back in his hometown, he gets caught up in a student demonstration against the Vietnam War. To his surprise, his sympathies are now with the students and a small group of Buddhists, led by an ex-Vietnam veteran wearing saffron robes and carrying a temple bell.

Krumnagel's conversion is completed by the violent confrontation that erupts around him as he talks to the former GI:

> He tinkled urgently, and a song of peace broke from the hushed throats of those courting life like lovers. To this murmured madrigal there was joined a truncated discordant percussive sound of voices, unmusical and strident, and ruthless. Across the square there burst a tidal wave of construction workers, roughnecks in working clothes, wearing yellow metal helmets, and waving American flags. They broke into a run when they saw the students, a slow sinister run like an infantry attack in a long-forgotten war. Their faces brooked no argument, and they had about them all the dignity of laboratory rats, trained to enter the little door with the Stars and Stripes painted on without question or hesitation, their minds uncomplicated by doubt, and therefore by humanity. The last bastion of reaction is never the officers, always the sergeants. Long after the officers have recognised the inevitability of change owing to the solidarity of the men, the sergeants are still there upholding a dead world, paying homage to witch-doctors and painted images, prey to the militant servility of their calling, yelling and shouting without respect for words or meaning. And here they were, on the double, flushed with the joy of activity, and drunk on hatred for all the infinity of human endeavour which lay beyond their comprehension.

Krumnagel exacts his revenge on the corrupt bosses who have betrayed him and the democratic ideals he holds dear in a climax reminiscent of the assassination in *The Manchurian Candidate*. This too would have made a great film. Walter Matthau wanted to play the central role, for which he would have been perfect casting, but the talks came to nothing. There were several other expressions of interest, but Peter was never very hopeful, 'because Americans are nervous with pictures like that, which show them in an odd light'.

The novel is rich in characterisation and comic incident, with an underlying serious point about the incompatibility of cultures. This was underlined by some of the different national responses to the book. Auberon Waugh, son of one of the best comic novelists in the English language, gave it a rave review in England and said that it was the funniest book he had ever read, which pleased the author more than the grumpy reaction of one American who said to him, 'Whoever heard of a police chief called Krumnagel?'

Peter replied, 'Whoever heard of a Chief of Staff called Eisenhower?'

The book has remained in print, and for me it is the most compulsive and stimulating read of all his fiction. Despite the black ending, the reader's sympathies are steadily drawn towards the central figure, as he changes from an unthinking grotesque into an avenger seeking justice.

In 1972 Peter and Hélène were free to marry at last, in a quiet civil ceremony on 17 June on the island of Corsica, attended only by the family. At the third attempt, Peter had found the right person to share his life, and they have now been happily married for thirty years. When one sees them together, it is hard to believe it has been that long, as the delight they take in each other's company seems still so fresh. At home they normally converse in French, and in company they slip in and out of French and English all the time.

Hélène told me that she had thought she would never marry someone who was divorced and who had children, but, she says, 'I don't live in the past, I live in the present, and Peter is quite an exceptional man, as an artist and as a human being. He's a wonderful father.'

Asked recently which had been the most enjoyable part of his life so far, Peter said, 'I've been married three times, but I feel that if it had been this one first, I would have been married only once. At the same time, I wouldn't have the same children, which I would regret, because I enjoy these very much.'

One obvious bond between Peter and Hélène is a shared sense of humour. Several of the figures who appear earlier in these pages told me that at dinner parties at his home, Peter would keep the entire table in an uproar with his stories and impressions, and the only person sitting there not laughing would be Suzanne. By contrast, Hélène's gurgling laugh sounds very like that of Judi Dench and is heard as frequently, whether Peter is regaling just a foursome or a much larger gathering.

The call of the opera drew Peter back into its world twice in 1973. The first time was for *Don Giovanni*, which Peter Diamand asked him to direct for the Edinburgh Festival; he also designed the sets and the costumes. The conductor was Daniel Barenboim, making his operatic debut, with a cast led by Roger Soyer as the Don, Geraint Evans as Leporello, and Heather Harper as Donna Elvira.

Peter provoked a storm of protest by restoring the original ending as written by Mozart and Da Ponte. 'It says in the script that Don Ottavio comes back with two officers, which means he's gone to Madrid to fetch the *due ufficiali*. I had Guardia Civiles of the time, with those strange hats on, measuring the hole through which Don Giovanni disappeared into Hell and making notes for their final report to Madrid. I thought that was completely justified, it's exactly what it says in the script. Everybody said, "Why did you do that?" But it's entitled by Mozart a "Dramma Giocosa", and to my mind if a man seduces hundreds of women it's not necessarily a tragedy.'

He did not relish the critics' overreaction to his restorations to *Don Giovanni* but enjoyed his work on the production.

In contrast, his second operatic commission that year was a nightmare from start to finish. Rolf Liebermann, who had moved from Hamburg to Paris, invited him to direct and design Massenet's *Don Quixote* at the Paris Opera, starring the great Russian bass, Nicolai Ghiaurov, but when Peter arrived the opera house was suffering its first ever musicians' strike. The orchestra had decided they wanted to be seen, not hidden away in the pit, so they worked to rule by playing very softly.

Whenever Peter asked for help in solving a technical problem, he was told: 'Demandez au Suisse!' There was an air of hostility and resentment that the new Intendant was not a Frenchman. Liebermann told Peter that when he took up his post, he discovered that there were nearly 3000 people on the payroll, many of them old men sitting in offices making lists; the waste was unbelievable. The paint and size were still made on a field kitchen from the Franco–Prussian War of 1870.

At one rehearsal, Peter watched in astonishment as the pianist, who was playing for the singers, suddenly looked into the wings and shouted, 'Madeleine.' She called again, but Madeleine was busy talking to somebody else. 'Madeleine!!' Finally, with an 'Oh', Madeleine rushed in. The pianist carried on playing, but stood up as she did so. Madeleine put on her glasses and sat down, and as soon as the first pianist left off, she picked up and carried on.

The mystified director exclaimed, 'What the hell is this?'

'Well, it's a union matter. One plays exclusively for the singers, and the other exclusively for the dancers.'

The French audience extended their hostility to the visiting director-designer. 'At the end when I came out there was a gale of booing, so I turned my back on the public. I heard a noise as if I had slapped every individual face simultaneously, and they all reacted together. "Oohh!!" It was like a very quick exhalation of air, in horror, and then the booing continued with greater intensity. I went off and came back, and again turned my back. Then I went and had dinner with my wife in a very good restaurant; by the end of dinner I'd forgotten all about it. I hate that opera house, I simply loathe it, and I've never been back.'

This was the nadir of his operatic experiences, and his future productions would be much more rewarding. Peter hardly felt he had escaped from that hyper-charged world when he appeared in Lew Grade's television spectacular, *Jesus of Nazareth*, directed by a man who began his career in opera – Franco Zeffirelli. Although he had branched out into stage and film direction, his operatic approach never really left him, which disconcerted Peter on the set.

'I was preparing myself as Herod to come into the arena and make a big thing about "Kill the children", pumping myself up into something enormous. Just before he said "Action", he whispered in my ear, "Darling, don't forget, this is the death of Boris (Godunov)." Nothing was further from my mind than the death of Boris. I had to say, "Stop. Stop for a moment, and let me concentrate." '

The cast included Laurence Olivier, Ralph Richardson, James Mason, Anthony Quinn, Ernest Borgnine, James Earl Jones, Christopher Plummer, Anne Bancroft, Ian Holm, Michael York, and Lew Grade's choice as Jesus – the much less well-known Robert Powell. He gave a moving performance but did not receive quite the same deference from his director as some of the more stellar names in the cast.

Peter observed this during one lunch-break. 'Zeffirelli was eating some pasta which was slightly escaping from his mouth before it was finally swallowed, and he was listening to Robert Powell, who was being frightfully intellectual, saying, "You know, Franco, I'm having trouble here, because I know that the physical human pain of the nails going in must have been excruciating, and I want to express the absolute physical agony of this, but temper it with another feeling of a kind of divine transport into regions which we are not usually able to penetrate, when it's sublimated into something quite different, and feeling goes and everything dissolves . . ." He went on like this until Franco suddenly stopped eating pasta, and said, "Darling, you are boring me, get back on the cross,"' which Peter, imitating Zeffirelli, pronounced 'croass'.

The television series was scheduled to run for a total of six hours, but the first cut was an hour and three-quarters longer than that; it was eventually trimmed back to six and a quarter hours. It was an expensive production but finally took $45 million from its worldwide distribution and showed a net profit of $30 million.

So Lew Grade was looking understandably pleased when Peter ran into him in Cannes, in the foyer of his hotel, and congratulated him.

'No, Peter, it's I who should be congratulating you.'

'No, no, no, nonsense, I only had a small part in that machine, it's you who were the animating force behind it.'

'Well, you know, when I have a success, I like to share it with all. When I have a failure, I think I've got shoulders broad enough to take the brunt myself. Actually, we're a bigger success than even I thought possible. Do you know who the Rabbi Tannenbaum is?'

'No, I'm afraid I don't.'

'Well, he's the leader of the Reformed Jewish opinion in the States, and he actually said that had this programme been available at the time, there is no need for the Crucifixion to have taken place at all.'

Peter laughed, and Lew Grade said hastily, 'No, no, I know why you're laughing. No, no, I'll take that back.' Peter said, 'He didn't mean it that way, he was just congratulating us.'

The television mogul could have been forgiven for getting a bit carried away. After the first episode was aired on Italian TV, the Pope ended his Sunday address from his balcony to the crowds in St Peter's Square by telling them that they should all go home and watch the second part of *Jesus of Nazareth* that evening. In his later dealings with the Vatican over his own television programmes, Peter Ustinov found their reactions just as unexpected.

His next film seemed to get screen comedy back on the right rails. It was his second for the Disney studios; his first, in 1967, was *Blackbeard's Ghost*, a piece of undemanding whimsy in which Peter, in the title role, does good deeds until he can sail off into the beyond. He added a few lines of his own: 'I suppose I'm the most unpleasant man on the Spanish Main, and the Portugee Main too, come to that.' It was a great success with children, and Peter found it fun to do, but his most striking memory of it is of Elsa Lanchester's arrival on the set, just after the death of her husband, Charles Laughton. 'It was the most hideous car that I've ever seen, an open Cadillac with fins, the colour of lingerie-pink, with all the seats embroidered in silver wire. I said, "Elsa, what are you doing with that?" She said, "I sold the Renoirs." Charles would have turned in his grave … He probably did! He loved those pictures.'

This second film was much more fun for him. In *One of Our Dinosaurs is Missing* he played a Chinese spy chief, Hnup Wan, pursuing a stolen micro-film, which is hidden in a dinosaur skeleton at the Natural History Museum in South Kensington. At one point the whole skeleton is stolen, and the truck carrying it is chased through the London streets at high speed.

The cast of British comedy stalwarts included Derek Nimmo, Deryck Guyler, Arthur Howard, Bernard Bresslaw, Roy Kinnear, John Laurie, and Richard Pearson. Joss Ackland played a Texan, and Helen Hayes gave a wonderfully comic performance as the nanny. Peter did his send-up Chinese accent, so that even his sinister threats got a laugh. Interrogating the captured Derek Nimmo, he says, 'If there's anything we can do to make you more comfortable, do not hesitate to . . . scream.'

He assumed a heavy Chinese make-up, but the whole characterisation was meant to be a parody, appealing to the Western rather than the Eastern sense of humour. Peter says he has always had trouble playing Chinese, because Chinese actors naturally want to play the part. 'But they don't realise that it's not funny if a Chinese says, "Oh, so sorry," it's only funny if it's our concept of what Chinese should look or sound like from fifty years ago. I wanted to put in a line when he's sitting alone with his hat in a warehouse, and suddenly an arrow penetrates his hat, and he says, "I have been expecting same." '

There were echoes of this performance six years later, when he played the famous detective in *Charlie Chan and the Curse of the Dragon Queen*. His casting then would prove to be even more controversial.

He was switching nationalities with each part at this time. In 1974 he played a thinly disguised Khrushchev to George Irving's similarly fictional Nixon in his own play on Broadway, *Who's Who in Hell*, directed by Ellis Rabb. It co-starred Beau Bridges as an idealistic young man who assassinates both leaders, during a state visit to New York by the reigning First Secretary of the Communist Party in the Soviet Union. The play is about the confrontation between these three characters in Hell, where an elevator goes up to Purgatory, and then on to Heaven, but it is always under repair, or does not work at all. There is a fourth character called Mr Pilger, a little American who is stuck between these elevators and who is desperate to make a final decision – 'I've gotta know where I'm supposed to go' – and he is like a lost spirit with these three.

Peter was a bit carried away by the Nixon/Watergate affair and now says, 'One has to be very careful not to be too excited by actual events. It was quite a funny idea, but I don't think it really came off, because you needed a large cast to make that convincing. It was too topical, and I think public opinion in America was too divided at that moment. Alexander Cohen was eager to put it on, and I didn't know exactly at that moment who would put me on in London. It came to Broadway, but it didn't last very long.'

The third of his films for Disney, in 1975, was *Treasure of Matecumbe*, which he enjoyed the least. It was about a manhunt in Florida, and in it Peter had to steer a small steamboat at speed through the Okefenokee Swamps, which he found unnerving. 'I had no practice in it at all, and you had to prejudge it by miles, so you would be at the right angle before you got there, otherwise you'd be too far away or too close. It was a miracle we didn't all end up in the water.'

He was struck by how different the Disney atmosphere was from any of the other big Hollywood studios. 'They were really geared for a kind of juvenile innocence, in terms of the audience. Even in the canteen, the list of desserts was far longer than that of entrées. I overheard a row between some elderly gentlemen draughtsmen, eating their fudge sundaes. "Well, it's your own damned fault, I told you not to make them rhinoceroses, but to make them hippopotamuses; because you got that goddamn horn to cope with, and you've got to put it in all different positions. You should have taken hippopotamuses and leave it at that, they's just as comic as rhinoceroses, but there isn't a horn to cope with." '

He was mystified by the enormous lifts at Disney, large enough to take a grand piano and part of an orchestra. But apparently when Disney built the studios, the financial backers had little confidence in the future of cartoon films, so if they failed, the buildings could have become the annexe to St Joseph's Hospital, across the road: the lifts were designed all ready for patients on trolleys.

In his next film, for American television, Peter was asked to play a Jewish delicatessen owner in Brooklyn, but he had some doubts about his ability to appear authentic in the role, especially to all the real Jews who would be watching him. However, the script was by Rod Serling (the last he wrote), who had an impressive record for screenplays that were both literate and entertaining, so Peter accepted the part. In *A Storm in Summer*, the shopkeeper has a small black boy parked on him, as part of a goodwill exchange scheme between the races. After an initial reluctance, he becomes so attached to the boy that he cannot bear the thought of him going back to his foster-home.

It was a very sentimental story, and Peter had to speak lines like, 'I lost my only son, flying with a lot of bombers over Stuttgart, Germany' – pronounced 'Goimany', but it was powerfully written and played. It drew wonderful notices and won Peter his third Emmy. He was surprised how well it has stood up. 'They showed a small clip in a retrospective of all the Emmys, and I must say I was very convincing, I looked disgruntled and unpleasant all the way through.'

Paddy Chayefsky, the creator of his next part, had an even more distinguished list of American TV credits than Rod Serling; Peter had met him in London during the war when they were both serving soldiers, and they had got on well. His TV play *Gideon* explored the relations between God and men, with dialogue written in an idiomatic American style, which Peter found difficult: 'God, are you kidding, leaving me in this situation with the enemy? Come on!'

But whatever his own reservations about these parts, either before or after, Peter now had American producers beating a path to his door, with offers to play similar parts in musicals. After Peter declined to take over from Topol in *Fiddler on the Roof*, Richard Rodgers wanted him for the title role in *Noah's Ark*. This had Noah talking to God in that same kind of familiar way: 'God – giraffes? OK, but two of them!?'

Peter hates the idea of appearing in musicals even more than he does that kind of dialogue. 'I know that I need more elbow-room than a musical allows. I know I'll go out of tune, I'll forget the music, I'll get the words wrong. By then, all the audience have got the records, and they can all prompt me; I'd much rather not be in that situation. Richard Rodgers said, "Peter, all I ask you to do is sing something, here now, for us. We just want to hear the timbre" – pronounced 'timber' – "of your voice."

' "I can't sing."

' "Peter, that's not true, we heard you sing before, we just want you to confirm our impression. Peter, sing anything, Happy Birthday to you."

' "I don't know the lyrics."

'Then he realised that I didn't want to do it; it was done with Danny Kaye and it lasted one night.'

More congenial to him was the part of the ancient American in the science-fiction film, *Logan's Run*, which was set sometime in the twenty-third century. It was directed by Michael Anderson, whose career had been so well launched by the early Ustinov films. Anderson originally approached James Cagney, who was ill at the time and declined. So he sent the script to his old friend, in the hope that it would persuade him to take the part.

'When he enthusiastically called and said that it was nice of me to send the script, but that he would have said yes anyway to our working together, I pounced into producer Saul David's office and proclaimed that single-handedly I had received the go-ahead from the great Peter Ustinov himself. We marched upstairs and informed MGM that the part was cast. And that was that. Peter's performance transformed the film into another realm, far beyond all my thoughts and aspirations. It remains the shining performance in a film that is still being talked about and studied as the return of the science-fiction genre of film that preceded *Star Wars* and that set the stage for the future.'

The screenplay was relatively faithful to the original novel by William Nolan, at least in outline. Some unexplained apocalypse has forced the human race to retreat to life in a huge biosphere near Washington, DC. To keep the population stable, life ends there for everyone at the age of thirty, in a fiery ritual in the Carousel, which is presented as translation into another life but is in fact an execution. 'Runners' who try to avoid this termination are tracked down by policemen and killed. Michael York played one such policeman, Logan, who decides to make a run for it himself, with his girlfriend Jessica, played by Jenny Agutter. When they escape outside the dome, they are amazed to find a very old man living in an overgrown Lincoln Memorial, alone except for a great number of cats.

Up to that point, the film is very much an action movie, but with the appearance of Peter Ustinov as the ancient survivor, wandering through the crumbling and ivy-encrusted Senate building, it changes gear into a philosophical discussion between the young and the very old. Their contrasting visions as characters are intriguingly reflected in the actors' different memories of the shooting.

Peter says he did no rewrites himself. Michael Anderson puts it slightly differently: 'Peter knew the Hollywood system better than anyone and rarely suggested script changes, knowing that they would have to go through a chain of command that was formidable. But we would confer often and make subtle changes that were always an improvement but without rocking the MGM ship.'

If they were subtle enough to slip past the studio heads, they seemed rather more major to Michael York. 'Everyone admitted the script needed some work, so what happened was we all input our own angle on this. I remember Jenny Agutter and I working every morning on dialogue, making it our own, inhabiting it; and seeing Peter just invent his character on the spot, as this wonderful old Southerner, tearing up what was there in the script, using it as a kind of guideline, and creating an entirely individual character. It was wonderful to see.'

That character was based on a chance meeting when Peter went on a visit to New Orleans. 'A man who was obviously very gay, carrying a cat on his shoulder with a leash, walked past me and said, as though to himself, "Well, what are you doing here?" I turned round and he just went on walking. He gave me a clue of how to play this.'

He enjoyed playing the part, but when he saw the design for his make-up he groaned to Percy Westmore, the make-up artist, 'Oh Lord, I know what this means, getting up at four in the morning to get all that done.'

The cheerful answer, 'No, no, Peter, I think we can do it in twenty minutes,' only depressed him even more.

However, he came to enjoy the results of the brief, but enormously effective, transformation. Most of the film was shot in the studio, apart from an exterior sequence in Dallas. During a break between takes in the Plaza there, the director and cast were sitting in the shade of big umbrellas, when some bystanders came up and said, 'Oh, you're making a movie?' Michael Anderson explained courteously, and then (shades of the visitors to the *Spartacus* set) they turned to Peter and asked, 'How long have you been in the business, old-timer?'

Jenny Agutter was entranced by his response. 'Peter Ustinov very benevolently became the oldest actor you could possibly imagine, well over a hundred with memories far beyond, and it mesmerised them, of course, and all the rest of us. It was so incredibly funny, not really sending them up, it was just using the moment – this was what they required, and this was what he fitted into.'

His cartoonist's pen was very active on this shoot, and he presented several sketches to his young co-stars. He devised a cat-game for Jenny Agutter, using cat words – catastrophe, catapult, catatonic – with drawings of the cat that went with the words. Michael York had one 'which shows him engulfed in cats, and Jenny and me looking suitably heroic, and it just says: "Sanctuary is a nutsy, fruitsy, cup-cake," which I think is a comment on the dialogue he was having to deal with.'

His creativity and relaxed attitude to the work in hand gained the affection and respect of both of them, but he was especially helpful to Jenny, as this was her first big American film, although she had a lot of stage experience, including at the National Theatre. 'What I appreciated was that if you're making films, you have to believe absolutely the moment you're in, and Ustinov holds you in that moment, and he gives you the moment. He makes you believe in him, and he makes you believe in the situation. Now our situations were completely ridiculous, but I was fully engaged in what he did. He made absolute sense of this person who'd never had company apart from the company of his cats.'

Michael Anderson knew the range and power possessed by his old friend and colleague. 'His ad libs in his march across the devastated streets, graveyards, waterfalls, and mountains on the

SANCTUARY IS A NUTSY, FRUITSY CUPCAKE

With Michael York and Jenny Agutter in *Logan's Run*

trek from Washington to the Logan Bubble City were priceless, and if I ever said anything it was to suggest he may be overdoing it. He was puzzled and I was wrong, because of course he wasn't. His silent performance at the end, when the very young people emerge from the sealed city and see the old man for the first time, reached audiences everywhere.'

Logan's Run was very successful at the time and has become a science-fiction classic, about which its director is regularly interviewed. It was one of the last major movies made at MGM and the last sci-fi epic made within the studio system. *Star Wars* and its successors have all been made by independent companies. Now there is talk of doing a remake of *Logan's Run*; if that happens it will be interesting to see if the new digital effects dwarf the characters, as they have in so many of the recent films in that genre. The 1975 *Logan's Run* won its only Academy Award for Special Effects, but the director did not allow them to overwhelm his actors or their performances.

Fifteen

1975–1980
From the loss of Nadia to
King Lear in Canada

After the death of Klop, Peter noticed an almost immediate change in his mother's approach to life, which both surprised and disturbed him. 'It was very strange, because she was awfully irritated by his passive attitude. She did everything she could to stimulate him, and as soon as he was dead, she became exactly like he had been. She suddenly didn't see any point in going anywhere any more, if he was no longer there.'

This upset him, as Nadia had always been so interested in everything her son had done, and had worked so closely with him as a designer in the theatre and on film. 'She was a very strong woman, who knew what she wanted, who was regarded with immense reverence and affection by people who knew her, because she had a kind of serenity that attracted all the rather effeminate elements of the ballet, who adored her. People like Bobby Helpmann were always around her. She had such inner strength that I found out that many people gave her the nickname "God" on our film set where she was doing the costumes.'

Now all that energy and curiosity seemed to disappear, which was saddening for Peter on his regular visits in her last years. She suffered from the same complaint as her husband, hardening of the arteries and the consequent circulatory problems. In February 1975 she fell into a coma, and Peter sat with her to the end. 'I put a little radio next to her, which was playing the Jupiter Symphony. A slight smile appeared on her face, and she said, "Mozart." That was the last thing she said.'

She died on 9 February, at the age of seventy-nine. Klop had been cremated, and Nadia had had a horror of that, but to her son's surprise she left instructions that she too should be cremated and her ashes buried in the same churchyard as Klop's in Eastleach. Her funeral was attended by a wide variety of people who had known her, including the head of MI5, Sir Dick White, who had been Klop's employer but was also a special friend of hers.

Peter says, 'She was really the best mother one could have, because she was entirely unpossessive, which is remarkable for somebody with only one child. She only worried when I was middle-aged, before she died, that I was "getting plump", as she put it; that was about the worst it could get. She was a most extraordinary woman.'

She had always been very proud of her son's accomplishments, so it was a pity that she did not live quite long enough to see him honoured by the Queen later that year for 'services to the arts' when he was created a Commander of the British Empire. The actual presentation of the ribbon and medal of the CBE took place in the British Embassy in Paris, in the presence of Hélène and a few friends. Appropriately for someone who is such an internationalist, Peter has also been honoured by ten other nations, from the Americas to Europe and the Middle East, and twice by UNICEF. (The full list is in Appendix Seven.)

The film studios continued to call, but few of his next movies made real demands on the Ustinov talents. On paper *The Last Remake of Beau Geste* ought to have worked. It was directed by Marty Feldman, who also appeared in it, together with John Cleese, Roy Kinnear, Ann-Margret, and Michael York. The latter was delighted to be back in harness with Peter so soon after *Logan's Run*. For Michael the actual making of the film was 'an enjoyable experience, despite everything. Things were going wrong on the film a lot of the time, poor Marty got sick, and we were in Spain, on the plain, where it rained all the time. Of course we were meant to be filming in North Africa, so that was not without its problems. I remember my final duel with Peter, making up lines on the spot.'

Marty Feldman asked Peter to play the sheikh, but he said he would be much better as the sadistic German sergeant in the Foreign Legion. For him, the director/star was not really funny;

'he was just terribly eccentric, with that face, and those extra-ordinary eyes like a chameleon. Marty was obsessed with directing, he used to direct when he was acting. You'd see him flying through the air, shot out of a cannon, and as he sailed by he'd say, "Move to the right." It was like working in a circus. I had to walk on one leg the whole time, peg-leg, then aim it and fire from it with a special attachment. One can be much funnier without going to those lengths.'

But even with those reservations, the film might have succeeded if the director had been allowed by Universal to complete it his way. The man who ran the studio, so Michael York was told, 'sat through the entire film poker-faced, didn't see anything funny in it, and had it cut down to pieces, so I think we were all mostly performing on the cutting-room floor. I wish there were a director's cut, but of course poor Marty is no longer with us to provide his cut.'

Quite a lot of time was lost during the shooting, waiting for the rain to stop, but it was not time wasted for Peter, who was sitting in his trailer, busily writing in longhand his autobiography, *Dear Me*. He gave it that title because there are frequent passages where he conducts conversations with himself, posing questions much more direct and challenging than most interviewers would dare to put to him, even if sometimes he declined to answer himself, about the failure of his first two marriages for example, mainly to avoid causing pain to any of his children.

The book was a great success in the English-speaking world and also in other languages – in Paris it was awarded the Prix de la Butte for the Best Autobiography of 1978. It has gone through a succession of reprints in paperback and still sells steadily, even though its author has so far declined to bring it up to date. There have been too many other books he wished to write instead.

His next film, *Purple Taxi*, co-starred Fred Astaire, Philippe Noiret, and Charlotte Rampling, and was made in French. It was a success in France, but despite the casting it did not create much of a stir elsewhere, unlike Peter's next one, with a much longer roll-call of big names.

Death on the Nile was the first time Peter assumed the moustache of Agatha Christie's detective, Hercule Poirot, but he made the character so much his own that he has played him another five times since, in the cinema and on television.

Albert Finney had preceded him as the Belgian sleuth in *Murder on the Orient Express* but had no wish to play him a second time, and the producer John Brabourne thought that Peter Ustinov would be the perfect choice. He had admired him ever since he had appeared as an extra in Peter's wartime film, *The Way Ahead*. John Brabourne had negotiated a four-picture deal with Agatha Christie's agents; he wanted no more than that because, he says, 'They're all the same story, just different locations.'

The Christie novels are stronger on plot than characterisation, so the films only work with all-star casts to sustain the interest, which was what Brabourne managed to assemble for *Death on the Nile* – Harry Andrews, Jane Birkin, Lois Chiles, Mia Farrow, Jon Finch, Olivia Hussey, I.S. Johar, George Kennedy, Angela Lansbury, Simon McCorkindale, David Niven, Maggie Smith, Sam Wanamaker, and Jack Warden. He had also obtained the services of one of the great legends of the movie business – Bette Davis, who had a reputation for being a bit of a dragon on the set, so the producer went out to the airport himself to welcome her. In the limousine on the way in, he asked her, 'Are you happy about the locations in Egypt?'

'Locations? In my day locations came to me.'

Angela Lansbury had worked with her once before, so she knew what they were all in for: 'The thing about Miss Davis was that she felt she was the only real professional among the lot of us. She had no time for people who were late on the set, or youngsters who didn't know their lines, or who didn't have their hair coiffed in time, or held up the make-up people; she'd make a tremendous fuss about that, so we were all terrified of keeping her waiting. She would be on the set ready to shoot at five minutes to nine, when the director had hardly arrived; that didn't matter, she expected everyone to be on their marks, ready set to go.'

Peter is not easily thrown by great divas, either in the opera house or on a film, but even he was a bit concerned when he heard at 8 p.m. that the schedule for the next day had been changed at the last moment, because one of the actors had ton-sillitis, bringing forward the big scene between him, David Niven, and Bette Davis. He stopped by his old friend's room to ask, 'Have you heard the news, David?'

'No. What's that, chum?'

He was very bright and cheerful, and Peter knew he was always expecting good news.

'We've got to do the scene with Bette Davis tomorrow.'

'Oh Christ!'

'Why?'

'I've never worked with her, but her reputation in Hollywood! . . . Oh God! She not only knows her script, she knows yours, and wants to know when you're rehearsing why you're not respecting a comma.'

'What!?'

'Yes, she knows it all, she's absolutely so thorough. God, that is absolutely the *worst* news you could have given me.'

Peter returned to his room, now really worried about this reaction from his normally very relaxed friend. It was very hot, so he stripped off to his underpants, laid the script open on the bed, and walked around, trying to memorise his lines.

'And, Madame, you are concealing something . . . No, that's not right. You knew Sir Hubert was going to leave you something . . . No, no.'

He eventually fell asleep and woke up in the morning still in his underwear; he had never changed into his pyjamas.

They had to leave early in the morning to reach the boat, and Niven looked as white as a sheet.

'What's the matter, David?' asked Peter anxiously.

'I didn't sleep a wink, trying to learn this. Oh God!'

They arrived on deck and began rehearsing. Bette Davis was smoking through a veil. 'We didn't know our lines very well. She didn't know any of hers at all. I looked at David, and eventually she threw down her cigarette on the deck, which is not a thing any yachtsman would do, and stamped it out with an angry foot, saying, "Oh Christ, I can't manage this shit. Goddamn it, I didn't sleep a wink all night. I knew I'd have to work with two professionals this morning." Funnily enough, we then all knew our lines at once.'

For Angela Lansbury, this was her first chance to work with the former brother-in-law she had met as an impressionable teenager; now as a seasoned film actress herself, she warmed to his gift for helping everyone to give their best. 'Peter is the first person to understand that to be able to play good comedy, you've got to have ease and relaxation among the crew – all of the artisans and the artists involved. It's lovely to be on a set with Peter, because he is full of bonhomie and jokes and fun and sweetness, and very, very considerate of other actors. He doesn't send you up, doesn't make jokes like Danny Kaye would have done, he's not that kind of performer. He's not a comedian in that sense, he's a wonderful comic actor, whose whole approach is through characterisation, not through funny tricks. It's his quizzical expression and his reaction to what's going on around him that's hilarious.'

Angela Lansbury was accompanied in Egypt by her husband, Peter Pullen-Shaw, who had been a schoolmate of the other Peter at Westminster. His professional name was now Peter Shaw, but Ustinov could not break himself of the old schoolboy habit of nicknames and always addressed him as 'Pulley'. The three of them and David Niven all stayed at the Oberoi Hotel on an island in the Nile at Aswan and most evenings would dine together, while Ustinov and Niven did a double-act, vying with each other as storytellers.

The one abrasive element in this happy scene was the savage tongue of the director, John Guillermin, whose coarse language shocked even the hard-bitten Bette Davis. She used to say, 'Oh, send him away to wash his mouth out.'

John Brabourne brought out Lord Snowdon to do some special stills photography, and when he started positioning himself to take the pictures, Guillermin ordered him off the set. Eventually the photo-session was arranged at a different Egyptian location. In an attempt to lighten the embarrassing atmosphere caused by this incident, Peter did some drawings, which were photocopied and given to all the members of the crew.

One was a caricature of Lord Snowdon, loaded with equipment, and John Guillermin stripped to the waist, with his trousers falling down, wearing his Australian hat turned up at one side (his usual dress when directing), shouting at the photographer-peer, 'Don't think I don't know about royalty, I directed fucking *King Kong*.'

The dénouement of this story took Peter by surprise much later when he was on another film set. 'Suddenly Viscount Linley appeared and in the background, encouraging him to ask me, was Princess Margaret. Her son produced the photostat and said, "Would you mind signing it? It hangs above my bed." I thought it was amazing that as a boy he'd had "fucking *King Kong*" hanging over his bed.'

Death on the Nile was a great success when it was released in 1977, and the Variety Club of Great Britain gave Peter Ustinov the Best Actor Award for his Poirot – a part he would return to four years later, with a different director.

When Clive Donner cast him in *The Thief of Baghdad*, he and Terence Stamp were both pleased to be working together again. Peter was also delighted by the casting of Pavla Ustinov as his daughter in the film. She was even more thrilled, 'mostly because I got to see him, which was rare, and we got to be father and daughter on a daily basis for several weeks! Roddy McDowall remarked how incredibly professional we were, because one would have never guessed we were father and daughter in real life. The minute Clive said "Cut" that was it. There was no socialising outside the set for us. Maybe our way of not being accused of nepotism? I don't know.'

They worked very well together and soon afterwards played opposite each other again for Channel 13 in the States, in scenes from several Ustinov plays, performed live on stage in Charleston, South Carolina. Pavla played all the women, including his eighty-year-old wife in *Photo Finish*. 'He would trick me during the performance by intentionally changing a prop cue – challenging me to improvise my way out of the situation. I loved that.'

They were both challenged when they appeared on *The Dinah Shore Show* on American television, at about the same time. They only discovered when they arrived at the studio that the topic was 'Fathers/Mothers and Daughters'; one of the other pairs was

Janet Leigh and Jamie Lee Curtis. 'At the end we had to play a game to prove how well we knew each other. Needless to say, Peter and I were at a disadvantage and we both knew it. So without being able to consult each other, since it was live television – we cheated (we had no choice) and won! They removed the parents and put three animals before each of us. The others had a kitten, a puppy, a goldfish, a canary etc. . . . I had before me a huge turtle, a six-foot-long boa-constrictor, and a very talkative parrot! We now had to guess, and write our answers on three pieces of paper, which of these our parents would prefer to take home and why. When Peter came back on stage, I dropped my papers on the floor. He picked them up and answered correctly. I asked him after the show if he read them and he said, "Of course. Incidents like this when one has to improvise an expected relationship bring one closer."'

Pavla felt even closer to her father when she watched him play Lear at Stratford, Ontario. 'I found the whole production remarkable and his performance very moving. I sat in the audience with Tammy and Andrea – his three daughters watching him as King Lear with his three stage daughters. There was something magical about that for me.'

Robin Phillips was the director, and he and Peter agreed on setting it in the 1850s, around the time of the Crimean War. This meant that in the early scenes Lear corresponded in costume to all the kings and emperors in Europe at that time, who on official occasions often changed into each other's uniforms. It emphasised some important mood-changes for Peter's interpretation of the King: 'On the heath, if he's in a filthy shift, it means something if he's been wearing glamorous uniform before, with a lot of medals. Also, when he's taken prisoner at the end, he's miraculously put into a French uniform, and the first moment of sanity is when he looks at his sleeve and asks, "Am I in France?", which would be an automatic reaction from somebody who is used to an English uniform and is suddenly put into something light blue and gold.'

The Fool was played by William Hutt as being the same age as Lear, sharing jokes that no one else understood and becoming dependent on one another. Peter had long wanted to play Lear, and he researched the various interpretations that have been offered up over the years. He soon found, like many of his predecessors, that the study is no substitute for the stage. 'You start off with those editions where over half the page is taken up by notes by professors, and you think some are rather peculiar, but others you treat with great reverence. I remember the phrase from the notes in the edition we used: "Kirschbaum, however disagrees with this." So whenever there was any difficulty, I invoked Kirschbaum. Then, when you're actually playing it, you have the illusion that you're going out to sea in a boat alone with Shakespeare. And that the professors are like bungalows disappearing into the distance.'

By the end Lear is exhausted, and Peter played the great cry of 'Howl, howl, howl, howl, howl' as though he had no voice left. 'I think it's by relying on pathos as a stepping-stone, not just on poetry and tragedy, that you can really move a modern audience, which you can't do by just bellowing or being poetic or choreographic. So I played it that way, for better or worse.'

For those who saw it, it was certainly for the better. His former leading lady, Rosemary Harris, thought 'it was a wonderful part for him. He had all the humour in it, and the madness and the tragedy of Lear.' She was staying with her friend Patricia Connolly, who was playing Cordelia, and also Viola in *Twelfth Night* that season.

Rosemary's daughter, Jennifer Ehle, was then about eight, and Patricia's daughter Emily was six. There was a big party after one performance of *Twelfth Night*, and Peter was invited, with the other members of the company. Because it was his night off, he was the first to arrive at 10 p.m., and the others only turned up at 10.30. The two mothers had left the little girls with instructions that if anybody came early, they were to hold the fort and entertain them until they got home. So they opened the door to Peter in their mothers' long dresses, wearing make-up. 'Being Peter, he wasn't at all nonplussed. They invited him in, sat him down, and entertained him. What he thought of these two little nymphets, I can't imagine; but only Peter would sit and be amused, and enjoy it all. He made them feel quite happy and very grown-up.'

He so took it in his stride that now he cannot even remember the incident, though the girls and their mothers do. But he was very thrown when his own son Igor suddenly appeared in his dressing room before a performance; Peter had no idea that he was even in Canada, and he was just about to go on stage for the opening scene.

'They'd called the five minutes, three minutes ago, so I said, "My God, what are you doing here?"

' "Oh well, I came anyway."

' "Yes, but I've got to go on the stage in a moment. You coming tonight?"

' "Yes, I've got a ticket."

' "Oh, wonderful."

'Suddenly he threw down an envelope, and I said, "Not now. What is that?"

' "I think you ought to look at it before you go on the stage."

'I looked at it, and there were pictures of a baby, even being suckled, with the breast slightly out of focus. "What is this?"

' "Well, it's mine, and in a way yours."

' "BEGINNERS PLEASE" came over the tannoy.

'I went on stage, realising I was a grandfather for the first time, and really found it difficult to concentrate on these three Ugly Sisters. He should have told me afterwards, but he felt now or never. Now she's twenty-two.'

He had such a happy time in the 1979 Stratford Ontario season that he agreed to return and repeat the role in 1980. Visually, it was exactly the same production, with some newcomers in the cast, but the atmosphere had changed, and Peter suffered two major disappointments.

The first was over the proposed television recording by the Canadian Broadcasting Corporation. It was all set to go, until the Canadian unions objected to the one Australian in the cast – the Cordelia, Patricia Connolly. They had no objection to the non-Canadian playing Lear, because his name was above the title, but Peter was furious and remonstrated with the union official.

'Explain to me the logic of doing forty-five Canadian actors out of a paying job on television, because there's one Australian actress. Does that make sense?'

'No, it doesn't, Peter, but that's the law at this time.'

One of the carrots to tempt Peter to return for the second season was the proposal to transfer the production later to London, but this too was doomed. Part of Robin Phillips' rehearsal process had been to make the cast play various games, which the first time around Peter had found interesting. But now, he says, 'You felt you were becoming part of a sect. Robin, instead of being another free spirit, just particularly gifted at his job, which was the way he held our attention at the beginning, became a kind of guru, asking to be followed in all sorts of decisions that were not necessarily ours. That's what led to the torpedoing of the whole initiative to take the Canadians to London. Many of them had accepted other jobs because he didn't warn them in time. It was a tremendous administrative cock-up.'

The whole thing ended with a great deal of acrimony. Duncan Weldon, whose management had planned to present *King Lear* at the Haymarket, had already built the sets at considerable expense, and the final act of this sad drama was played out in the law courts. Peter sued for breach of contract, as a matter of principle, but finally settled out of court for a modest sum, not wanting to penalise the Stratford organisation for the short-comings of its director, who was at loggerheads with them anyway and soon departed himself.

The upshot was that British audiences were denied the opportunity of seeing the only Shakespearean role Peter Ustinov has played or ever wanted to play on stage. He had already declined Falstaff, and Prospero never appealed to him, although he would seem admirably equipped to play that magician. When I reminded him that he did play Caliban on radio, he just laughed and said, 'Oh, on radio anything's possible.'

King Lear was not quite his farewell to the theatre; there was still his appearance in his own play, *Beethoven's Tenth*, to come; but apart from that, his stage appearances since have been limited to his one-man show, or acting as narrator in performances involving music of various kinds. These engaged more and more of his attention over the next two decades.

Sixteen

1979–1982
From *The Hermitage* to
The Marriage

The Russian line in the Ustinov ancestry has always been important to Peter, and his interest in Russian history and culture has become stronger as he has grown older. The Olympic Games were to be held in Moscow in 1980, so the American television network NBC, who had acquired the TV rights to the Games, in association with a German producer called Lothar Bock, invited the BBC to make a major documentary about the treasures of the Hermitage Museum in Leningrad. Owing to the international situation at the time, the BBC had grown a little wary about such co-production deals, so their Head of Music and Arts, Humphrey Burton, invited Derek Bailey to direct it under the banner of his own independent company, Landseer Films.

The presenters were already fixed to be Peter Ustinov and Natalie Wood. The American film star spoke fluent Russian; born Natasha Virapaev in Siberia, she had learnt the language at her mother's knee. Derek Bailey had worked briefly with Peter a couple of times before on television, filming him on the set of *Billy Budd* and revisiting Westminster School with Russell Harty, but this project was on a much bigger scale.

The filming in Leningrad took four weeks. Peter was present for the first two, and Natalie for the second and third, so they overlapped by one week for the scenes involving them both. The scripts were written by Derek Bailey and his arts historian researcher, Judy Marle, although there were also spontaneous conversations between the two presenters as they walked through the endless galleries of the Hermitage, sometimes almost lost in the milling crowds of tourists.

The collection is so vast that a visitor intent on seeing all of the 2,500,000 objects, including 8000 paintings, would have to walk at least thirteen miles to visit all 350 rooms. So the film-makers were faced with a succession of difficult choices.

The director knew how Peter could seize on an inspiration, and he retains one very clear image of him, in 'a wonderful gallery which is covered with paintings by George Dawe, the English portraitist of the late eighteenth and early nineteenth centuries, of Russian generals of the time. I suggested to Peter that instead of doing a commentary to camera, it might be fun if he were just to walk down there, thinking himself into the mood of the time and humming to himself the *1812 Overture*. First take – straight away.'

On another occasion in the film he is suddenly confronted by a series of large Rubens canvases, prominently featuring his characteristically over-endowed female voluptuaries. Peter's eyes twinkled as he said, 'Oh dear, here we go again!'

One of Catherine the Great's court composers, Paisiello, wrote obscure operas, which have never since been performed. The production team dug out the score of *The Pretentious Pundit* and chose 'the coughing duet' for Peter and his son Igor to sing. They performed it in eighteenth-century wigs and costumes on the stage of the little theatre in the Winter Palace, accompanied by a small orchestra. It was a difficult piece, and the singers had to cough on the note. After stumbling through one unsatisfactory rehearsal, Ustinov Senior had to remind Ustinov Junior that it was all very well to make beautiful sounds, but it was more important to hit the right notes. The final filmed performance was hilarious, but failed to rescue the opera from its former and well-merited obscurity.

The film was made when Leonid Brezhnev was at the helm of the Soviet Union, so the British crew were lumbered with a KGB minder as official interpreter. Derek Bailey shuddered as he recalled that this man 'used to become terribly depressed and get very drunk and melancholy, when he would go and wake up Peter to talk in the middle of the night'.

Peter's satirical eye for Soviet bureaucracy almost got the better of him when he spoke at a dinner for everyone connected with the filming – British, Americans, Germans, and Russians. He praised the formidable women attendants who kept watch on the galleries and their visitors, suggesting that if they had been present in 1917 the revolutionaries would have handed in their rifles to them, instead of storming the Winter Palace. 'No wonder the Germans failed to get through during the Second World War siege, though they have at last managed it through Lothar Bock and his associates.' This last sally raised few laughs from the Russians in his audience.

Ironically, shortly after the film was completed, the Russian tanks rolled into Afghanistan and America responded by boycotting the Russian Olympics. NBC's motive in commissioning the film had consequently disappeared, so they put it on the shelf. But it was well received when it was aired by the BBC.

Peter enjoyed appearing with Igor in Leningrad. When he moved to Israel, the location for the movie *Ashanti*, he received a letter from his eldest daughter, asking if she could join him there. Tamara's first marriage to Chris Parr, the Director of the Glasgow Traverse Theatre, was breaking up, and she was in need of a complete change. Her father said that of course she must come out. So she spent about ten days with him, 'and got my head together about where I was going back to live. It was wonderful, and it really helped. In a situation like that he was very helpful, he'll be there when you need him.'

Peter enjoyed her stay just as much. 'I must say we had a lot of giggles. We got to know each other better than we had before.'

In *Ashanti* Peter played an Arab slave-trader, pursued by Michael Caine in search of his kidnapped wife. Peter's distrust of his previous four-legged mounts was now transferred to the camel that he had to ride across the desert in this adventure movie, which made few other demands on his talents.

This was but the lull before the challenging intellectual storm of *Einstein's Universe*, which he was persuaded to do by Nigel Calder, the science writer and broadcaster. It was about space and time, and included a sequence between Peter, as a centenarian on earth, and his twin brother, who had been in space for years and remained exactly the same age as when he left. Peter was intrigued by the whole concept: 'I understood the Theory of Relativity for about three minutes after we had finished, and after that I forgot it and couldn't understand a word of it again.'

He enjoyed the whole experience, with the exception of one expedition to a remote American location, which for once the BBC organised with less than its usual efficiency. He had to fly to New York and take a domestic flight to Odessa, Texas. There, he was told, he would be met by another means of transport and taken to an observatory high in the Texan hills. He expected to find a car waiting, but when he disembarked with his bags there was no sign of one. He feared momentarily that he was going to be marooned for ever in Odessa, until an old man approached him.

'Is your name Unisock?'

'Probably, yes.'

'I've been waiting for you. I'm going to take you to the Observatory, is that right?'

'Yes, that's right.'

'Come on.'

They walked to a one-engined plane, and the man said, 'Throw your bags back there, can you find your own way up in there? I'm the pilot, I'll be sitting there.'

As they took off into the Texan hills, the pilot's conversation made his passenger increasingly nervous.

'I'm eighty-five years of age, I do this job as a hobby, and the BCN – what is it, BCN?'

'BBC.'

'Oh, is that what it is? Well, they got in touch with me through their agent in El Paso, and they suggested you might want to fly there. I've retired a long time ago, but I do this for my own pleasure. I own the plane, it's probably the last one I ever will own.'

Peter said, 'I couldn't concentrate, I was looking at everything he did in case he had a heart attack. I thought, eighty-five! Christ, the law of averages! I made them take me back by car.'

In all his world travels as performer and UNICEF ambassador, Peter must have flown by as many different airlines as almost anyone, but he has developed a marked preference for pilots who are younger than he is.

If that trip frightened him, the next film he made for the BBC frightened the viewers even more. This was *Nuclear Nightmares*, which speculated on four different ways that nuclear war could break out without anyone being able to control it. The programme took no sides in the East–West ideological divide, and when it was screened at UNESCO headquarters in Paris, the Soviet delegation was amazed by its political neutrality. They said they could find nothing to quarrel with in it; it was the general terror of all civilised people, and they wanted it shown on Russian television. That never happened, but for its presenter, 'It was one of those many things which I loved doing at the time, provoking the lobby that suggested the Cold War was inevitable. I was just delighted that we could show this film and that the Russians were amazed by the impartiality of the West.'

He was brought back to earth with a bump in San Francisco, the location of *Charlie Chan and the Curse of the Dragon Queen*. The mutterings of Chinese actors in Britain about him in *One of Our Dinosaurs is Missing* swelled to an uproar from the Chinese branch of American Equity about him playing Charlie Chan.

When the filming was threatened by certain non-theatrical elements of the Chinese community, the Mafia stepped in and offered their protection. Peter was told, 'Frank wants to know whether you'd be able to come and have dinner with him on Saturday, an Italian restaurant, just the greatest food, where you can eat as much as you like for five dollars.'

Peter demurred. 'It would be easier for us if he invited us on Sunday, because since we are on location Saturday is accepted as a working day, and I don't know when we finish.'

'I'll ask him and bring back the noos for ya tomorrow.'

The next day the spokesman came back and said, 'No, Frank can only do Saturday. It's Saturday or nothing, because Sunday he goes into jail.'

When the film opened in the States in February 1981, the protests went up several notches; Asian-American groups denounced the Ustinov portrayal as 'a racist and degrading stereotype'. Several TV stations in San Francisco and Los Angeles refused to run commercials for the film, and the Association of Asian American Artists took out newspaper advertisements accusing the production company, American Cinema, of 'robbing Asian Pacific Americans of dignity, pride and human qualities'.

When Richard Lederer, its marketing vice-president, counter-accused the protesting groups of practising censorship, one of their organisers, Mr Forest Gok, denied it, saying, 'It's not news or public affairs, it's a money matter. We want to show it's bad business to promote racism.'

The bemused actor at the centre of this ethnic furore tried to cool the atmosphere, pointing out that in some forty-six previous films featuring Charlie Chan, only two of them had cast Chinese actors in the role. He commented mildly of the San Francisco protesters, 'I think these people were slightly lost. Many of them look in their mirrors and see Chinese but they aren't Chinese. They can't speak Chinese. I told them we were really in the same position. I'm as English as they are American, and I'm as Russian as they are Chinese. Now where does that leave us?'

The film arrived in Britain just as his new play, *Overheard*, opened at the Theatre Royal in the Haymarket. Set in a small unnamed Balkan country, the action takes place in the British Embassy, where the ambassador and his wife (Ian Carmichael and Deborah Kerr) have grown bored with each other. When a dissident poet bursts in seeking asylum, he quickly seduces both the ambassador's wife and his secretary, played by Tamara Ustinov. The actor who played the defector, Aharon Ipale, was described by the author simply as 'bad' but by the director, Clifford Williams, as 'a pain in the neck'.

Author and director met to discuss it at the Berkeley Hotel, and the latter asked, 'How do you see these people?' Peter promptly drew impressions of them on the hotel notepaper, but said there was no necessity to cast like his drawings. While he was doing this the telephone rang, and after a conversation in Italian, Peter turned to Clifford Williams and said, 'I've got to get a move-on now, because I've got to go to Rome.'

'Oh, what have you got to go there for?'

'The Pope wants me to play tennis with him.'

Ian Carmichael had been contemplating retirement to York-shire, 'but you don't turn down a play by Peter Ustinov, opposite Deborah Kerr, at the Haymarket, and I certainly enjoyed the experience. We thought *Overheard* was overlong, and Clifford and I suggested to Peter some specific cuts. But Peter would say, "No, no, I'll go away and rewrite it." And the new version would be even longer.'

Tamara told the director, 'He's always like this, you must cut it yourself.'

The question of length, and the procession of directors down the years pleading for cuts, had been such a constant refrain that I pressed Peter on his reluctance to oblige. 'Usually there was a very good reason for keeping them in, for the logic of the play's construction. But now I've begun to think that everything that's ever been written is a tiny bit too long with the exception of a Japanese haiku, which is just about the right length. One of which I'm inordinately fond was written by a woman in the eighteenth century. "Of the infinite steps to my heart, he scaled one, perhaps two." That's all. I think it's the most divine cruelty.'

Clifford Williams, a noted Shavian director, tried to stop himself worrying about whether this Ustinov play was too long by remind-ing himself, 'They said that about every play Shaw ever wrote.'

The pre-London tour, which took in Billingham, Richmond, Bristol, and Brighton, drew packed appreciative audiences, keen to see the latest Ustinov play and its two stars who were so well known through their films. The playwright's professional judgment on them was that 'Deborah Kerr was a marvellous actress when she was being soft, but perhaps because she had done so many films she felt constrained to talk much louder than was necessary in the theatre. Carmichael was rather conventional but very good.'

Once again, he had exerted no influence in the casting of his daughter, so he was particularly pleased by her performance:

'Tammy was absolutely marvellous in it, as a very short-sighted secretary, who could never distinguish whether a door was shut or open, and always tried to enter beside the door, then had to come back to feel for it. She was the epitome of a resilient British secretary with some sort of defect.'

The plot mechanism hinges on the fact that the embassy is bugged, and the ambassador's knowledge of that to misinform the eavesdroppers to win the day, and his wife back, at the end. The author's enthusiasm for both the structure and the message of his play seemed to be shared by audiences, both in the provinces and in London, where it ran for six months.

But this was despite the critics, not because of them, as their response ran the full gamut from denunciation to disappointment. For Michael Coveney in the *Financial Times* it was 'a quite appalling evening, dreadfully directed by Clifford Williams and containing as much life and contemporary appeal as a stuffed dinosaur'. Irving Wardle in *The Times* thought it 'all carefully assembled and dramatically lifeless'. Milton Shulman admired some of the performances in the *Evening Standard*, but his conclusion was that 'for all its talk about Marxism and defection, this is really a slight, romantic comedy that can hardly be numbered amongst Mr Ustinov's more profound efforts.'

In the *Guardian* Michael Billington took a different view from Michael Coveney, saying that 'the piece is given the full Haymarket treatment in Clifford Williams' tony production.' But even he thought the play was flawed. 'The old charge remains true: that Ustinov is better at describing what divides countries than what unites individuals ... He seems to observe countries through a sharp microscope and people through a hazy telescope ... One just comes out wishing that Ustinov's characters had one half the blithe waterfall-wit and abundance of their astonishing author.'

Tamara thought it was a shame that her father could not act in the play in London, 'because I think if he'd been in it, it would have been more of a success than it was'. That opinion would seem to be borne out by the fact that when he did appear in *Overheard* on German television, as the dictator who seeks asylum at the end, the play was greeted with acclamation.

The author was spared the immediate impact of the unfavourable British reviews, as he left London two days before the opening night, to begin shooting his next Poirot film.

By the time they were sent on to him in Majorca, he was fortunately more preoccupied with breathing life again into Agatha Christie's most famous detective. He was pleased to be rejoined by Maggie Smith and Jane Birkin, and the newcomers to this Christie story were Colin Blakely, James Mason, Diana Rigg, Roddy McDowall, Sylvia Miles, Richard Vernon, Nicholas Clay, and Denis Quilley.

Anthony Shaffer was the scriptwriter for both *Death on the Nile* and *Evil Under the Sun*, and for the new film the novel's setting 'somewhere off Devon' was translated to the Dalmatian coast although, in a switch of location which so often seems to happen with films, it was actually shot mostly in Majorca, where the director Guy Hamilton lived. The period was also moved back to the 1930s and the music of Cole Porter, with evocative watercolour illustrations by Hugh Casson for the opening credits.

Peter was keen to add the scene where Poirot enters the sea in a voluminous pre-war bathing suit, more for dramatic than costume reasons. 'We wanted a break in the film: the form is as rigid as an interview, with Poirot asking all the questions and not being able to put on a bravura performance until the very end.'

He had also been giving more thought at this time to the novelist's view of the hero's foreignness. 'Agatha Christie only made Poirot a Belgian because someone told her that there were too many French detectives around. With another stroke of the pen she could easily have turned him into a Luxembourgeois. On the printed page Poirot is no more Belgian than Major Thompson is English. In language terms we probably see him as one of those foreign schoolmasters whose English is *too* correct – all very fluent and fluid and quite artificial. Remember that Poirot only puts the simplest words into French, the complex ones are always left in English. He remains very avaricious, very honourable, and very deeply in love with himself.'

Although he thought that the story was not as interesting, nor as tightly directed, as *Death on the Nile*, it was chosen for the

Royal Command Film Performance of 1982. He was naturally asked then how many more times he would play Poirot, and his reply was cautious. 'Perhaps one more, if the production team wants it. They come at roughly five-year intervals and that's just about right for me.'

The John Brabourne/Richard Goodwin partnership did want it, but he only played Poirot once more for the big screen. By then, however, Poirot had become so associated with the Ustinov portrayal in the public mind that he would subsequently play the character in three more films for American television.

He took a break from filming by returning to the opera, at La Scala, Milan, where he directed two-thirds of a Stravinsky triple bill – *Mavra* and *The Flood*. Despite La Scala's reputation for being a difficult place to work, Peter found it very hospitable after his treatment at the Paris Opera. 'It's the only place I know where they call you Maestro from the moment you're woken at the hotel in the morning – "Otto e mezzo, Maestro" – to the moment you retire to bed. I find that most reassuring.'

Peter has enjoyed a number of happy creative experiences in Italy, but not all of them have exported successfully. La Scala was keen to stage all the Mussorgsky operas, including *The Marriage*, of which only one act exists, and that was only scored for piano. As forty minutes of music was not enough for a whole evening, Peter's help was sought. He wrote a play around it, inventing a sleazy provincial opera company who gather for the sixth year of rehearsal of the first act, because the second act has still not arrived. The stage was stacked with bits of sets from *Lohengrin*, *Aida*, and other operas, and in Milan Peter played Rimsky-Korsakov in Italian, wearing a long beard and a naval uniform. The concept delighted the Milanese, and Peter said it was 'the best press I've had for a long time'. He was then invited to take *The Marriage* to the Edinburgh Festival in 1982.

He was dismayed when it was bitterly attacked there, because its origins were not properly explained. The Festival publicity omitted to mention that it had been commissioned by La Scala, with very specific requests, 'so they thought it was a new play of mine, in which I was just so lazy that I put a whole opera in the middle of it, without any reason'.

Irving Wardle was one of the reviewers who did know the terms of the commission from La Scala, and he leapt to the author's defence in *The Times*, blaming the Festival for billing it 'as a main event. As a sideshow, appealing equally to the theatre-going and musical public, it would have had queues snaking round the circuit tent village or any other modest venue. They would have got their money's worth from Ustinov's scarf-swathed performance as a superannuated stage manager, from seeing the fine musician Roger Vignoles playing a hen-pecked rehearsal pianist, and from pro-longed sketches of delicious comic-writing – such as the stage manager's grovelling courtesies to a top-grade Tsarist audience, coupled with a catalogue of Tsarist taxes for anyone thinking of asking for his money back.'

Wardle's long article, championing the Ustinov case against the savaging from the other critics, ended with a handsome *mea culpa* on behalf of his fellows: 'We are always telling him that he could do better, and bemoaning the slapdash work of such a talented boy. When he does make the attempt, we regress to the little girl in the Beerbohm cartoon and complain "Oh, Uncle Peter, why cannot you always be wholly frivolous?" *The Marriage* is one answer to that; and it could only have been made by someone with a generous heart as well as matchless talents.'

The failure of *The Marriage* was unique to that Festival. Apart from its earlier acclaim in Milan, it has since succeeded in Bonn and the text has recently been published in Germany, with drawings by the author.

Brickbats in Edinburgh were mere irritations, compared to the tribulations that were about to beset him on his next major venture into film production.

Seventeen

1982–1986
Memed My Hawk, Beethoven's Tenth and *Ustinov in Russia*

In the previous forty years in the film business the name of Peter Ustinov had become familiar as an actor, writer, director and producer – sometimes in all four capacities at once – but he bitterly regrets getting sucked into carrying out a fifth function as financier on *Memed My Hawk*.

It was certainly not his original intention, and everything looked promising at the beginning. The book on which his screenplay was based was by Yasher Kemal, a Kurdish writer who had been considered for the Nobel Prize several times. Peter's old friend Herbert Lom joined the cast and, after their enjoyable time together in *Evil Under the Sun*, so did his newer friend Denis Quilley, with an eagerness that startled his agent when he rang and told him, 'You've been offered a part in a film in Yugoslavia called *Memed My Hawk*, which is going to star and be directed by Peter Ustinov.'

'I'll do it.'

'Well hold on, it's not a marvellous script, I don't think, and it's not a very good part.'

'It doesn't matter, if Peter's there, I'll do it, just for the pleasure of being there with him.'

He and Michael Elphick played a couple of Turkish bandits, Simon Dutton was Memed, who leads the bandits against the tyrannical Abdi Aga, played by Peter Ustinov, and Herbert Lom was a competing crooked landowner. But there was a much bigger financial drama going on off-camera, when his backers left him in the lurch.

The first Peter knew of this was when the technicians' wives began ringing up to tell their husbands that no money had come that week, rapidly followed by calls to the actors from their agents. To stop the plugs being pulled on the film, the director resorted to paying the salaries out of his own pocket.

As the costs escalated, Peter's lawyer in Yugoslavia came to him and said he should declare himself bankrupt, which he flatly refused to do. 'We found a man who was willing to put up the money to buy it out as a tax loss for his company. We came to an arrangement with the bank to absorb some of the loss, but they still insisted I had to pay out something like £180,000, apart from having paid out all the crew on location in Yugoslavia. It was a nightmare! Also I had to try to direct the film under those conditions!'

His professionalism was such that even highly experienced actors like Denis Quilley had no inkling of Peter's problems until afterwards. 'Unbeknownst to us, and certainly to me, he was directing and starring in a film during the day, which is already enough for two men, and spending every evening phoning LA, London, Switzerland, and everywhere else, trying to raise a million quid. Peter put in many thousands of pounds of his own money to keep the production going, while still doing the fundraising. The point about that is, that all during that period you would never have known anything was wrong. He never lost his sense of humour; he was the same entertaining and amusing and calm person that he was all through *Evil Under the Sun*.'

This echoes the memories of the cast of *Billy Budd*, when the pressures of Peter's multiple duties never showed either, but at least on the earlier film he was not also dipping into his own pocket to keep things going.

Peter shared the real nature of the problem with no one, but Herbert Lom knew him well enough to know that something was up; he also knew that Peter was spending a lot of time on the telephone. 'I noticed when he had a difficult phone call the night before, he had twice as big a breakfast as usual. He had a lot of big breakfasts on that film.'

Denis Quilley found his directorial style very relaxed and easy.

'He waited to see what you bring, what your natural response is, and then gently nudges you a little way in one direction or another, nearer to what he has at the back of his head. He never says, "I want you to play the part like this." He'd say things like, "This scene might be funnier if you both wore your fezzes," to Michael Elphick and myself.'

Although he admired the performances of both Herbert Lom and Peter Ustinov, Quilley thought the film was flawed and did not really work.

Peter was disappointed too in its lack of a coherent style. 'There were too many different accents, but one couldn't really rectify that, because we were shooting on a shoestring, we had no money to pay for anything. Eventually we opened at the Minema in Knightsbridge,' – which was tiny – 'and ran there for two weeks. Then we had a gala opening at the ABC in Shaftesbury Avenue, but it didn't seem satisfactory. The German version was excellent, simply because they had it all dubbed, with Germans speaking every part, which gave it a consistency that it never had with us.'

Peter never recovered the money he put into the film and ended up deeply out of pocket. It was a very upsetting experience for him, and it took him seven years to clear the outstanding debt. Apart from the severe financial penalty that he incurred, it was our loss that *Memed My Hawk* was the last film to bear his credit as director.

But, just as before, when his way seemed temporarily blocked in the theatre he turned to film, so now he transferred his energy and talent to his twenty-first full-length play, *Beethoven's Tenth*. Many of his plays have a rich vein of fantasy running through them, and some are based on an inspired flight of the Ustinov imagination that could only work in the theatre of illusion, not in the world of cinematic realism. Here he speculated on what would happen if Beethoven reappeared at the age of 212.

He explained why in a programme note to set the scene:

All those who have lived on this earth are still present in some form or other, whether it is as mere ash, bone, earth or as a molecule or quirk in a living person. That is, or should be, a consolation for death even in those who reject the comfort of a conviction in the soul's immortality. There are those exceptional cases like Beethoven and Shakespeare, Molière and Mozart, Pasteur and Pavlov who are more present today than during their own lives, either by virtue of music, words, a mere bottle of milk, or indeed the motivation of a dog biting a milkman.

It was this feeling that immortals are just out of sight, out of earshot, which led me to imagine the effect on a family obsessed with somewhat mundane problems of a visit by just such a great figure of the past, not in the form of a ghost or a spirit, but in a remarkable, palpable and indeed boisterous form. Stephen Fauldgate is a reputable music critic whose special study outside the contemporary scene is Beethoven. He is fastidious in his choice of words and selection of sentiment. His son, Pascal, writes facile symphonies in menacing profusion. His wife, Jessica, an erstwhile mezzo-soprano, gave up her career to make peace between the two men in her life. She is not helped much by Irmgard, an Austrian au pair, whose childhood was spent with Beethoven's death mask over her cot.

The stage is set for a visitation, and even if imaginary anguish is replaced by moments of real pain – humanity, honesty and humour are the winners in the end.

When Irmgard conjures up the composer, his arrival is heralded by a thunderous knock on the door like the opening chords of his Fifth Symphony – pa-pa-pa-paaah.

The critic is discomposed by the appearance of the subject of all his studies, which rapidly disrupts the household. Some of the composer's sallies have a particular edge, coming from the mouth of the actor-author playing him.

Ludwig What is there to be concerned about in your father? In my experience, critics have always been more than able to look after themselves.

Pascal He's not a critic at heart, you understand, but a failed composer.

Ludwig There is nothing unusual in that.

After Beethoven is fitted with a hearing aid by a local doctor, the critic sits him down to listen to his complete works on disc. Surveying the shelves of review copies, he exclaims, 'You mean critics get presents these days – as well as bribes?' When Pascal asks him if he is deeply religious, Beethoven replies, 'I am deeply superstitious. From the outside, it looks exactly the same.'

The author strongly identified with the composer. 'I feel that Beethoven is always more constipated than Mozart, because you can always feel the effort of the composition with him, but he is the most moving to me as a person. I find him absolutely fascinating.'

To portray the man himself on stage, he shaved off the beard that had become one of his most instantly recognisable features, and in a curly wig he looked astonishingly like the paintings of Beethoven.

As Sheridan Morley pointed out in his enthusiastic review in *Punch*, he was well matched by the 'Levinite music critic wonderfully well played by Robin Bailey as the Laurel to Ustinov's Hardy, and from that moment forward the two of them go into a sustained double-act of such massive humanity and charm as to be unmissable and unbeatable'.

In the *Observer* Robert Cushman also zeroed in on this now long-established partnership. 'Mr Ustinov moves slowly around in a cloud of dust, occasionally going into nervous spasms which leave his head and hands vibrating long after your ordinary limb would have called it a day; his uniqueness is to be simultaneously febrile and lethargic. He is cunningly matched here against the trim, barbed urbanity of Robin Bailey, an actor still coming into his kingdom. (As he says, accurately and with superlative timing, "You are a great man and I am merely rather important.")'

Michael Billington took a similar line in the *Guardian*, concluding that 'the play brings a touch of erudite intelligence and verbal grace to a West End currently steeped in witless nostalgia.'

But these three critics were swimming against the tide of what Sheridan Morley denounced in his review as 'some of my loonier daily and Sunday paper colleagues' who were less than welcoming to this latest Ustinov brainchild.

This in no way diminished Peter's affection for the role and the play. In 1983–4 he took it to Berlin, to the Nederlander Theater in New York, and on a tour of the USA; and in 1987–8 he played it in German at the Schiller Theatre in Berlin, where it was a huge sell-out success. Some German critics said it was uncanny and they felt they really were in the presence of Beethoven.

In 1995 he revived the play at the Chichester Festival Theatre, in a production by Joe Harmston, with John Neville as the critic. The audiences there loved it, but, Peter sighed, 'The critics didn't like it any more than they liked it the first time. I never understood it.' John Neville relished the renewal of the acting relationship they had established thirty years earlier in the film of *Billy Budd*. 'Peter and I had a good time. Of course it was a very good role for me. It was great fun to play. Off stage we slipped into the roles of two Deep-South, very redneck, right-wing senators – which we still do to this day. It was a pleasure playing opposite him – and no different from film. I think the audiences expect him to be funny and are possibly surprised at the depth of emotion he can play.'

Other actor friends also caught occasional glimpses of the more serious and emotional elements in Peter's make-up. His daughter Tamara was in a special position to know, from both the professional and personal viewpoint: 'I think that there's a melancholy side to him that you don't see and that the acting is a wonderful vitamin boost for him; the applause and the response from the audience gives him enormous reassurance. I don't think he'd like me to say it, but I do think there's a sad side, and quite a low-key side, to him as well, and the acting is a wonderful lift for him.'

In one of our many long talks, I asked Peter whether he accepted that there was a streak of melancholy in his nature. 'Yes, I think that's true. It's probably something atavistic, which comes from a long Russian background. My grandfather was exiled from Russia and sold his estates; he came to Württemberg and then to Palestine, and I'm sure he had the same instinct. I think there is a degree of melancholy that is attached to distance, a degree of fatalism too.'

So is his prolific comic invention a way out of that melancholy?

'Yes. I think it started as a defence mechanism at school. Because I started life, born in London, as a small foreigner, and I've really been a foreigner everywhere ever since, because I'm ethnically filthy and proud of it. I don't think I could have done half the things I've done unless I had been and had my toe in various camps.'

In his history of the land of his forebears, *My Russia*, published in 1983, he philosophised about the emotional outlook of its people, some of which he believes he has inherited:

The Russians are deeply attached to their miseries as well as to their joys. Their literature and music have made an artistic pleasure of sadness. The well of melancholy is bottomless, and laughter is a close relative of tears. Russian exiles suffer more from the absence of this pungent perfume of sorrow than other exiles seem to miss whatever they have left behind, and they try to recreate it wherever they go. In order to understand the Russians, it is worth knowing that no other people speaks so shamelessly of the soul, not for want of a better word, but because it is a correct description of that aching void which is not a void at all, but a nerve sensitive to everything.

If they seem stiff and unsmiling in their official guise, is this not an act of voluntary discipline to eradicate an erratic and searching spirit? It is the only country I know in which a policeman will write out a ticket for a dirty car. What is this if not one of the many efforts to eliminate an age-old tendency towards sloth and idleness instilled by the frigid winters and immensity of the country?

The book tells the story of the growth of Russia from the time when it was ruled by Rurik (862–879), up to the present. Some reviewers accused the author of being an apologist for Stalinism, when in fact he was trying to explain it, not excuse it. He even had a small contretemps in public with his publisher, when he appeared on BBC Television with Harold Macmillan to discuss the book.

Just before the programme went out, the interviewer asked

Macmillan, 'Do you mind if Tony Benn appears with us?'

'Who's that?'

'Tony Benn.'

At that moment the programme went on air, and the former Prime Minister said, 'Oh no, I'd rather have Khrushchev.' As the discussion began, he said to Peter, 'I can't tell you how pleased I am to be head of a publishing firm that is publishing your very interesting book about Russia, which I read with the greatest interest up to about 1900, perhaps a little later, and after that it becomes Soviet propaganda.'

'Oh, I don't think that's true. I think if I'd written the book thirty years ago you would have said you thought the book was awfully good until about 1870; after that it's all Soviet propaganda.'

Macmillan said, 'Well, I daresay you're right.'

Peter recalled, 'At that moment Benn came in and supported me of course, and he never realised it was Benn. He treated him just as somebody who had a different point of view.'

Macmillan was added to the gallery of Ustinov impersonations, and he said the clue to capturing him 'was to talk as though you had a cathedral in your mouth'.

The book provided the basis for the six-part television series that followed it, *Peter Ustinov's Russia*. It was produced by John McGreevy's Canadian film company, and shooting began during the brief regime of Konstantin Chernenko as General Secretary of the Soviet Union. The necessary permissions to film were obtained without the endless delays and arguments endured by previous documentary crews, so Peter received two separate visitations by the British and American cultural attachés, asking how he had managed it all so quickly, and had travelled to so many different places right across the country.

He could not resist saying to them, 'By not consulting you as to how it should be done.' He had just knocked on doors and asked, and in most cases people simply agreed.

One of the techniques used in the series was for Peter to meet various historical figures – Ivan the Terrible, Peter the Great, Catherine the Great, Alexander I, Dostoevsky, and Tolstoy – all played by Russian actors. The tricky one was Lenin, which the Soviet authorities indicated would not be looked on so kindly. 'I explained that I had studied Lenin quite a bit before this, and one or two things about him amazed me. For instance, he said he would rather have written the *Appassionata* sonata by Beethoven than any of his political achievements; he had a regret that he wasn't able to do something more creative than talk and theorise.'

He came up with the suggestion that he encounter the young Lenin before the revolution, which they accepted. They found a young actor named Orlov who resembled him, prematurely bald with red hair and a little beard. In the film they met on a staircase, where Lenin was running away because he was convinced this man Ustinov was a Secret Policeman trying to ensnare him. Peter assured him that he wasn't but that he did know something about his writing. Lenin at once became positive and expansive about what he was trying to do.

Their conversation ended with this exchange:

Ustinov Go upstairs, lock yourself in, you won't have any more trouble from me, because I'm interested in history, and not at all in arresting you or doing anything disagreeable. Time alone will show whether you succeed or not.

Lenin Thank you for making me such a challenge, it makes me all the more determined to succeed.

Ustinov Good luck, I shall watch the result with interest from far away.

Before the shooting had finished, Chernenko died and the succession passed to Gorbachev, so the series was made at a crucial moment in the history of the country. Peter's sensitive antennae for a national mood made him very conscious of the changes that were coming. This prompted him to write a very different book from the previous one, with a not dissimilar title – *Ustinov in Russia* – about his experiences whilst making the TV series, illustrated by many of the photographs the crew took on their travels. It is a much more personal, and therefore more accessible,

With Hélène. 'I've been married three times, but I feel
if it had been this one, I would have been married once'.

On location in Dallas for *Logan's Run*. Michael Anderson, Michael York, Michael Anderson Jr, Peter Ustinov and Jenny Agutter. 'How long have you been in the business, old-timer?'

Beethoven's Tenth, with John Neville as Stephen Fauldgate. 'You mean critics get presents these days – as well as bribes?'

Opposite: Hercule Poir
views a Christmas parc
with suspicio

Sir Peter Ustinov at Buckingham Palace, 1990, with Tamara, Hélène and Andrea. Tamara Ustinov: 'Andrea and I decided we looked like air hostesses in our specially bought hats!'

On holiday in Israel in 1978, photographed by his eldest daughter.

His two younger daughters, Andrea and Pavla.

With Andrea and son Igor on the set of *The Last Remake of Beau Geste*.

Hélène trying to curb the commercial acumen of a jewellery vendor on the Ganges at Benares. 'He has just produced his trump card with, "Come on lady, you are old enough to wear this jewel". We are still laughing.'

The keen tennis player, here playing against the British No. 1, Bobby Wilson.

With Natalie Wood at the Hermitage, St Petersburg, 1979.

The Chancellor of Durham University confers an Honorary Doctorate of Laws on Mikhail Gorbachev in an Athens Hotel, 1995, returning the honour paid by the former Russian leader to members of the Issyk-kul Forum in 1986.

Opposite: Wit Arthur Miller at th first Issyk-kul Foru in Kirghizia, 198

The one-man show in Prague, 1991.
'The greatest after-dinner speaker in the galaxy'.

book than *My Russia*, but taken together they say a lot about his attachment to that country and to its people. He was to become a much more frequent visitor in the years to come.

One of the most significant occasions was the following year, in October 1986, at the invitation of Chingiz Aytmatov, the Kirghiz novelist and playwright, who has narrowly missed winning the Nobel prize on three occasions, and became a Soviet diplomat and later ambassador to Luxembourg. He grew very close to Gorbachev when he first came to power, and together they conceived of a link between Russian intellectuals and selected representatives of the West. Their hope was that it might continue even if everything went wrong with the new Russian Revolution and Gorbachev was unable to put an end to the Cold War. The Russian leader insisted that culture was the basic springboard of understanding.

In addition to Aytmatov and Ustinov, the international group of fourteen included Arthur Miller, James Baldwin, and Alvin Toffler from America; the French Nobel laureate Claude Simon; Augusto Forti of UNESCO; Alexander King, the President of the Club of Rome; Afework Tekle, the Ethiopian artist; the Cuban novelist Otero; the biologist Federico Mayor Zaragoza from Spain; and Yasher Kemal, the author of *Memed My Hawk*, who was still admired by Peter despite the ill-fated film of his book.

They gathered by Lake Issyk-Kul in Kirghizia, under the towering mass of the Tien Shan mountains on the Chinese border. They talked for three days about their various approaches to the problems of the age, and produced a slim manifesto of their conclusions and speculations about the next millennium, which was forwarded to both General Secretary Gorbachev and President Reagan. The Soviet leader responded quickly and invited the whole group to meet him in Moscow.

Peter had just got home to Switzerland, where he was telephoned by Gorbachev, asking him to return.

'But I haven't got a visa.'

'It will be issued you on arrival, and Aeroflot will be informed that you're travelling without a visa.'

To his astonishment, this breach of the hitherto inflexible Soviet bureaucracy worked, and he was whisked to the Kremlin to join the others.

The delegates were told that they had just an hour, but the meeting in the Kremlin was allowed to run on for nearly three hours. Gorbachev chaired it unaccompanied by advisers or assistants, only interpreters, and he listened to each of the visitors before offering his own views. He astonished his foreign listeners by saying, 'Politics needs to be nourished by the intellectual in each country because he is more likely to keep the human being at the centre of his examination. Any other concentration is immoral.'

He convinced them that he genuinely wanted to reform the whole Soviet system, but they found it difficult to relay that message to the outside world at that time. No American newspaper or national magazine would print the articles offered by Arthur Miller or Alvin Toffler, and some of the British press attacked the alleged gullibility of Western intellectuals in allowing themselves to be duped by the Kremlin.

Peter was most anxious that the Issyk-Kul Forums should continue. A second followed, but the third occurred in the middle of the uprising, so he invited the group to Vengen in the Swiss Alps, where the hotel proprietor was a great enthusiast for the whole idea. There were new participants, such as the Swiss playwright Friedrich Durrenmatt, and return visitors, like Arthur Miller. Peter chaired the session and footed the bill, including the cost of the simultaneous translations, 'which was very expensive, but I thought it was worth it, because it was such a good idea, I didn't want to let it perish'.

Spain hosted the fourth one at the University of Granada, and Peter hopes that that will not be the last time we shall hear of the Issyk-Kul Forum. His hopes have not always been fulfilled. In *Ustinov in Russia* he wrote, '*Glasnost* is the opening of a window. It has been attempted often, but has rarely got as far as Gorbachev has already taken it. For the sake of peace, for the sake of Russia, for the sake of all of us, he must be allowed to succeed.'

In 1987 many other people shared that hope but, like other Russian leaders before him who tried to reform the system from the top down, Gorbachev was toppled from power with the task unfinished.

The use of power is something that has long intrigued Peter as a writer, and he now pursued that interest in a series of major television interviews.

Eighteen

1984–1989
From *Peter Ustinov's People*
to *The Disinformer*

While he was completing work on *Ustinov in Russia* Peter was approached by Seamus Smith of Radio Telefis Éireann about doing a series of major interviews with world leaders. He thought, rightly, that the combination of Peter Ustinov and Irish television might open some doors more easily than regular political interviewers for much bigger national networks.

The list of eventual subjects included many of the major figures in the Middle East – King Hussein of Jordan, Yitzhak Rabin of Israel, and Yasser Arafat of Palestine. Peter was just as intrigued by former leaders like ex-President Jimmy Carter, 'because he was by his own admission not a terribly effective President, but he made astonishing contributions after he'd finished being President, with an organisation that is far more efficient than the State Department or the Pentagon. He has a think-tank in the local university, which is devoted entirely to his studies of various people. When he went to Haiti for Clinton, and to Bosnia later, he was given a full briefing by his university about local customs, local prejudices, things that the State Department never really bothers to do. So he was very well informed and astonished the locals.'

All these programmes were revealing, but the most momentous, by an extraordinary accident of timing, was the one with Indira Gandhi. When he arrived in Delhi in October 1984, tensions were still running high after the storming of the Golden Temple at Amritsar, sacred to the Sikhs, just four months earlier. In the gun-battle between the Indian Army and the militants demanding their own Sikh homeland, more than 700 of the separatists had died.

The subsequent threats to the Prime Minister's life led to tight security.

The Irish camera crew followed her to a huge rally in Bubaneswar, and Peter interviewed her in a very noisy Russian helicopter.

He watched the rally from the back of a raked grandstand, and as Indira Gandhi was waiting for the crowd to stop chanting 'Zindabad Gandhi', he saw her beckon an officer and speak to him, pointing in Peter's direction as she did so. By the time the officer had climbed up the steps to reach him, the crowd had fallen silent as he relayed the Prime Minister's message to her guest: 'In case you should need the toilet, it is under the building.' He was touched by her consideration of his possible needs.

Peter told her later that he recognised in her another only child; he could spot every symptom. It was obvious in her case that she was the only child of a particularly exceptional and remote father, whom she adored and wanted to emulate. She only saw Pandit Nehru rarely and was left very much to her own devices as a child, as Peter had been.

As they flew back from the rally, they filmed Indira Gandhi looking out of the window with the Himalayas in the background, a striking last image of her. It was 30 October.

The next morning was scheduled for the main set-piece interview at 9 a.m., in the garden of her official residence at 1 Akbar Road. She had selected a large shady tree under which the two of them were to sit and talk. The cameras were set up and locked off, and Peter was wired up ready by the sound recordist. They waited for the Prime Minister to come through the gate in the hedge, where two Sikhs stood on guard. At 9.15 she had still not appeared. Then they heard what sounded like shots, quite close. The Indian cameraman said reassuringly, 'We are a very young people, and when there are fireworks left over after a national holiday, they can't resist letting them off at any old time.'

Almost immediately there was a burst of machine-gun fire, and it became clear to everyone that this was not harmless fireworks. One of her Sikh bodyguards had shot the Prime Minister with his pistol as she approached the gate, and as the Gurkhas ran to the rescue a second Sikh sprayed her with a burst of automatic fire. All this was heard but not seen by the waiting television team, which was agonising for Peter.

'Then there was a pause of about seven minutes, and suddenly a second burst of machine-gun fire from further away, and that was a settling of accounts by the Gurkhas, who killed one of the two Sikhs in the guardroom. People said to me, "Why didn't you rush to see what was happening?" I said, "First of all, I was linked by a cable and couldn't really move; and second, our garden was immediately invaded by Gurkhas, looking for other political assassins, aiming at everyone and no one." I thought it wiser to stay still; we had enough damage already.'

Then two Indian Army officers appeared and demanded, 'We want to see the film in your camera.'

'There isn't any, we haven't shot anything.'

'All the same, we want to see it.'

'Well, there's nothing to see. I did a sound-recording imme-diately after it happened, because I thought there might be some-thing in the quality of my voice, when I'm still under the shock of what happened, which I can never reproduce.'

They demanded to hear that and then said, 'We still want to see the camera.'

Peter argued again, 'What good is it, when I tell you we shot nothing?'

Their inability to understand the technical process of filming only heightened their emotional tension at what had just hap-pened, and the officers shouted at him, 'Oh, don't be so difficult, we've been very good to you, we've allowed you to shoot here. All we want to do is take the film out of the camera, look at it, and just put it straight back again.'

Next to appear was an old man with a shock of white hair, Mrs Gandhi's *chef du cabinet*, who said, 'Why are you still here? Can you not see this is a moment of national tragedy? Why are you here to invade our privacy? Go away, go away.'

That was easier said than done. The crew packed up all the film gear and went to the gate, but an Indian colonel with a huge moustache stopped them, saying, 'What are you doing here?' and sent them back. The *chef du cabinet* came out again and said, 'Can you not take a hint like civilised people, must you haunt our every moment at this time of lamentation and woe?'

But the army had sound reasons for holding them all there, as Peter quickly understood. When he was interviewed later by NBC, CBS, and the BBC, he told them that it was quite clear they were kept in the garden so they could not spread rumours; they were only released when the news was general knowledge. The army needed to delay the announcement until they had deployed troops to try to prevent reprisals against Sikh property. Even so there were riots and bloodshed.

Soon after Peter got back to his hotel the telephone rang.

'Mr Ustinov?'

'Yes.'

'This is Bellamy, from the British High Commission. There's a rumour going round that there was a British film crew involved in this morning's nastiness.'

'No, there was no British crew; there was a German continuity girl, and two technicians from the Republic of Ireland.'

'Oh, oh, yes, well, that's hardly our business. Did you notice anything you think we ought to know?'

'No, I really didn't notice anything I think you ought to know.'

'Well, is it too much to ask you if it occurs to you that you think we ought to know anything, to let me know?'

'I'll let you know straight away if I think there's something you ought to know.'

'That's very good. Oh, don't go, don't go ... Would you be free to have lunch with the High Commissioner?'

'Yes, but you'll have to fetch me, because I can see from my window they are burning cars all over the place, and there are dead Sikhs lying in the road, and I can't possibly cope with all that alone.'

'No. We'll send the Commission car for you. One o'clock, would that be all right?'

The Rolls-Royce arrived, flying the British flag, and Peter was driven through streets littered with the dead Sikhs and burning vehicles he had glimpsed from his hotel room. When the door of the High Commission was opened by a Sikh in a red turban, Peter instinctively pushed him back into the building. The other lunch guests were already gathered, including Princess Anne, who was there for the Save the Children Fund.

They all went out into the garden for an alfresco lunch. 'I remember it started out with avocados filled with prawns, and there was an awful smell in the air, which I remembered from the war, of burning plywood, the sweet smell of wallpaper and other things, which hung over the whole town. Bricks kept falling into the garden, and there was a very high hedge, which occasionally gave a bit. It was a nerve-racking lunch. Suddenly there was a particularly loud outburst of catcalls, a shower of stones fell not very far from us, and the whole hedge sagged enormously. I was eating my avocado, and I said to the British High Commissioner, "Er, is this anything to do with you, sir, do you think?"

' "Well, I sincerely hope not."

'There was a sudden stillness at the table, and then Princess Anne's voice rang out: "I was particularly impressed by the quality of Indian quarter-horses."

'I thought to myself, what the hell are you doing here? This is nothing to do with you, it's not your world. You've asked for it by wanting to interview Indira Gandhi.'

He flew back to England the next day and agreed to carry some exclusive photographs taken of the mourning crowds around the body prepared for cremation, which he delivered into the hands of the *Daily Mail* representative at Heathrow Airport. His own itinerary was as tight as usual, and he was due to speak at the Royal Naval College at Greenwich the next evening. Concerned at getting his dinner jacket pressed in time, he bought an electric iron in the tax-free section when the flight stopped at Dubai and pressed his evening suit himself. 'I appeared on time at Greenwich, and was able to tell them the whole story, which appalled the admirals.'

Peter has a deep and abiding interest in history, but this was the first time in his life that he was actually present when history was being made in such a dramatic and tragic way. He was still in a state of shock two days after the killing; when he attended the wedding of Lord Brabourne's daughter, Amanda, the film-maker had never seen him so shaken.

The memory remained strong when he returned to India nine months later to finish the programme with her son Rajiv, who had succeeded her and who was also destined to die at the hands of a fanatic. The traumatic experience in Delhi did not put him off making programmes about the political systems and personalities of other countries, but he was relieved to turn his mind for the moment to the more sanitised crimes conjured up by Agatha Christie.

More cheering news in 1984 was the announcement of an Emmy nomination for the first of his television music documentaries, *The Well-Tempered Bach*, a German film that paved the way for a series of TV films about great composers, which he presented in the 1990s.

In 1985–6 he made a trio of Poirot mysteries in rapid succession for CBS Television, the first of which was called *Thirteen at Dinner* and was set in London. Jonathan Cecil played his English sidekick, Captain Hastings, in all three; it was eighteen years since he had acted in *Halfway Up the Tree*, but Peter greeted him warmly like an old friend. The rest of the cast included Faye Dunaway, Bill Nighy, and John Stride. Inspector Japp was played by David Suchet, who would later adopt the Poirot moustache himself, in a long-running series made by London Weekend Television for the ITV network.

Since Hastings has all his scenes with Poirot, Jonathan Cecil spent a lot of time in Peter's company either shooting or, for rather longer periods, waiting to shoot. He remembers one occasion: 'It was a bitterly cold night and we were filming on the Embankment, and the lighting was causing problems. We stood there in the cold, and it's one of the few times I've seen Peter getting really impatient and angry. They said, "All right, you guys, hold on, we'll be with you in a minute," and Peter groaned. But when the director came up and said, "We're ready for you," only I, standing next to him, knew he was getting really quite angry, because he didn't let on to the crew. He was the perfect gentleman in this way, but he hadn't much time for temperamental stars. Faye

Dunaway could be quite difficult, arriving late, coming out of make-up, objecting to things. I remember someone saying, "Faye, you can go now," and Peter said, "That's fortunate," in a quiet voice to me.'

This was all of a piece with the consideration he showed for the lesser stars in the firmament. On the second film, *Deadman's Folly*, which was shot in West Wycombe, one of the actors was Gerard Healy. When he arrived on set, Jonathan Cecil introduced him to Peter, 'because I used to be a supporting actor to Gerard's leading man, and I was concerned he should be treated properly. We had to pass in the background, while these three characters had a short conversation, and the director, Clive Donner, said, "Now, Jonathan and Peter, don't overact in the background when you're going past, because we want to hear the dialogue." Peter said, "What else can I do if I have to compete with Mr Healy?" I thought that showed his generosity of spirit.'

On one of their Sundays off, Peter nipped over to Dublin to do some post-synching on his Russian TV series and returned with presents for the leading ladies. Jonathan Cecil was impressed by his observant eye. 'He'd chosen a folk-weave scarf for each one, and he'd noted their complexions, so they were exactly right, and I thought that was a wonderfully gallant gesture.'

He soon learnt to follow Peter's lead on the script, 'because Agatha Christie writes terribly flat dialogue, and as filtered through some Hollywood hack it's even worse. So unless there were some salient facts for the murder mystery, I used to learn the substance of the scene, but not the actual words, then I'd wait to see what Peter threw at me, and I threw it back. We played the actual scene as we'd improvised it in rehearsal. Those dreadful scenes at the end where Poirot sums up and goes on for ever, he rewrote those completely. He was dazzling.'

The last of the trilogy, *Murder in Three Acts*, starred Tony Curtis as the unhinged murderer. Here again, the summing-up was so badly written that Peter rewrote it entirely and put in some jokes. He said he couldn't bear the detective moralising like a clergyman, so he tried to make it teasing and mischievous. His sense of humour kept the crew amused during the long night-shoots, as he imitated animals and musical instruments. When the name Jeffrey Bernard cropped up in conversation, Jonathan Cecil remarked, 'It's astonishing he's still alive, the amount he drinks. He's had pancreatitis three times.' Peter's instant response was, 'And *once* even on the Station.'

He had one more appearance to come as the Belgian sleuth before he bade farewell to the part, but his identification with it had now spread around the globe. In 1986 he paid a visit to China to make a documentary film about that country, where he was already known to the authorities for his audiotapes about the Forbidden Palace, which he had recorded for tourists in three languages – English, French, and German.

Chinese Television transmitted *Death on the Nile* in honour of his visit, 'with the result that when I turned up in small provincial towns the concierge of the government rest-house would say, "Ho, Pollo."'

The other purpose of his visit was to show the flag for UNICEF. He had been involved with that organisation since 1968, at the instigation of Leon Davičo, a Yugoslav who was their representative in Geneva. He began by hosting some charitable events, and then on a visit to New York was recruited by the head of UNICEF, Henry Labouisse, as the second UNICEF ambassador, the first one being Danny Kaye. When Labouisse retired, he was succeeded by Jim Grant, an American born in China, the son of a missionary. As Peter says, 'He therefore had a very balanced view of the world. On one occasion he took me with him to Washington, to argue the case with the Senate Subcommittee not to cut their contribution to UNICEF, and we managed it quite well. I used to smoke in those days, and I smoked cigars. I was offered one by a notorious senator who was opposed to UNICEF. I looked at it and said, "You're smoking a Havana."

' "I trust you're not going to hold that against me."

' "Well, that depends on your attitude towards UNICEF." I meant it as a joke, but he was evidently used to that kind of threat. We had a pretty truculent time, but ended by persuading them that UNICEF was really very important.'

When Jim Grant died he was succeeded by Carol Bellamy,

another American and formerly a leading Democrat politician in New York State. She took a much more belligerent line in pursuit of rights for those without them, and UNICEF became a more militant agency as a result. Peter found her very good value.

One of his aims for the organisation has been to dispel the many misconceptions about its work in the field. When he arrived in China in 1986 there was a great outcry in the Western press about the abuse of human rights in that country, in particular charging that girl children were being allowed to die in crèches there. 'They didn't know what I already knew: that before this outcry China had asked UNICEF to oversee all their crèches, to teach them how it should be done, which I thought was an extraordinary open gesture and an admission of defeat.'

He was also alerted to another serious health problem in China, which UNICEF helped to solve. Chinese factories were capable of manufacturing the most complicated serums and vaccines, but they had no technical means of keeping them at the right temperatures for distribution across this huge country. Until UNICEF brought in special polystyrene carriers, something like 25 per cent of Chinese-manufactured serums and vaccines had to be thrown out by quality control, because they had lost their effectiveness before they could be used.

Over the years, Peter has been round the world for UNICEF, with particularly important trips to India, Pakistan, Thailand, Guatemala, Jordan and Kenya. In the Philippines he met an elderly midwife, who told him she was brought up in the old school and never had any failures with her babies, but she couldn't work with only one pair of forceps, which was all that UNICEF had supplied. Her request for extra forceps was quickly granted.

For all Peter's multilingualism in European languages, in many countries this was of little use with the children, so he quickly invented a universal means of communication with them, which never failed. He would get down on his hands and knees and bark like a dog at them, running through his repertoire of canine impressions. After momentary bewilderment at this unexpected performance, the children would invariably shriek with delight at this new game, and would soon be clambering on his back. 'The game has to stop when there are eight of them on your back, with a line forming to climb on. You have to think of something else very quickly. It never stops working, but then they become greedy and want all sorts of other things. In Fiji I did a Flamenco singer and they loved that, they were killing themselves with laughter.' As an international emissary, his diplomatic style is unlikely to be confused with anyone else's.

He sees this work as a great challenge and a stimulus. 'Actual contact with the Third World as I have in UNICEF is to my mind absolutely invaluable. If you have the opportunity of achieving a little success in your life, it raises your responsibilities, it doesn't diminish them. I've never seen the laurel that is comfortable for me to rest on. They're just spurs to further excitement.'

In the summer of 1987 Peter donned the waxed moustache again for his last appearance as Poirot, in *Appointment with Death*, made for the cinema and shot in Israel, with a cast including John Gielgud, Lauren Bacall, Carrie Fisher, Jenny Seagrove, David Soul, and Hayley Mills. The director was Michael Winner, who has a reputation for blowing his top and shouting at people. Hayley Mills was astounded when he told Lauren Bacall, 'He was directing the film, not her, and until she was directing it she'd better shut up. She was just gobsmacked and didn't retaliate; she could have sent him from there to kingdom come if she'd decided to.'

Hayley Mills observed that this kind of boorish behaviour seemed to have very little impact on Peter, who just let it roll off him, like water off a duck's back. He disapproved of the director's strong language but responded with a joke. Filming at night in the Old City, they had the occasional problem with passers-by. When one white-garbed figure wandered into view, wearing a transparent burnous, Michael Winner screamed, 'Cut! Fuck you, what are you doing there in that shot?' Peter said, 'Do be careful. It's Jesus.'

He was more concerned about the inadequacies of the script, which was nowhere near as good as *Death on the Nile* or *Evil Under the Sun*. The major compensating factor for him was the presence of John Gielgud, whose perfect manners were as legendary as the director's lack of them. Peter thought he was marvellous in what should have been a wildly inappropriate part, 'because the last thing you'd really cast him as was a British general, and yet his ignorance of British generals made him very good. He had a line to me in the script, "Do you think I was wrong to deploy so many men on the left flank?" Then his eye would search the stratosphere. That's exactly what a British general would have said, I think, without knowing any more about it than Gielgud.'

After six Poirot stories, Peter shook off that image and now had a second chance at a part he had lost years before – Detective Fix in *Around the World in Eighty Days*. Mike Todd had wanted him for his star-studded production of the Jules Verne story in the 1950s, but Twentieth Century-Fox were so worried about the threat to them from his revolutionary new wide-screen Todd-AO process that they refused to release Ustinov from his contract. To add insult to injury Fox tried to make him take the role of sidekick to a blind detective played by Van Johnson. He refused, and a lawsuit ensued, but Peter succeeded in getting out of his contract. So when NBC produced a TV mini-series of the same story thirty years later and offered him the same part, he jumped at it, and his Detective Fix was soon in hot pursuit of Pierce Brosnan as Phileas Fogg.

The end of 1988 heralded a particularly happy period from a family point of view. On 28 September the new Benois Museum was formally opened in a house that Peter's great-great-grand-father Nicholas Benois had built near St Petersburg, more than a century earlier. All the surviving members of the Benois and Ustinov families were invited, and 160 turned up – too many to fit into the group photograph. Peter took Hélène and all his children except Pavla. (Her friend John Houseman was dying, and she felt she couldn't leave him at that time.)

It was Tamara's first visit to the land of her ancestors, and she was introduced to lots of cousins she had never met. It was the biggest family gathering any of them had experienced and was treasured by them all.

Four months later Peter's immediate family came together again on 1 February 1989 to watch him installed as one of the fifteen

Foreign Associate members of the French Academy of Fine Arts. He was elected to the seat formerly occupied by Orson Welles – another extraordinarily versatile and creative figure in the performing arts, but whose early brilliant success sadly was not, unlike Peter Ustinov's, sustained into later life.

The new member was welcomed by the architect Roger Taillibert, who traced his previous achievements and praised him as 'an inspiration to the Theatre'. At a reception later Peter was presented with his sword of office, which was the work of his sculptor son, Igor, and his jewellery designer daughter, Andrea. It was ornamented with the symbols of his many skills and activities – theatrical masks of comedy and tragedy, pens, musical notes, a microphone, the UNICEF logo, and an aeroplane.

The same year marked the release of his next film, *The French Revolution*, in which he played Mirabeau to Klaus Maria Brandauer's Danton, directed by Robert Enrico. It was made in French, and in the end nearly everybody was dubbed. The whole experience was an unhappy one for Peter, as it broke all his cardinal rules of film-making.

'It was directed in a way that makes my blood boil. They had students as extras, who were eager to learn and were malleable, and the whole thing was orchestrated by assistant directors saying, "When he says *Vive la Révolution* you all cry at once, and then when something else happens, oohh – depression." The result was that watching the film was of no interest whatsoever because the whole crowd were dead, they were all looking anxiously for cues. These things are terribly important, especially if you're going to do a film about the French Revolution, because the really vital part is the people and their reaction. You have to spend much more time with the people and less with the principals.'

In between all these filming trips and his travels for UNICEF, he managed to complete his first major works of fiction since *Krumnagel* in 1971 – two novellas, which were published in one volume, *The Disinformer* and *A Nose by Any Other Name*. The first was inspired by the *Spycatcher* case. When he told Mrs Thatcher that he was writing the story of a man who was jealous of Peter Wright, the Prime Minister commented, 'He's not worth it.' The author replied, 'How would you know? You've never had a book banned by someone like you.'

The novella takes a wicked delight in showing up the fallibility of the intelligence community, when an ex-MI5 agent, Hilary Glasp, mischievously invents a mythical terrorist group, 'Martyrs of the 17th September' (which seems an almost uncannily prophetic name now). Real terrorists descend on London to liquidate these interlopers; four of them are killed by the Anti-terrorist Squad, and Hilary finds his own life at risk as the whole thing escalates and he is advised to seek refuge abroad.

In one passage the hero pokes fun at his former superiors:

He still remembered with annoyance being called before Sir Aubrey Wilket, then head of MI5, in order to be briefed on his new mission, back in the Fifties.

'You are to go to Persia, in order to use your undoubted talents to help destabilize the government of Dr Mossadeg. You doubtless know the situation out there as well as I do.'

'I know the Iranians are attempting to get rid of the British oil interests.'

'Who's doing that?' Sir Aubrey had barked, fearful that he might have missed something vital in the situation.

'The Iranians.'

'Who are they?'

'They used to be called Persians.'

'Used to be? Used to be? Listen to me, young man, as far as I am concerned, they still are the Persians, and always will be. I am sick and tired of their constant attempts to confuse the issue. What an absurd idea, to change the identity of peoples after aeons of history? Is my wife's cat a Thailandic cat? No sir, it is not. It is a Siamese cat, and will be for the span of its natural life. Is my mother's dog – yes, I still have Mother – she's ninety-six, God bless her – is her dog a Beijingese? Not as far as I'm concerned. It's a particularly disagreeable dog. I don't see why it should be encumbered by an unpronounceable breed as well.'

The second novella, *A Nose by Any Other Name*, has a different target for the Ustinov satire. Eastern-European immigrants to the USA, Professor Ramaz Atoulia and his wife Ala, have a daughter, Thamar, who on her twenty-first birthday leaves home, has a nose operation, and marries an apparently all-American guy, Bruce Connaby. Their child is born with a distinctive nose like her maternal grandparents. Eventually Bruce has to own up that he too had a nose-job from the same surgeon, for the same reason. The disclosure of their mutual deceit and common origins repairs their marriage rift.

The comic style reinforces the author's serious point about the folly of trying to deny one's own racial identity. The stories sold quite well, but probably reached their biggest audience through Peter's reading of them on the BBC's *Book at Bedtime*, with his matchless repertoire of voices making the radio broadcasts sound like a large and distinctive cast.

That gift for storytelling was about to be given full rein in the next decade, as he launched a long and successful run of his one-man stage show.

Nineteen

1990–1992

From 'The One Man Show' to Chancellor of Durham University

The idea of *An Evening with Peter Ustinov*, as his one-man show was billed, had been born as long ago as 1962. During the Dublin rehearsals of *Photo Finish* one of the Gaiety Theatre stage-crew died in an accident, and a benefit performance was quickly assembled in aid of his family. Peter agreed to do the first half, in which he came on and talked about some of his earlier film and theatre experiences. The second half had the old Irish actor-manager Anew McMaster doing scenes from Shakespeare. The contrast between the two styles could hardly have been greater – McMaster in full orange pancake make-up performing in traditional declamatory style, and Peter chatting to the audience in as relaxed a manner as if he were just at a dinner table with a few friends.

His fellow actors, Paul Rogers and Edward Hardwicke, never forgot that evening in Dublin, recognising it as the progenitor of his full-length one-man show when it opened on 21 March 1990 at the Theatre Royal in the Haymarket. The audience was packed with old friends and colleagues, from Angela Lansbury and Molly Daubeny to John Brabourne and Natalia Makarova, as well as his family, including his daughters Tamara and Andrea. Pavla could not be there, but she has now watched her father give that show in other countries in several different languages and says, 'I can't even begin to understand how he does it.'

Typically he makes light of the technique involved, saying that it is really a reversion to his earliest days at the Players' Theatre, with one modification: 'I usually have the auditorium slightly lighter than normal, so I can see faces and appear to dwell on all of them. I sweep across the public the whole time, like a searchlight in an American prison-film, and they have the illusion, I hope, that I'm looking at each one of them individually. The trick is to make an auditorium seem smaller than it really is.'

His stories ranged from his childhood up to his recent travels, and his impersonations of actors, politicians and royalty had been honed and polished over many years of enlivening film locations and stage rehearsal rooms; for good measure he threw in some of his impressions of musical instruments. The critics raved about the performance, from the *Daily Express*, which acclaimed him 'the greatest after-dinner speaker in the galaxy', to *The Times*, which wished it were longer and that he would 'go on talking until the small hours'.

Every other actor in the business wanted to see it, let alone the general public, so the sold-out scheduled run of six weeks was extended to nine, with queues for returns throughout that period. After a short break, he then took the show on a three-month tour of New Zealand and Australia. The whole world began clamouring to see it. In 1991 he added San Francisco and Prague; in 1992 he took it to Australia (again), Hong Kong, Kuala Lumpur, Singapore, Chicago, and on a tour of Germany. In 1993 he went on a second tour of Germany; in 1994 to Athens, Vienna, and Hong Kong, interspersed with a return to the Haymarket and visits to Edinburgh, Nottingham, and Birmingham. His last appearance in the show, so far, was in Toronto in 1995, where one performance was recorded by John McGreevy for television and transmitted in two parts in the UK on BBC1 in December.

Keeping a show fresh over such a long time is even more of a challenge when the performer is alone on stage, as John Gielgud found with his *Ages of Man* Shakespeare recital in the 1950s. His solution was to ring the changes on the speeches that he included, and Peter did the same with his choice of stories. 'I know roughly the milestones, but it's different every time. It depends on the public reaction. Suddenly I get an idea during the show, which seems to me apposite or right, in which case I'll change my direction for a moment, but I have certain milestones, which I recognise when I come to them.'

I caught up with the show at the Haymarket in 1994, which was the very first time I met Peter in person. I wanted to interview him for my biography of Ralph Richardson, and he suggested that I came to his dressing room at about half past six, to give us plenty of time before he went on at 8 p.m. To my initial dismay his car was late in collecting him and he didn't arrive at the theatre until about ten to seven. But he cheerfully, and most illuminatingly, talked to me about Sir Ralph for nearly an hour, until it was I who was getting nervous about the imminence of his curtain-up. Having shared a couple of platforms with him since, I have observed the same relaxed demeanour right up until the moment we walked out on stage – the welcoming applause triggers his adrenalin, and he slips instantly into performance mode, with never a hesitation, verbal fluff, or any groping for the right word. His comic timing is a joy to behold.

I asked him recently whether, like most other actors, he follows a pattern for the day when he has a stage performance in the evening. 'No. I used to be able to do almost anything, to really squander my energy. I would have a cup of soup or something, just before going on, and it wouldn't affect me at all. But nowadays this has all changed. I don't need any special preparation, because I'm not nervous, I don't have what the Germans call *lumpenfever*, which is stage fright. So that doesn't worry me at all, but I feel better if I don't think of anything in particular beforehand. I like to get to the theatre early, so that I can waste a bit of time. I think, as I'm growing older, these bits of time to waste are more and more important. Once I'm on the stage I don't notice any great strain, except perhaps in my voice, or something imponderable like that, but actual strain I don't really notice. I could go on for a long time without worry, I have a great deal of stamina in that sense. But now I do have to have a rest beforehand.'

He is unlikely to revive that particular show, as diabetes has severely restricted his mobility. This began to affect him in the mid-1990s, and he has found it increasingly difficult to climb steps or to walk any distance. At airports he now needs a wheelchair to reach the gate and the support of a stick to get on stage. This is frustrating for a man who used to play a very competitive game of tennis and who has shared a court on occasion with world-class players.

If he felt tempted to bring back *An Evening with Peter Ustinov*, he would have to overcome the opposition of his wife. When I asked Hélène whether he might do it again, she said most emphatically, 'I hope not.' She worries about him doing too much and travelling too much, but he must still rank high in airlines' Frequent Flyer categories.

The accolades from press and public that greeted the opening of the one-man show in 1990 were swiftly followed by a more personal one from 10 Downing Street. A letter arrived at the stage door of the Theatre Royal from Mrs Thatcher, asking whether Peter would accept a knighthood; if so, she would recommend the appointment to the Palace for royal approval. The public announcement was made in the Queen's Birthday Honours on 16 June 1990.

For the investiture several months later, Peter was permitted to take three guests, and he was accompanied by Hélène, Tamara, and Andrea. He was proud to be honoured but could not fail to see the humorous potential in the occasion. 'I was kneeling in front of the Queen, and she is tinier than one ever imagines. I've seen her often on television, but when I actually see her again in a room, she seems minute. She lifted this enormous sword, looking at it with a kind of trepidation through her glasses; she put it on one shoulder and lifted it, and moved it very carefully, seemingly hypnotised by something on the ceiling, and lowered it perilously on the other shoulder. At that moment I had a vision that this procedure must be due to the fact that the time before me she'd thought that she could go from one shoulder to the other without lifting the sword.'

He had no time to share this mischievous vision with his sovereign, as there were several hundred other people waiting their turn at Buckingham Palace. Having safely dubbed him Sir Peter, the Queen smiled and said, 'How nice to have you here under these circumstances.'

'It's very good of you, Ma'am, I love being here.'

'Where have you been recently? We haven't seen you.'

Peter started to say, 'I've been in New Zea—' and was pushed out of the way by the next knight in line.

The Ustinov family all went off to lunch afterwards with a friend of Peter's who was also knighted that day, Ronald Grierson, but even that brought a note of surrealistic humour, when the main course arrived: 'grouse, lying manacled on our plates. It was the last thing any of us wanted to see at that moment, and we left all the grouse,' or 'grice' as Peter pronounced it in his best upper-class English accent.

Becoming Sir Peter Ustinov in his seventieth year was never likely to affect his general irreverence towards those in authority, and as if to prove the point he published in the same year *The Old Man and Mr Smith*, in which God and the Devil return to earth and have a series of witty and provocative debates in various Western and Eastern countries. Their arrival and their supernatural powers cause general consternation, especially their ability to disappear at will whenever someone tries to arrest or kill them.

The issues raised in the book are so stimulating that the reader accepts the fantasy and is carried along by the ideas, as well as some wickedly barbed jokes. When Mr Smith tries to tempt the Old Man into visiting Rome, he refuses, on the grounds that he's 'not nearly well enough dressed for the Vatican'. They get caught in the Israeli–Palestinian crossfire in the Middle East, are followed by Holy Men in India, have to levitate in a hurry out of the White House, and also out of the reach of a Japanese mega-millionaire who is trying to patent the secret of eternal life.

After their visits to various faiths and denominations they have one last exchange of thoughts before returning to their celestial and infernal homes:

They looked at each other with affection and amusement, as equals. It was, curiously enough, Mr Smith who became grave first.

'There is just one element I would like to clarify,' he said.

'Yes.'

'There is so much condemnation in the various holy writs about praying to false gods, to idols with feet of clay, all that internal propaganda, publicity put out in favour of one belief at the expense of all others. This seems to me entirely erroneous, in that it is belief itself which is important, not the objects of belief. Belief entails a lesson in humility. It is good for a man's soul to believe in something greater than himself, not because he magnifies his god, but because he shrinks himself to size. Now, if this is so, a primitive man who worships a tree, or the sun, or a volcano derives the same benefit from his act of moral prostration as a cultivated man would do before the god of his tradition, and the effects on the worshipper are identical. It is the act of worship which is important, at no time the object of that worship. Heresy?'

'All I can say is that which is self-evident to everyone except a theologian. Since I am everything, it follows that I am the clay of the false god's feet, to say nothing of the volcano, the tree, the sun. There are no false gods. There is only God.'

'Many heretics have been burned and hideously tortured because they worshipped false gods. They should have been congratulated for worshipping at all.'

'Don't. Please don't ask me the impossible, a comment on the imperfections of the past. I am not in the mood to rake up the embers of conflicts in which convictions won battles over doubts. Remember only that mankind is united by its doubts, divided by its convictions. It stands to reason that doubts are far more important to the survival of the human race than mere convictions. There. I have said too much already.'

'You do not think ill of me for bringing up the subject?'

'I would have thought ill of you if you had not.'

The Old Man stretched out his hand, and touched Mr Smith's shoulder. 'Why are you good to me? So tolerant of my lapses? So eager for my welfare?'

Mr Smith answered with a simplicity which was disarming. 'You forget I was trained as an angel.' And as a barely audible afterthought, he added, 'Sir.'

Like all the other Ustinov novels, one cannot read it without thinking that it would translate into a brilliant film, with the right cast and director. The Germans have a script ready, which Peter thinks is very good, and a German composer has written an opera about it. Peter was going to play God in the film, and he wanted Bob Hoskins as the Devil, a most intriguing double-act, but nothing has come of it yet.

However, it is his daughter Pavla's favourite among her father's books, and she says she would love to be in a position to make it into a film, so perhaps the prospect is not entirely lost.

The Old Man and Mr Smith is also Hélène Ustinov's favourite. Apart from its entertainment value, the book gives a clear insight into the author's view of organised religion, first inculcated in him at school and then developed during his extensive world travels, which he expounds in a very personal way: 'I think that religion is a temperamental matter, a geographical matter, a seasonal matter, and to do with climate. It's very difficult to imagine a great Roman Catholic seminary north of the Arctic Circle; it's very difficult to imagine a bleak Puritan meeting in Sardinia; and the whole Orthodox East has a definite flavour to it, which is different from the others, and which suits it temperamentally. But as far as religion's concerned, the teaching is precisely the same.'

That book, like most of his others, revolves around a series of journeys, as do several of his television documentaries. Peter was soon off on his travels with another film crew. John McGreevy, who had directed his programmes in Russia and China, now made *Ustinov on the Orient Express*.

They used the same technique that Peter had invented earlier, of him running into historical characters impersonated by actors – the arms-dealer Sir Basil Zaharoff, Ernest Hemingway, and the Duke of Windsor when he was still Prince of Wales, accompanied by Mrs Simpson. 'It was a very interesting diversion. I'd never felt as silly in my life, in this train that throws you left, right and centre, because the springing is exactly as it was in those days. You have to dress for dinner, which I think is absolutely absurd on a train; while trying to adjust your black tie, you're flung from one side of the small toilet to the other. Like hearing about the Indian quarter-horses, you begin to wonder what you are doing there, when you could be at home.'

This is a reflection that has crossed his mind on more than just those two occasions over the last six decades of his extraordinarily multi-faceted career. But since his favourite word is 'serenity', as he told one newspaper questionnaire, he does not dwell for long on those disquieting thoughts. He gets impatient with journalists who ask him why he bothers to write novels that only sell moderately, when he could be doing something else. He writes them because he wants to, and because there are certain ideas that he can only express in that form. Besides, with his books he enjoys complete freedom of expression, with none of the interference that so often occurs in the film world.

Several of the films of which he is proudest fared only modestly at the box office. One of them was *Lorenzo's Oil*, a true-life medical drama about a strange and rare disability for which nobody seemed able to diagnose either the cause or the cure. All the children stricken with it fell into a paralysed condition and died. The story traces the struggle of a couple, played by Nick Nolte and Susan Sarandon, who refuse to accept that nothing can be done for their small son, and embark on their own research programme into the disease. They eventually find a formula for treating it, derived from rapeseed oil.

Their stubborn determination irritates many of the other afflicted parents, as well as the medical professionals they consult. Peter played a highly regarded consultant, whose caution makes him plead for more time to research the formula properly, and he movingly conveys the dilemma of a man torn between his professional ethics and his personal sympathy.

The authenticity of the film was largely due to the fact that the Australian director, George Miller, was also a doctor, whose interest in the subject was medical as well as cinematic. Its impact on medical opinion was considerable, as the real boy in question survived. At the end of the film, a long list of names of those who did not underlines how unusual that was.

For audiences more used to seeing Peter Ustinov play larger-than-life characters, it was a revelation to see him register emotion by only the slightest twitch of his mouth, or by the look of pain in his eyes. It was his experience of working with Susan Sarandon on this film that added her to Maggie Smith on his personal list of favourite leading ladies, joining that select group that began forty years earlier with Deborah Kerr, Rosemary Harris, and Diana Wynyard.

His sensitivity to people and to places often leads him to respond in a spontaneous way, which can be both engaging to the many and disconcerting to the few. These simultaneous opposed reactions have occurred more than once at Durham University, beginning when he was installed as Chancellor in 1992. He succeeded Dame Margot Fonteyn, whose ballet shoes he had painted for the *Sleeping Beauty* his mother designed back in 1938.

He confessed in his column for the *European* newspaper:

That it was a great responsibility I knew in advance, but I could not guess at the pervasive atmosphere of the place itself. Now that it is over, I can admit to having abandoned my formal speech after the dress rehearsal in the Cathedral, where I was exposed to the magically warm atmosphere of a place which, by virtue of the Gothic splendour, could so easily have remained cold.

The singing of the choir, the fanfare of sundry brass instruments, the clear diapason of the organ, all contributed to bring life to the ancient stones, creating an envelope for the ritual at once majestic and miraculously accessible or, as I put it, at once human and super-human. The whole short, almost terse, affair, struck a balance which once again made me conscious of a sharpened focus. An appreciation of the past lends credibility and confidence to a vision of the future.

In one of his ad-libbed references to his own past, he remarked that his father would have been so pleased to see that he had managed to scrape into a university at last. 'I noticed consternation among the professors in the half-darkness, but it was too late, wasn't it, and I've been there ever since.'

An incoming Chancellor is awarded the privilege of naming his own recipients for an honorary degree, and Fred Zinnemann was overwhelmed to be told that he was to be so honoured, more than thirty years after the making of *The Sundowners*. But after a while Peter received a letter from him, saying, 'I am writing to you to refuse the honour, much against my better instincts, but I'm too old now. I can't move up to Durham, my wife is in a wheelchair. I'd better stay here and wait for the end. This was a wonderfully flattering gesture, but I'm not in a position to make use of it.'

So without telling Zinnemann, the new Chancellor made arrangements for the mace and the other ceremonial necessities to be brought south, and he conferred the film director's honorary degree in his apartment. 'The wife was sitting in her wheelchair; he had shrunk with age and in this hat he looked much too small for it. He was terribly touched, and then he died shortly afterwards.'

Peter has since conferred honorary degrees on Mikhail Gorbachev, the German President Roman Herzog, Glenda Jackson, Leon Davičo, and Prince Charles. The preparations for the last of these ruffled one set of bureaucratic feathers, when Peter had to have lunch with the man who represented the Prince's interests in that part of the country. This individual was dismayed by Peter's response to his opening question: 'Could you tell me roughly what you're going to say tomorrow?'

'No.'

'Good God, man, do you realise it's twenty-four hours to go, and you still can't tell me what you're going to say tomorrow?'

'No, that's the way I work. I'm terribly sorry, I don't know exactly what I'm going to say. I have to take myself by surprise, otherwise it doesn't work. It would be unfair to Prince Charles if I tell you something now, and it won't happen to be the truth.'

'Very well. In that case would you mind telling me roughly what you think of the Prince?'

'I think he is a highly intelligent man, who must therefore suffer tremendously on occasion. I further think that we always talk about human rights in reference to those who don't have any, which is quite correct. But we tend to forget those that have them all but are not allowed to use them.'

'Oh dear! I hope you're not going to upset the apple-cart.'

The conversation went steadily downhill from that point, at

what Peter says was the worst lunch he has ever had in his life. It ended with his being told, 'You say you've just been to South Africa and had a working arrangement with Mandela. It may interest you to know my brother has just left South Africa for good, because of the corruption.'

By now Peter was so incensed that he could not stop himself replying, 'Oh, in that case I hope he takes some of the corruption with him.'

He made the university promise him that he would never have to sit next to that man again. But he had not yet come to the end of being patronised by him.

At the ceremony he said exactly what he meant about the Prince of Wales, who looked suitably appreciative. 'I said, "I'm dying to hear what he has to say about many subjects, not because I could conceivably agree with him, that's neither here nor there, but I believe he has the right to express himself, just as anybody else, and I certainly have the right to listen to what he has to say." The sun came out behind him at that moment, and his ears became transparent, he seemed to glow. The public reacted with great enthusiasm to what I said. On the procession out, this loon was sitting on the aisle, and I suddenly felt a little tug on my sleeve as I passed. He said, "Well done," as though in some mysterious way his influence had told.'

In the years since 1992, the university staff have come to accept that Peter has his own way of doing things. The expansion of student numbers has meant that instead of just one graduation ceremony, at the last count Peter presided over twenty-three separate congregations in five days. In the beginning the professors reassured him that he need not worry about making the same speech each time; although they had to attend them all, the students graduating would only hear it once. He in turn reassured them, 'If you think I can possibly remember what I said from one to the next, you're very much mistaken.' He ad-libs his remarks there in exactly the same way as he does in his one-man show or in his after-dinner speeches.

This spontaneity comes in useful when responding to the students. Some of them are so quick off the mark that they say 'Thank you' before he has uttered, 'Congratulations.' Two of them recently said, 'OK.' The dress code is fairly elastic too. 'One of them came wearing a strange hat, a knitted skullcap which looked as if it had come from an African protestor; I was wearing my mortarboard and I said, "Snap!" '

He takes his responsibilities to the university very seriously, as the Vice-Chancellor, Sir Kenneth Calman, told me: 'He's a marvellous figure to have as the formal head of the university. His most visible public role is presiding at our degree congregations. He attends as many of these as his numerous other commitments will allow, and we estimate that in his first ten years as Chancellor he must have shaken some 25,000 hands. His speeches are always a sheer delight for the graduates, their families and friends – and the staff. Gaining a degree may be a serious business but we don't like our ceremonies to be solemn and self-important. Sir Peter brings a mixture of wisdom, food for thought about serious issues in the world, and a generous helping of humour. One of his key messages is the importance of respect between generations. He tells the new graduates that he is very positive and optimistic about the future achievements of youth, and, turning to the parents, observes that the younger people will make good the mistakes that the older ones leave behind.'

But Sir Kenneth points out that his involvement and initiatives go much further than that. 'When he met members of our Institute in Middle Eastern and Islamic Studies, during a visit to cut the first turf on the site of their new building, they were enthralled to hear of his personal conversations with people like Yasser Arafat, King Hussein, and Prime Minister Rabin. At Ushaw College – a Roman Catholic theological college affiliated to the university – he entranced them with accounts of his visit to the Vatican and its museums, on which he had just made a television series. He took part in a student theatre production as a voice on the radio, recording his part with the student producer during his visit for use the following term. He was a keynote speaker at the History Society 2000 Conference, an annual event organised by students, and spoke of his hopes that in the new millennium people with varying culture, backgrounds, political, and religious allegiance could learn to live together with their differences. On that same theme, we are currently involved with him and the Ustinov Foundation in developing his initiative for linking up academics, writers, politicians, other public figures, and the media throughout Europe and further afield on the subject of prejudice.'

When the university wanted to establish a Ustinov Institute, it took Peter a long time to figure out what it should be, until it came to him that it should study the history of prejudice, from Northern Ireland to the Middle East and many points beyond. As word has got out along the international university grapevine, other universities have indicated a wish to join in, including those of Warsaw and Haifa. The sensitivity of the whole subject is revealed by Peter's own reservations about the latter application, having said, 'I won't go to Israel until Ariel Sharon is put back in his box. I have described him as a bull in search of a china-shop.'

Another part of the Foundation's work ought to prove less controversial – the relief of noma, an African disease similar to leprosy, which could be eradicated by a policy of immunisation. This aspect of the Ustinov Institute's plans has already attracted the interest of the universities of St Petersburg, Vienna, and Berlin. For someone who never went to university himself, Peter Ustinov has had a remarkable impact on the academic world, both in Britain and further afield.

That world has not been slow to acknowledge it. As long ago as 1958 he was awarded the Benjamin Franklin Medal by the Royal Society of Arts. This honour is conferred annually, on a citizen of the USA or the UK in alternate years, who has 'forwarded the cause of Anglo-American understanding in the fields of arts, manufactures and commerce'. Peter was not around to receive it then, and it was not until March 1997 that he was actually able to accept it in person, when he chaired a lecture at the RSA by Roger Coleman of the Royal College of Art, on 'Breaking the Age Barrier'.

In his introduction of the speaker, he said, 'I'm very flattered to be asked to be here tonight, because I regard myself as one of the ageing population in urgent need of consolation by Mr Coleman. During my lifetime I've seen design develop terribly quickly. I remember flying by Imperial Airways from Paris to London in 1936. You were seated in an enormous club chair, worn in places, with hair coming out of it and not at all comfortable. In front of you was a speedometer nervously going between 75 and 110 mph. As a schoolboy I was riveted by this, but it was like the old motor cars. There was no design attached to them at all, dials and things were put arbitrarily all over the place, but nowadays you're more and more conscious of design.'

To prove his point, again in a very personal way, he went on: 'Roger Coleman and I were recently invited to Buckingham Palace, along with all the Rectors and Chancellors and Vice-Chancellors in England and Scotland, all in our costumes. I was awfully jealous of the delegation from the RCA, because the rest of us all wore heraldic things in very obvious colours. I was dressed in the most absurd red robe with a jagged golden line, which looked like the sort of thing down which drunkards had to walk when taken out of their cars by the police. Roger and the others from the RCA were dressed in the most ravishing outfits. They looked like characters out of *A Midsummer Night's Dream*.'

Then he made a particular plea. 'We were talking about education. Government ministers and the opposition all talk about education as being a tremendous priority, but none of them suggests that to be successful it should be entertaining – a stimulus to the imagination, so that one educates oneself with some guidance from a good dog.'

Stimulating the imagination has been a lifetime occupation for Peter Ustinov, though it is a burden he carries lightly. When he thanked Roger Coleman at the end of that evening at the RSA he remarked, 'On my seventieth birthday I told my children that the time had come when I really must decide what to do with my life. My son said, "You're quite right, but don't hurry." '

Twenty

1993–1997

From *Ustinov Meets Pavarotti* to *The Love of Three Oranges*

In the last decade of the twentieth century the Peter Ustinov we saw on the screen was more likely to be appearing as himself in TV documentaries, rather than as another character in a cinematic drama. He was far from giving up acting, but more interesting projects were being offered him by the programme makers for factual television, several of which were about the world of music.

One that he found intriguing in prospect, but which did not quite come off as he had hoped, was a conversation in 1993 with the Italian tenor Luciano Pavarotti. It was set up by a Norwegian producer, Bjorn Benko, who had also been involved in the Ustinov interviews with Rabin and Arafat. Eventually, however, Peter had to take the project away from him, 'because he hadn't the experience. He's a middle-aged Norwegian who had the right ideas, but has no technical knowledge of how to carry them through and loses control of them.'

The programme was made for German television but was also transmitted in other countries, including Britain. However, the timing was not particularly auspicious, as Pavarotti was in the process of an acrimonious divorce. Although the two men had never met before, they got on very well. Peter was anxious to keep their conversation as spontaneous as possible, without a lot of discussion beforehand. Unfortunately, his Irish producer was not exactly attuned to his presenter's sometimes oblique approach.

Peter tried to open out their filmed talk by saying, 'Don't you think in interviews, silence is a terribly important thing, it may be embarrassing for the onlooker, because nothing happens, but it's the exploration of people's silence that interests me.'

The singer brightened and got as far as, 'That's a very good point, I tell you ...' when they were interrupted off-camera by a voice saying, 'Ask him about his muther.'

Peter snorted with frustrated laughter as he complained to me, 'He'd done the same thing when I interviewed Ted Heath. When I said, "Yachting, now that's a solitary thing. I think probably your relation with the sea is terribly important ...' again I got, "Ask him about his muther." The call *always* came at the wrong moment.'

But despite these hiccups the Pavarotti programme went down well with the audience, and the *Guardian*'s TV critic, Nancy Banks-Smith, devoted the whole of her column to rhapsodising about it: 'Pavarotti, wearing something slimming in black, was in his swimming pool blowing happy fountains like a whale with whiskers. Peter Ustinov, who favoured tight turquoise, bobbed alongside. It was a buoyant sight. Pavarotti took a call on his mobile phone. Ustinov, who is not lightly upstaged, claimed to be taking a call from the mafia; "What I done to you? Na-thing!" he whines, diversifying swiftly into Peter Lorre. "It's Palermo on the line," he hissed. Pavarotti laughed hugely and sank. *Ustinov Meets Pavarotti* (BBC1) was extraordinary. How many interviews can you remember in which the subject was having a good time? ... And there's another thing. Great stars are on their guard, they roll their eyes at you like racehorses, but this one was being amused by a star in his own right. Ustinov was so entertaining that it gave a whole new force to collapse of stout party.'

His next Italian subject was on a much bigger scale and went unexpectedly smoothly, given the subject – *Inside the Vatican*. It helped that Peter already had a good relationship with Pope John Paul, whom he had met during the celebrations at the Year of the Child in 1979, when they talked about their mutual passion for tennis. A few months later the Pope sent him a message via Cardinal Magee, who was passing through London: 'Tell him that if he comes to Rome in the near future not to forget his tennis racquet.' (This was the call that had so impressed Clifford Williams when it interrupted their conversation about *Overheard*.) Unfortunately the assassination attempt a little later left a gunshot wound that put paid to the papal tennis, so they never had the game they had promised each other.

But their rapport overrode some of the objections lower down the hierarchy to the television plans. The freedom of action Peter was given mystified outsiders. When the series was given a big première screening in Vienna, the first question to him at the press conference beforehand was, 'Mr Ustinov, you have been divorced two times and you are not a Catholic. Why did they allow you to do this film?'

'Perhaps for that reason,' was his diplomatic answer.

He left it at that, but during the filming he was never once asked about his beliefs and kept his own counsel about what they were. He had one difficult moment right at the beginning, when he arranged a dinner to warm the atmosphere. Among his guests was an American archbishop who had been put in charge of PR at the Vatican, after he saved the Pope's life from an attack by a madman in the Philippines. Another guest was a Scottish bishop who suddenly stopped the conversation with the pronouncement, 'Well, I still think the Church has been far too indulgent in the matter of Galileo.' His American colleague said impatiently, 'Oh, come on.'

The television treatment was based on the work of a Canadian historian who had prepared the way, but most of the actual script was written by Peter on the spot, sitting in the Vatican gardens. 'It was very difficult to do, because we had to give the impression, like all modern investigative journalism, that although you had to be reverent, at the same time you cast a certain amount of doubt on the efficacy of what was being done in modern times. Would it last? So I put the emphasis on humanity, that if the Church didn't forget humanity, there was a chance the Church would go on for a long time; but that in its history it has always shown that when it forgot that, it had a rocky period.'

It was as well that the Scottish bishop was not around when they shot the scene where Peter met Galileo, in the person of a German actor of Italian origin, and told him, 'I've got some news for you which I think will interest you. The Vatican has exonerated you of all blame in the matter. Your reputation is as clean as it ever was.'

Galileo looked at him in astonishment. 'Is that true? When did this happen? It must have been five, no, ten years after my death?'

'No, it was quite recent.' The two men both collapsed in laughter, almost out of control. Finally Ustinov said, 'May I drink to your health?'

'No', Galileo replied, 'I would rather drink to the sun.'

The Vatican authorities were very pleased with the final results, which were screened in many countries. One of the most contentious locations led to a remarkable spin-off later. The film-makers asked to shoot in the tomb of St Peter, two levels below the High Altar, which had never been allowed before. The Vatican agreed to let them in, against the fierce opposition of the man in charge of that area, Cardinal Noë, who severely disapproved because it broke with tradition. When he was overruled, he pleaded, 'I can't stop you from doing this, but once you do, Ustinov, *con molto reverenza, con molto spiritualità?*'

Peter did his best to oblige, doing his commentary in what he called his 'shrouded voice, and it turned out to be quite effective and interesting'. But he was surprised to receive a fax subsequently from another cardinal, reading: 'Dear Ustinov, we are very grateful to you for your contribution to the Vatican. Now we want to enlist your contribution once more. We are planning for Radio-Televisione in Pacem' – Vatican Radio/TV – 'together with our collaborator Radio-Televisione Monte Carlo, the first talk show from St Peter's Tomb.'

This idea developed into something much more ambitious, which proved to be beyond the producers' capacity to deliver. There were several hook-ups with other countries, including one to Shimon Peres in Jerusalem; they tried for another with Helmut Kohl but failed to get him. Peter co-hosted with a man from Radio-Televisione Monte Carlo, and caught a terrible cold because the Vatican insisted on his introducing the programme from outside St Peter's.

The Diplomatic Corps were all involved, and an African Ambassador was asked to speak in the programme, but they were all unused to the ways of television. 'He'd prepared his whole speech on about eighty tiny sheets of paper, like telephone pads, and he started reading them; but he didn't know where to put the ones he'd already finished, and suddenly a gust of wind blew them all over the place. We had the sight of other members of the Diplomatic Corps, who thought they were below the level of the camera, hunting for them while he went on talking, but he got stuck as after page 14 came 18. It was the most enormous shambles you can imagine.'

The absolutely key communication on such big outside broadcasts is between the production control room and the presenters, but the latter were left totally in the dark about where the producer was going next. Peter asked his colleague, 'What do we do now?'

'I don't know.'

'Well, are we in Tel Aviv, or are we here?'

Peter shook with laughter as he told me, 'Nobody knew where we were. Eventually the man said to me, "Let me ask you a personal question. Are you a Catholic?"

' "No, I'm not, I'm really not anything, but I was born a Protestant."

' "Oh well, that makes the whole thing perfect, I'm Jewish!" '

It was a relief to Peter to put himself in surer professional hands for his next television appearances. The first was an adaptation of Dickens' *The Old Curiosity Shop* for the Disney Television Channel, produced by Greg Smith and directed by Kevin Connor. It was shot in Ireland, where Peter has always enjoyed working, and he announced that he was so enamoured of the country he was thinking that from now on he would write his name as U'stinov. He played the old grandfather, addicted to gambling, who spent all his money on it and then seized his granddaughter's pocket money. It was a long part, and he made the most of it.

The second was a two-part documentary in celebration of Haydn, for the American Public Broadcasting network, produced by EuroArts Entertainment and directed by Derek Bailey; it was fifteen years since he and Peter had last worked together on *The Hermitage*. The original treatment was written by the pianist Israela Margalit, who was also the soloist in the Haydn Piano

Concerto in D. Derek Bailey then produced the first draft script, which Peter transformed into his own style in a rapid longhand. At the end of each day's shooting the two men would repair to Peter's room and spend the next couple of hours agreeing the script for the next day. Then the PA and the autocue girl were summoned, and by about eight o'clock in the evening everything was set for the following day. In less experienced hands that kind of last minute rewriting could have been a recipe for disaster but, with Ustinov as his presenter, Derek Bailey enthused, 'That was a great way of working.'

In the films Peter walked through a series of ornate rooms and corridors in the Schloss Esterhazy, opening doors to discover the musicians, playing various works by the composer. In the Farewell Symphony at the end of the first part, he walked through door after door, explaining all the players' exits until just the last one was left. His serious passages were interspersed with a vocal impersonation of the Empress Maria Theresa, and a facial imitation of the gargoyles on the castle walls. He mimed taking wine from a statue representing Autumn and grimaced at its imagined taste. He appeared to doze through the Surprise Symphony, awakening with a start at the crash of the drum 'surprise'.

Three years later, in 1997, Derek Bailey directed *Peter Ustinov's Mendelssohn* in a similar style, and this time the subject offered Peter the opportunity of reviving one of his earliest and funniest impersonations. Mendelssohn's Scottish Symphony was dedicated to Queen Victoria, and Peter quoted from her diary in his best falsetto, with pursed lips, in an impression that would have been familiar to many wartime habitués of the Players' Theatre.

In between these two musical tributes, he travelled further afield for a pair of documentaries about Thailand and Hong Kong, with his regular collaborator John McGreevy. He was reasonably content with the Hong Kong film, but less so with the one on Thailand, which he found more difficult than he expected. The background information had been prepared for them by an American who had lived there for a long time, but Peter thought much of it was very suspect. They also sailed up the Irrawaddy and filmed in Burma, which 'wasn't particularly difficult, but it was very interesting, because one is always conscious that it's a ridiculous regime, just like any South American junta with nothing but generals. There is a general who is Minister of Hotels.'

But his consciousness that the country was as sinister as it was ridiculous was reinforced by one of the locals who told them, 'The golden era of Burma was in the fourteenth and fifteenth centuries; we are now in our Stone Age.' For his own safety they did not quote him in the programme.

Thailand and its people captured Peter's affections, and he and his wife now fly there every Christmas Day to spend three weeks in the tropical sun, always staying at the same hotel. One of its attractions is that he finds it easy to write there. 'It's very Buddhist and that's charming, and also its water is clear enough for you to be up to the neck in it, and decide it's time you cut your toenails.'

The other part of its appeal is that, unlike the rest of Asia, it has never been colonised by any European power. He has more ambivalent feelings about India, partly because of his rejection of that glorification of the British Empire he was fed at school.

So it was with some glee that he appeared in *Stiff Upper Lips* in a parody of the British Raj, set in the India of 1905. That was not all it parodied, as any viewer of the Merchant/Ivory films would have realised. In Rome a boy throws open a window, to be faced by a brick wall, and the old butler pees in the soup as a gesture of protest. A more subtle satire on *Death in Venice* seems to have escaped most people's attention. At the end a young man announces in the church in the Isle of Man that he can't go through with the marriage to the young girl, as his Cambridge room-mate is his real and secret love.

Peter played a tea planter who made love to Prunella Scales, with a line to which he added the adjective – 'You are the most lovely, breasts like half-filled tea bags.' She was playing the aunt in the film to her real-life son, Samuel. One of the make-up girls, after seeing them hugging each other, asked her, 'How long have you known Sam West?'

'Oh, about twenty-six years, he's my son.'

Prunella said, with great amusement, 'She thought I was trying to pull the juvenile!'

She and Peter were both pleased to be working together again, and Samuel West remembers that time as a very special experience. 'Apart from playing elephant polo with him in the film, I remember particularly an evening at a tea plantation in the Ootacamund highlands, miles from the nearest hotel, where Sean Pertwee, Georgina Cates, Bertie Portal, and my mother and I were treated to an evening of Peter's stories till way past midnight. We had to stay on the plantation in order to get up to film early next day, but no one was in any hurry to go to bed, and though fuelled by nothing stronger than tea, Peter was inexhaustible. I can't remember saying more than a dozen words all night, and none of us wanted it to end; it was one of the happiest evenings of my professional life. Or of my life, in fact.' Quite a tribute from one of the rising stars of the Royal Shakespeare Company, with many happy evenings under his belt in the theatre as Prince Hal, Richard II, and Hamlet.

The film, released in 1996, did not do as well as it deserved, in the view of Prunella Scales. This was Peter's forty-first appearance in the cinema, so he was now philosophical about the success or otherwise of his movies. He was less so about his more recent career in the opera house, so he was both pleased and a little apprehensive when the Bolshoi invited him to direct Prokofiev's *The Love of Three Oranges* in Moscow in 1997.

His chief problem, once again, was with the set. The young designer from Odessa came up with a complicated system of three hydraulic bridges, controlled by computers, whose rise and fall had to be precisely timed with the movements of the singers. Peter's faith in the concept was hardly enhanced when he was told on arrival that there were not enough Russian experts to build the contraption, so it had been contracted out to the Yugoslavs. There was no sign of the bridges until two weeks before the first night, so the director was struggling until then to choreograph over a hundred people on a flat stage, so that it would all work when they were on the four different levels envisaged. Without them, 'it looked like the rush hour on the Underground'.

When the bridges finally arrived from Belgrade, they rose as planned, but then, with an awful grinding noise, two of them stuck. The singers and dancers refused to go on them, because they looked too dangerous. In an attempt to break the incipient strike, Peter climbed up with his walking stick to the topmost bridge and stood there, alone, doing his best to look imperious. The company applauded his bravery but still refused to follow his example. So he had to descend, more slowly and a bit sheepishly.

'Then some of the women, bless them, noticed that I looked unhappy, and they're a very emotional people anyway, so in twos and threes they ventured on to the bridges, going out on them as though they were testing water. When there were about eight of the women on the bridges they began to chide the men, saying, "You're cowards, all of you men, cowards." The men said, "You come down here, and we'll show you how much we're cowards." Eventually the men were shamed into going on the bridges, and the situation was saved.'

The real saviour was the old stage manager, a former colonel who had had a distinguished career in the war and was a chief engineer at the battle of Kursk, one of the last great tank battles between the Red Army and the Wehrmacht. He told Peter technical details about the hydraulic bridges in Russian, and although he barely understood either the technicalities or the stream of Russian, it all sounded so authoritative that Peter trusted him. When Peter needed him he called out, 'Colonel,' and the old man would arrive, wearing his medals on his suit.

By the end Peter was totally dependent on him, as four days before the end of rehearsals the designer walked out on Peter. 'He had a calculatedly splendid exit line – "You will find that I am too expensive a toy to play with in this manner" – but it was in Russian, and my Russian is not perfect, so the whole effect was spoilt because I had to wait for a translation, and by then he'd gone.'

At the dress rehearsal nothing worked, but on the first night everything went like clockwork. When the director was dragged on stage to join the cast for the curtain call, the first person he saw was the stage manager. 'He came towards me as though we were behind the Nazi lines and had closed the pincers, gave me an enormous bear-hug, and kissed me on the mouth, which was a sacrifice I was willing to make in the circumstances.'

There were two personal hiccups on the way to that triumphant opening. During rehearsals Peter was forever being asked to sign handwritten slips in Cyrillic, and if he stopped to try to decipher them someone would shout, 'We're holding the lift for you,' so by the end he was just signing whatever was put in front of him. Before the dress rehearsal he was waiting for a magician to come and show them his tricks for one of the scenes. Eventually, in exasperation, he demanded, 'Well, where is the magician? What is this? I asked for a magician.'

One of the assistants said, 'That is quite correct, but it was you who signed the paper forbidding him access.'

'What!? Well, give me another paper to sign, and I'll say it's all right.'

'It's a very good idea, but he's already gone, furious.'

He was allocated four tenors to choose from, but three of them were very jealous of each other, so they never appeared, claiming that they were all ill. But fortunately the fourth tenor, a young man of twenty-six, was a wonderful actor, even though his voice had not properly formed yet, and he had an enormous success in the part. Peter only discovered later that, to support his wife and baby when he was not singing, Sergei Gaidei was driving a taxi to make some real money.

Of all the operas he has done, Peter is proudest of this production, and it has certainly received the greatest acclaim. *Izvestia* headlined its notice, 'Englishman saves Bolshoi.' To be accused of being English there, of all places, struck the director as very paradoxical.

Two years later the Bolshoi brought the production to London, for just two performances, in August 1999, and experienced some difficulties fitting everything on to the stage of the Coliseum. One bridge worked, one was static, and there was no room for the third. The weather was very hot, and the Russian company complained bitterly about the lack of air-conditioning in the dressing rooms, which they were accustomed to at home.

The other opera brought by the Bolshoi was *Boris Godunov*, in a conventional production that was respectfully received. But the British response to *The Love of Three Oranges* was ecstatic, with

Martin Anderson proclaiming in the *Independent*, 'It was one of those productions you dream of: relentlessly funny, thrillingly paced, magnificently sung and played ... Sir Peter Ustinov's production grabbed every fleeting opportunity for wit with such dizzying wanton invention that it almost outpaced the audience's ability to take it all in: laugh a moment too long and you'll miss the next gag, on stage, in the subtitles – you didn't know where it would come from. And Ustinov's imagination fills every inch of space, the chorus of Cranks commenting from overhead walkways, while the Bolshoi dancers, with comically extended buttocks and bellies, waggle on and off stage below them like agitated chickens ... Those of us lucky enough to catch it came out with our heads whirling with giggling delight.'

The period between the two triumphant openings in Moscow and London was a very fertile one for Ustinov the music-lover. He wrote a new script for Saint-Saëns' *Carnival of the Animals*, which he has performed on German TV and in various European concert halls, and has recorded on CD. For a musical production of Molière's *Le Bourgeois Gentilhomme*, he wrote a narration, including a whole new third act, which he performed first at the Garmisch Strauss Festival and has also recorded on CD. Another of his CDs was the narration he wrote and recorded for Richard Strauss's last, unfinished opera, *The Donkey's Shadow*.

To top off this burst of musical creativity, he began work on the narration for Beethoven's only ballet, *The Creatures of Prometheus*, which he first performed in Germany at the end of 1999 with the Latvian Chamber Orchestra and has given on several occasions since.

With his long affection for this particular composer, both on the stage and the concert platform, it is no surprise to learn that his only remaining ambition as an opera director is to stage *Fidelio*. He shares the intensity of Beethoven's later antipathy to Napoleon; and his own passion for individual freedom, allied to his stagecraft and musical knowledge, would make him a seemingly inspired choice to produce Beethoven's only opera.

Twenty-one

1998–2000
From *Planet Ustinov* to
The Salem Witch Trials

If you wanted to make a television series based on Mark Twain's nineteenth-century journal of his travels, *Following the Equator*, who better as a guide to retrace his footsteps than that inveterate modern traveller, Sir Peter Ustinov? So reasoned Granada Television when it offered such a series to Channel Four, for transmission in 1998.

It was Peter who needed persuasion to do it. His first reaction was 'Who's going to see this? Nobody's heard of the book, nobody feels very strongly about Mark Twain.' The British producers sidestepped that problem by entitling the series *Planet Ustinov*, which he found slightly embarrassing, but the American co-producers naturally screened it in the States under the title *In the Steps of Mark Twain*.

The British director Michael Waldman had his own ideas about the structure of the series, which did not entirely tally with his presenter's. On this project, Peter did not enjoy the same amount of creative freedom that he had experienced with John McGreevy. 'Michael Waldman had great sensitivity, but it didn't always coincide with mine. I liked working with him, but with the other films I was more or less responsible for the actual content; here I rewrote a lot too, but it didn't always fit in with his cut.'

Their journey took them from the Pacific islands of Hawaii, Kiribati, and Fiji, down to New Zealand and Australia, back up to India, and across to Mauritius and South Africa. They travelled in big ships, small ships, and canoes; in airliners, light planes, and helicopters; in luxurious trains and rail-workers' trolleys; and at one point Peter was carried in a litter up 199 mountain steps by six strapping Fijians as if he were a tribal chieftain. He could walk short distances for the camera, but that kind of climb was now impossible for him.

The series took him to out-of-the-way places and strange locations that were new even to this seasoned traveller. In the book, Mark Twain described his visit to the Tasmanian penal colony at Port Arthur, which was a byword for brutality to convicts transported there between 1830 and 1880. It has been preserved as a tourist attraction, though it can hardly fail to depress the spirits of any visitor, however interested in history – as it did those of both Mark Twain and Peter Ustinov.

In the forbidding prison chapel, the pews looked like small individual horse-boxes, with high backs and sides, so that the men could not see each other, only the chaplain in the pulpit. Those in the solitary block were not allowed to speak to other prisoners and had to answer prison officials with just 'Yes' or 'No'.

Filming here allowed Peter to draw on his reserves of sardonic humour. 'I was in the pulpit, and I said, "Can you imagine when the clergyman stood up and said, 'We will now sing hymn number 118.' Can you imagine the roar, the release, the proof that people still had the capacity to talk and sing words more complicated than yes and no?" It was the most awful, heartless, grim system, these penal colonies, they undermined every iota of human dignity. That was fun to do, because with an empty church you could evoke all that in a very powerful way.'

There were many lighter moments in the series, but since the intention was to see how the world had changed in the hundred years since the American writer's visit, much of it was bound to be deeply serious and thought-provoking. For Twain's successor, the biggest surprise came when he met Nelson Mandela for the first time, in a filmed exchange that was never transmitted.

Mandela told him, 'I want to thank you for the strength you gave me in prison.'

'What?' Peter replied in disbelief. 'What are you talking about?'

'Yes, when we left Robben Island and went into prison on the mainland, things were easier, and we were able to see films and television. We saw your series about Russia, and I thought to myself how extraordinary, with the temperature of the time being so anti-Russian, that you were able to get away with dwelling on human prospects.'

Peter was dumbfounded. 'In other words, he's the first person that I've met who fully understood what I was up to. I was extraordinarily flattered and honoured by this, but it would have looked like an absurd self-advertisement to put that in the programme.'

Robben Island, like Port Arthur, is now on the tourist circuit, but unlike the Tasmanian penal colony, it remains inhabited by a curious mixture of residents, living in the little township that has grown up around the prison buildings. Now living there side by side are some of the ex-convicts – hardened criminals who have no wish to go back to the mainland again, former political prisoners who are exhausted by their political life, as well as some of the ex-warders who have chosen to retire there.

On the day that Peter visited the island, the first school opened for all the children of these three groups. 'It was so extraordinary, that the atmosphere of peace and reconciliation had spread even to Robben Island, and they were all now talking to each other and discussing old times.'

Peter also attended some of the tribunals of the Truth and Reconciliation Commission, chaired by Archbishop Tutu, and was impressed by how different their atmosphere was from any court presided over by a judge. The archbishop said to him, 'I was never really called to the Church, it was not a vocation in my case; I just thought it was the one place where a black boy could be on equal terms with a white one. Only later, when I was already in the Church, did I begin to believe. And so now shall we pray together for a moment?'

Peter raised with Archbishop Tutu what he saw as a paradox of the historical divide in South Africa.

'Both you and the Boers seem to be extremely Christian, which makes the whole of your conflict odder. The Afrikaners seem to be more Pharisaical in their attitude and seem to say, "Thank you God, for making us unlike the others. If there's anything we can do to help the others, you only have to tip us the wink." Your sense of religion is much more choreographic and symphonic, with a lot of gesture and choral music. It seems to me to be rather incongruous that you're both such ardent Christians.'

'Don't be too hard on the Boers.'

'Really!?'

'Yes, you know, like many minority people who believe, rightly or wrongly, that they are surrounded by a more powerful majority, they take refuge in the idea that they are a Chosen people, and after all it's not the first time in history this has happened.'

Peter thought this comment 'very clever, generous, and at the same time reflective and true'. This spirit of forgiveness was embodied most dramatically in the attitude of Nelson Mandela, who astonished Peter again by telling him, 'I am grateful for my twenty-seven years in prison, because it allowed me to meditate deeply on the human condition, and I maintain that every young person of either sex who wishes to make politics his or her career should be compelled to undergo the same discipline. Since I've come out of prison I've had no time to meditate.'

The willingness to forgive the injustices of the past in South Africa was so unique in Peter's experience of other divided societies that he wound up his visit there by observing to the camera, seated at the top of Table Mountain: 'The success or failure of the Third Millennium will depend on how much we are allowed to forget, in comparison with how much we are incited to remember.'

Questions of justice also engaged his attention in 1998 at the wider international level. The World Federalist Movement, of which he has been President since 1992, was asked to spearhead the UN vote in Rome on the creation of the World Criminal Court. 'We all thought it would have difficulty passing, because of American opposition. Yet 120 governments voted in favour, with 21 abstentions, and 7 against.' The seven included such unlikely bedfellows as the USA, China, Iraq, and Iran.

Peter may be disappointed by such opposition, but he is no longer surprised. He presided over one AGM of the Federalist Movement, arriving direct from the Pacific. On the agenda was what should have been the uncontroversial vote on the Convention of the Rights of the Child. It had already been signed by every country in the world except three – the Cook Islands, Somalia, and the United States. 'I was able to bring the happy news to the Federalist Congress that there were now only two countries left, because the Cook Islands had just decided to sign after all.'

The Federalist Movement now has a small secretariat at the UN headquarters in New York and works closely with the national UN Associations in individual countries. 'Our aim is to make the UN more democratic if we can and to help materially by bringing non-government organisations into it. The first NGO was the Red Cross, which came into being when a Swiss gentleman walked across a battlefield by mistake and suddenly saw with his own eyes what a wasteful, cruel occupation war is. No elected government would ever have had the mandate for founding such a thing as the International Red Cross; it had to be the idea of one man, which caught on and gradually spread and is now gratefully accepted by all governments as a means of protecting prisoners of war and so on.'

The Ustinov view of justice struck a more mischievous note in his novel *Monsieur René*, first published in Germany in 1998 and in the English-speaking world the following year. It is set in Switzerland, and the protagonist of the title is a seventy-year-old widowed and retired hotelier, who is the Permanent President of the International Brotherhood of Concierges and Hall Porters. Partly out of boredom and partly out of principle, he conceives a plan to use the hotel network's knowledge of the indiscretions of their guests to expose their immoral or criminal acts. Its unexpected success arouses the suspicions of the Swiss police, and Monsieur René has to use all his hotelier's guile to outwit them and rescue his new love, fellow conspirator Agnes, from a triple murder charge.

The author's long familiarity with the ways of the great international hotels and their staffs brings the ring of authenticity to the story. Television Suisse-Romande has optioned the book for a film, to be made in French. The title role would seem ideally suited to be played by its creator, but he insists it requires the services of a younger actor.

At the Cheltenham Festival of Literature in 1999 he read the seduction scene between René and Agnes, which delighted his packed audience as he conjured his characters off the page.

Peter draws a sharp distinction between writing novels and plays. 'Because I'm trained in the theatre, I tend to think more strongly of character. Writing a play is a much more difficult craft than a book, because in a play it's essential to know what *not* to write, and that's something that many of the greatest novelists never learnt. When novelists try to write plays, they very often overwrite, because they don't trust actors very much, and they want to be sure the ideas get across. You would have thought Dostoevsky was the ideal playwriting talent with his sense of the dramatic, but he never wrote a play, he couldn't. Dickens wrote wonderfully funnily and well about theatrical people, but he could never write a play, because he was used to a different kind of format. In the theatre it's like running for a new election every night, you're hoping more people like it than don't, so playwriting is a terrifying discipline; books are not supposed to be read at one go, otherwise the bookmark would never have been invented.'

Although he says that as a playwright he is not consciously influenced by other writers, his preferences are interesting. 'I'm devoted to Christopher Fry, for instance, though I could never write like that; his background is so different that I find it very interesting. I admire Alan Ayckbourn a lot because he does something that is desperately needed in England, and yet nobody else had the gift to do it; it's really very traditional, and yet with a twist it's not traditional at all. I admire Michael Frayn. I'm not as intrigued by Harold Pinter, though it's an interesting form of ambiguous theatre, which started with Ionesco. I don't care for Tom Stoppard's endless punning, because I think it will date terribly.'

And Samuel Beckett? 'Now there I'm really defeated, because it doesn't really reach me. Maybe it should, but I feel dissatisfied.'

But he also believes that writers should be left alone to plough their own furrow, and he has not forgotten his abortive exercise in organised collaboration with other leading playwrights, not long after the war. The idea was borrowed from the American Playwrights Company, a highly successful producing organisation formed by Maxwell Anderson, Marc Connelly, Sidney Kingsley, Elmer Rice, and Robert Sherwood, to put on their plays in the States.

The British quintet who set out to emulate their success consisted of James Bridie, Benn Levy, J.B. Priestley, Terence Rattigan, and the youngest of them all was Peter Ustinov. 'We met for the first time in Priestley's flat in Albany, and everything seemed to go quite well until Priestley said, "Well, gentlemen, I think we ought to make up our minds that from now on our plays are going to express the right ideas." James Bridie said, "May I make a comment here? I've made what little money I have in the past by expressing the wrong ideas, and I think it would be fatal to my chances of success if I changed my horses in midstream."

'We resolved to meet again, but with the problem still in the air. The second time we met in Priestley's home, we came up against the thorny problem – what happens if one of us has an enormous success, from which the others are bound to benefit up to a point, and the rest of us, for the time being anyway, have no success whatever? Benn Levy, who was the legal mind of the five of us, said, "Perhaps we should have some guidance here, from somebody who's had a great deal of success and knows how it is to deal with it. Perhaps, Terry, you would tell us what you do in this case?"

'J.B. Priestley interrupted by saying, "I think I ought to remind my fellow writers that I too have had my share of success."

'We never met again. It was absolutely impossible.'

Peter has always read widely from the literature of many countries, and he puts high among his favourites Gogol, Gorky and Chekhov from Russia, Guy de Maupassant from France, and Eric Linklater from Britain. 'They are all accessible authors. If there's anything I cringe from, it's affectation; literary affectation is the worst of the lot, because it impresses a lot of the critics. Many of the famous writers have frightful affectations, which drive me up the pole – Thomas Mann, for instance, with his endless convoluted sentences, I hate that. I love a mixture of whatever poetry you can find inside you, and a common touch. Perhaps that comes from the theatre, because if you're putting more or less ordinary people on the stage, you can't embellish their dialogue and make them lyrical; unless you're Irish when they all talk that way. Sean O'Casey was extremely lucky.'

The acting roles that were offered to Peter in his late seventies continued to be diverse and highly rewarding to do, even if some of them were quite small. He played the Walrus in a new TV version of *Alice in Wonderland*, in 1998, with Pete Postlethwaite as the Carpenter; and the following year he had just one day's filming for *The Bachelor*, for the man who had directed him in *Stiff Upper Lips*, Gary Sinyor. 'I enjoyed that enormously because I played a very unpleasant old American, and it got rid of a whole lot of inhibitions in me. When I wash my hair I look exactly like Henry Hyde, the man who was the thorn in Clinton's side during those embarrassing hearings in the Senate about his "affair" with Monica Lewinsky.'

He added another British monarch to his royal assumptions in 2000, with his crotchety old William IV for *Victoria and Albert* (described in the Prologue), which was screened by the BBC in 2001.

By then he was in Canada, working on a television version of the Salem Witch Trials that was based on the actual transcripts of the proceedings, not on Arthur Miller's play *The Crucible*. Peter thought the treatment of the text was very well done, and he only made slight changes to it. The Governor of Massachusetts is very interested in all the latest scientific theories and suggests that science might have an explanation for witches. Peter relished his character's stiff-necked riposte: 'You're a man of science, are you, Governor? Well, let me say this about science. It has about the same effect on witchcraft as a jet of urine into the ocean, by which I mean of course we all know it to be rank, and to be tepid, but it soon loses its personality in the ocean, when it's confronted by the far greater waves of faith and godliness. It always has been that way, Governor, and I daresay it always will be.'

The Governor was played by Alan Bates, who told Peter, 'You

won't remember this, but you offered me a part in *Billy Budd*, which I refused because I wanted to play Billy and nothing else.' He was right; Peter had no memory of that at all. 'But Alan was far too accomplished already to be as spontaneous as Terence Stamp was. For that part I needed somebody who isn't sure of anything and is surprised by everything and has a certain degree of innocence.'

Innocence was not much in evidence on the Salem shoot. Shirley MacLaine had not acted with Peter since 1964, and he found her more difficult than she had been in *John Goldfarb, Please Come Home*. In one scene he had to supervise her hanging after she was found guilty of witchcraft. She held up the shooting for hours, because she had to be naked. It was not that she minded stripping off; it was that when her clothes dropped off, she said they did not do it elegantly enough; they should do it more fluidly. So all the seamstresses had to put weights in her petticoats, and the delay meant that it was three in the morning before everyone got back to their hotels.

Peter pointed out, 'If you're going to strip her naked, people are not going to be looking to see how the clothes fall! Oh she was terrifying and old-fashioned in her insistence. She'd say, "No, it's still not right, put another weight in there." Weight soon became spelt W-A-I-T of course. The next day one of the men was supposed to rush at me with the idea of attacking me personally, and when he attacked me the director said, "Don't try to resist." I said, "In that case I'll need time out, so that I can have weights put in my underwear, because my desire is to jump up," and I got applause from the crew.'

He was nearly as disconcerted by her conversational style. She was sitting in the box for the accused, with another actress, and just before they started shooting, she leant towards her Inquisitor and said, 'We have decided we want to fuck you.' Peter deflected this by saying, 'I'm afraid that until four I'm rather busy.'

Despite these moments, he enjoyed his meaty role, and he shows no sign of giving up film-acting. Retirement is quite clearly not a word that figures in his vocabulary. 'Forces beyond my control will retire me sooner or later. I don't see why I should assist them; and working in the garden isn't really my thing, it's bad for my back. I'm always surprised with these film offers, at this date, especially as I'm limited to how far I can walk. In *The Salem Witch Trials*, thank God, I hardly had to move at all, I was nearly always sitting.'

In 2001 he celebrated his eightieth birthday, showing few signs of making any concessions to an age when many people have given up working a long time before.

Twenty-two

2001–2002
Sir Peter Ustinov at Eighty

As 2001 dawned, Peter was unsure of how his eightieth birthday would be celebrated, but his earlier predictions to me were spot on. The French did fail to raise the finance for their proposed TV programme, and the Germans did put on a spectacular tribute in Berlin. The details were kept secret from the recipient until the day. He was not even consulted about the guest-list, though all the immediate family were there except Pavla, who was editing her latest film. 'But she'd been to Berlin before, when I got an award for Lifetime Achievement; I was very glad she was there then, because she's one of my lifetime achievements.'

The Vice-Chancellor of Durham and the Provost of Stockton-on-Tees both flew to Berlin for the tribute, and many others were there in spirit. 'There were goodwill messages on the screen which absolutely staggered me – from Gorbachev, Havel, and one from the Dalai Lama, which was the last thing I expected. It was a wonderful occasion, and afterwards, as I sat there with relatives of mine who had come in from St Petersburg, suddenly there was a voice behind me.

' "You don't know me, but I'm the British Ambassador here."
' "Yes?"
' "Well, there's no getting away from it, you're a big star in *these* parts." '

The show was presented in a large theatre, and televised by ZDF, the German equivalent of BBC2. There was another evening on ARTE, the arts channel shared by Germany and France, which was a retrospective of his life, 'and frightfully funny and good, because they took me round places that had haunted me, like Westminster, and my prep school, which is now a supermarket, selling Continental soups!' That part of the evening ran for ninety minutes, and they also screened one of his best films – *Lola Montès*.

Peter even received a charming and surprising birthday gift from the German police. In 1999 he did his last long drive, from Berlin to Geneva, with only one break of half an hour for a brief nap in the car. He has always liked to drive fast, but this time he got a ticket for speeding between Basel and Freiburg, because they said he was driving at 197 kilometres an hour in a zone that was restricted to 120.

As he said, with a shrug, 'Well, obviously at that speed, I didn't see the restriction, and it was at night, I wasn't hurting anybody. To prove the point, I got a picture of myself at the wheel, of absolute sublime idiocy, looking so cretinous with pleasure at going so fast, that I willingly paid the heavy fine. I told this story on air during my eightieth birthday programme and said, "I paid it without complaint because I was in the wrong, but I very much regret that I couldn't keep the photograph." At the end of the next week I received the photograph with the compliments of the Karlsruhe police, saying, "You deserve this, after all your efforts." '

He has since had to have an operation on his eyes and cannot judge distances as well as he used to, so he has decided regretfully to give up one of the most enduring passions of his life.

The British recognition of his birthday was, in comparison, very muted. Nicholas Garland, the chief cartoonist of the *Daily Telegraph* and a long-time admirer of Peter Ustinov since their collaboration on *Photo Finish*, told me back in 2000 that he would remind his editor of this important milestone to be reached on 16 April 2001; his suggestion of a major interview to mark the occasion was then passed on to the sister paper in the group, the *Sunday Telegraph*.

They contacted Peter and said they planned to mark the occasion with a long feature in the Review section, 'but only on condition that no other paper did it. Could I guarantee to fend the others off? There were no others. I said yes, and then at the *last minute*, when I'd made all the preparations, cleared the decks for this, they said, "No, it's all right, because you've done a broadcast now with John Bird, and we'll publish that." So the Garrick invitation was a very nice gesture after the majesty of Berlin.'

It had to be a belated gesture in the finish because, despite the best efforts of both Peter and the Garrick Club, they could not find a window in his busy schedule until 14 October 2001, but the six months' delay in no way diminished his appreciation of their thoughtfulness. Fellow playwright Sir John Mortimer proposed the toast with an elegant wit; Sir Peter Ustinov responded by thanking him for his remarks, saying with a smile, 'I loved the bits particularly that had nothing to do with me.'

He thanked the members for inviting him to bring his wife on this occasion and told his wartime story of the Club gates being closed against the possible invasion by hysterical women fleeing the bombs. He followed this with stories of David Niven, the Prince of Wales at Durham, his Bolshoi Opera production, and the British Ambassador's remark to him in Berlin.

Hélène confided to me that she was as daunted by the prospect of being the only woman allowed to be present as she was mystified by the English love of men-only clubs; but she enjoyed the occasion and was touched by the sight of the happy photograph of Peter and her smiling at each other, which adorned the front of the menu card for the evening of celebration.

The various Peter Ustinov shows continued to tour throughout 2001. He took Beethoven's *The Creatures of Prometheus* to Ankara, where he performed it in English, but the entire audience seemed to be equipped with the Turkish translation, 'and they understood every point, registered at exactly the right moment. We had to give two performances of it, with a very good orchestra.' He has now also recorded that show on CD, which went straight into the German best-seller lists.

In November he was in Prague, narrating Mussorgsky's *Pictures at an Exhibition* and Saint-Saëns' *Carnival of the Animals.* Herbert Lom was in Prague at the same time, and he attended the performance. He said wonderingly to me, 'I don't know why he does it, that's the puzzle to me. A man who has done so much, why does he travel from Budapest to Prague, with all the discomfort of having to be carried upstairs – just for the applause? He certainly doesn't do it for the money.'

When I put this to Peter, he looked at me in surprise. 'I enjoy them, and I'm defending something I've done myself, of which I'm rather proud.' This confirmed his daughter Tamara's belief, and my own observation, of the lift he still got from performing. There was talk of him bringing one or more of these shows to the BBC Promenade Concerts – which would have been a long overdue debut for them in the country of his birth.

The writing slowed just a bit. He used to pen a weekly column for the *European* newspaper, which was syndicated in other languages in Europe. When that paper folded, he thought that was the end of that. But then he received an agonised call from the offices of the *Courier* in Vienna, saying, 'Where's the article?' So he did one column a month for them – a thousand words a time in English, which they translated into German.

He had no new play on the horizon but did not rule out the prospect of one. Or any other books? 'You never know. When you start, all sorts of juices begin to flow that are dormant. I wouldn't be surprised,' said with a happy smile of anticipation.

He had lost little of his creative energy and had few complaints about the onset of his ninth decade. 'I find actually getting old is fascinating. I don't find it a handicap. I can't walk as easily as I used to, but I'm having time to think now, and I really feel I've changed a gear into something where I'm capable of better things than I used to be. This may only be an illusion, but it's a very pleasant one.'

His legs may have been slower, but his mind was as quick and inventive as ever. He expressed disappointment when I finally ran dry of questions at one of our last long sessions, and genuine pleasure when I came up with a whole lot of fresh ones at the next. Others occurred as I neared the end of writing this, and he never ceased to surprise me with his answers, which were often amusing and endlessly thought-provoking.

His contribution to the gaiety of nations has been incalculable, and because he has expressed it through so many different media he is impossible to categorise. Other actors may have done as much on the stage, or on film, or on TV, or on record; other writers may have given us as many plays, or screenplays, or novels, or travel books, or articles; but no single person has done so many of those things all together, moving from one to the other without seeming to pause for breath.

He may have paused a little more often in his eighties, but we can still read the books, watch the films, and listen to the recordings. It is also high time that some of his plays were revived in Britain, which deserve to be seen by new generations – either in the West End or at the National Theatre – as they are regularly in Russia and Germany.

He was born with so many gifts that it is pointless to try to evaluate them in any order of relative importance, but it is hard to disagree with his wife Hélène, when she says, 'It's wonderful to be able to make people laugh.'

Epilogue

After the final revisions to the hardback edition of this book had been despatched to the printers in mid-2002 I asked Peter if there was any chance that he might be in England when it was published in September. He replied, 'Oh, I wouldn't miss that little shindig for worlds.'

As the date approached, the Weidenfeld and Nicolson publicity department was besieged with requests for interviews by the press, radio and television. To fit everything into the six days of his visit, we each did a number of them separately, and a few together. After the marked lack of British interest in celebrating his eightieth birthday as the Germans had done so spectacularly, Peter was touched by this upsurge of enthusiasm two years later, and he agreed to a demanding schedule of interviews and speaking engagements.

The two literary luncheons in London sold out immediately they were announced. I knew that he never decided in advance what to say, and watched him appraising the audience before he rose to speak. The *Oldie* luncheon at Simpson's-in-the-Strand had him following Dickie Bird and Norman Wisdom. The former cricket umpire spoke for twice his allotted time, and the audience was amused to hear his Yorkshire accent also issuing from the Ustinov mouth, 'because sitting next to Dickie Bird is contagious: I can't break myself of t' abit'.

The following day at the Savoy Hotel he gave a quite different speech, and was rewarded with a standing ovation at the end, which our *Daily Mail* hosts told me was only the second time this had happened at one of their luncheons, the first having been for that other veteran actor-knight, Sir John Mills.

But what pleased me most was arranging for the Peter Ustinov debut at the National Theatre, where our Platform conversation filled the Olivier auditorium. Appropriately, we were occupying a Russian set, as the Tom Stoppard trilogy *The Coast of Utopia* was running that week. But when we went onstage for the prior soundcheck I realised it was going to be a long walk from the upstage doorway to our chairs at the front. So I asked, 'Peter, do you want to come on with your stick, or in the wheelchair?' (which had borne him through the backstage labyrinth).

'Oh,' he said, 'it will be much quicker in the chair, and I'm now very used to people seeing me in it at airports.'

However, when we entered I heard a surprised intake of breath from the audience seeing him unexpectedly chairbound, which was immediately drowned by the welcoming applause. But his disability was forgotten within seconds as he launched on his first story, generating that laughter which Peter always affectionately referred to as 'the most civilised music in the universe'.

There was a long line for the book-signing afterwards, and some of his more elderly admirers were charmingly optimistic of recognition. One imposing lady announced, 'We last met when you were just nineteen,' and another remarked, 'You sat next to my husband on the Centre Court at Wimbledon in 1957.' Peter assumed his most beatific smile, in pretended remembrance; this obviously happened to him all the time.

A couple of months later on a Sunday afternoon in the Floral Hall, Covent Garden, I saw him cast his spell over the very young. He was narrating his script for Saint-Saëns' *Carnival of the Animals*, with the soloists of the Royal Opera House. The children loved it and stood and cheered at the end. Peter was called back for a second bow, and clutched the nearest pillar for support. He told me afterwards that he actually needed it, but he made them think he was just fooling for their benefit, and they shouted with laughter.

The Saints and Sinners Club of London have the admirable custom of making a large donation to the charity nominated by the guest speaker at their Christmas lunch. In 2002 it was Peter, who gratefully passed the money to his own foundation, which helps needy children around the world, such as those suffering from Noma Disease in West Africa, and South African orphans who have lost both parents to Aids.

This time he flew in to London from Berlin, where he was dubbing the soundtrack for his part in the Martin Luther film. The following week he was off to Vienna for talks with the University about his Institute studying the History of Prejudice.

In 2003 the first German edition of this book was published, and to my delight it went straight into their bestseller lists. When I telephoned Peter in Switzerland, he had just returned from a tour of Germany with his concert appearances, and as soon as I said, 'Oh Peter, you'll be pleased to hear that our book is doing very well in Germany,' he groaned in mock-horror, 'Don't tell me, people have been bringing me copies to sign wherever I went!'

Sadly, that tour proved to be his last. His legs had become increasingly troublesome, and towards the end of the year they required daily hospital treatment. I assumed that would mean he and Hélène would have to forego their annual departure to Thailand on Christmas Day, but when I talked to him a few days beforehand he replied cheerfully, 'Oh yes, we're going as usual, it will be fine.'

That was the last time I spoke to him. On his return in mid-January he was whisked straight from the airport to hospital in Geneva. I telephoned Hélène every couple of weeks, and could tell by her voice how worried she was. He was diagnosed with heart trouble, and was losing a lot of weight.

On Sunday 28 March 2004, he breathed his last. The official announcement of his death the following morning flashed round the world, and the tributes poured in from all those countries he had visited in his many roles.

UN Secretary General Kofi Annan praised his 'compassion, conscience and character', former Prime Minister Sir Edward Heath said, 'There has been no one else in our lifetime to compare to him. There was no greater laughter-maker on any stage in the world.' Chancellor Gerhard Schröder wrote to Hélène, describing him as a 'role model for us all, not only as a great actor and artist, but above all as a man with a great heart, spirit and humour'. Peter might well have responded with wry humour to the press release from an African pressure group headed 'Ustinov Death a Great Blow to Ethiopians', but he would surely have been touched by the heartfelt comment from Carol Bellamy, the executive director of UNICEF: 'The children of the world have lost a true friend in Sir Peter Ustinov,' she said. 'Sir Peter had a magical way with children and an inimitable way of making their problems matter to people all over the world. He was one of UNICEF's most effective and beloved partners, a man who exemplified the idea that one person can make a world of difference.'

The following Saturday St Peter's Cathedral in Geneva was packed for the funeral. Hélène and her sister were accompanied by all of Peter's children and his grandchild. His old UNICEF friend Leon Davičo gave the Address. The music was by Peter's favourite composer, Mozart, but the most haunting moment of the ceremony came when the violinist Ivry Gitlis advanced to the coffin playing a lullaby his mother used to sing to him. At the end the congregation filed out past the bier and the family, as they paid their last respects. Afterwards the interment took place in the little churchyard near the house with its beautiful views which had been home to Peter for so many years.

He always said he would never retire voluntarily, as one day he would be forced to do so involuntarily. That day didn't come until shortly before his eighty-third birthday. For more than sixty years he brought happiness and laughter to millions of people all over the world. He had so many gifts, and he shared them all with us until the end. We shall not look upon his like again, but our lives were the richer for having known him, either in person as I was so privileged to do, or watching him in performance, or by reading him on the page.

The book is now closed, but his memory will live on in all of us.

Acknowledgments

I am hugely indebted to Sir Peter Ustinov for agreeing to let me write his biography, and for talking to me at such length and so frankly over the last three years. On each of his visits to this country he has gone out of his way to reserve several days at a time for our conversations. Not only have these sessions been enormously informative, they have also, as I hope I have captured in this book, been incredibly entertaining. I am grateful too for the help I have received from his family, in particular his wife Hélène, and his daughters Tamara and Pavla.

I have consulted as many of his friends and colleagues as I could reach – in person, by telephone, fax or letter, and several of the more distant ones sent me their memories on audiotape, to ensure that they did full justice to such an important figure in their lives. For their time and thoughtfulness I would like to thank: Jenny Agutter; the late Jean Anderson; Michael Anderson; Lord Attenborough; Derek Bailey; Tony Benn; Lord Brabourne; Judith Buckland; James Cairncross; Sir Kenneth Calman; Ian Carmichael; Jonathan Cecil; Petula Clark; Lady Daubeny; Christopher Fry; Nicholas Garland; the late Sir John Gielgud; Sir Peter Hall; Edward Hardwicke; Rosemary Harris; Frank Hauser; Sir Edward Heath; Antony Hopkins; Deborah Kerr; Angela Lansbury; Moira Lister; Herbert Lom; Hayley Mills; Sheridan Morley; John Neville; Denis Norden; Frank Novak; Denis Quilley; Paul Rogers; Prunella Scales; Terence Stamp; Eric Till; Samuel West; Clifford Williams; and Michael York.

For their help with my research I am indebted to James Barber at the Yvonne Arnaud Theatre, Guildford; Susan Bennett at the Royal Society of Arts; Diana Devlin for the correspondence with Sir Lewis Casson; Keith Seacroft at the University of Durham; the Study Room staff at the Theatre Museum; and Thalia Verganelis for research in New York.

Sir Peter's London agent Steve Kenis, and his staff, have been most helpful with the chronology of his career and in keeping me up to date with his busy itinerary during my work on the book.

I owe special thanks to Ion Trewin for commissioning the book and for his most helpful suggestions at every stage; and to his staff at Weidenfeld and Nicolson for all the care they have taken in producing it.

If it were not for Sarah Smyth's original invitation to interview Sir Peter for the Cheltenham Festival of Literature, I might have missed the opportunity to embark on writing his life; and without my wife Aileen's unfailing interest and support, not to mention her keyboard skills, I doubt if I could have finished it on time.

John Miller, 2002

Permissions

The passages quoted from Peter Ustinov's books are included by kind permission of Michael O'Mara Books for *Add a Dash of Pity*, *The Loser*, *Frontiers of the Sea*, *Krumnagel*, *Ustinov in Russia*, *The Disinformer*, and *The Old Man and Mr Smith*; and of Macmillan London for *My Russia*.

Where there are alternative spellings for names in other languages, the author has in general followed the usage of Peter Ustinov in his writings.

Theatre

Stage roles

Date	Play	Role	Theatre
1938	*The Wood Demon*	Waffles	Barn, Shere
	Mariana Pineda	Police Chief	Barn, Shere
1939	*Bishop of Limpopoland* and *Madame Liselotte Beethoven-Fink*		Players'
	White Cargo	Doctor	Aylesbury
	Rookery Nook	Harold Twine	Aylesbury
	French without Tears	French Professor	Aylesbury
	Goodness How Sad	Seal-trainer	Aylesbury
	Pygmalion	Colonel Pickering	Aylesbury
1940	*First Night*	Rev. Alroy Whittingstall	Richmond
	Swinging the Gate (revue)		Ambassadors'
	Fishing for Shadows	M. Lescure	Threshold
	Diversion (revue)		Wyndham's
1941	*Diversion No. 2* (revue)		Wyndham's
1944	*The Rivals*	Sir Anthony Absolute	Garrison tour
1946	*Crime and Punishment*	Petrovitch	New
1948	*Frenzy*	Caligula	St Martin's
1949	*Love in Albania*	Sgt. Dohda	Lyric, Hammersmith and St James's
1951–2	*The Love of Four Colonels*	Carabosse	Wyndham's
1956	*Romanoff and Juliet*	General	Piccadilly

1957	*Romanoff and Juliet*	General	Plymouth, New York, and US tour
1962	*Photo Finish*	Sam Old	Saville
1963	*Photo Finish*	Sam Old	Brooks Atkinson, New York
1968	*The Unknown Soldier and His Wife*	Archbishop	Chichester
1973	*The Unknown Soldier and His Wife*	Archbishop	New London
1974	*Who's Who in Hell*	Boris	Lunt Fontanne, New York
1979	*King Lear*	Lear	Stratford, Ontario
1980	*King Lear*	Lear	Stratford, Ontario
1983	*Beethoven's Tenth*	Beethoven	Vaudeville
1983–4	*Beethoven's Tenth*	Beethoven	Nederlander, New York, and US tour
1987–8	*Beethoven's Tenth*	Beethoven	Schiller, Berlin
1990–5	*An Evening with Peter Ustinov* (one-man show)		On tour
1995	*Beethoven's Tenth*	Beethoven	Chichester

Playwright

Date	Play (first performance)	Director	Theatre
1942	*House of Regrets*	Alec Clunes	Arts Club
1943	*Blow Your Own Trumpet*	Michael Redgrave	Old Vic
1944	*The Banbury Nose*	Norman Marshall	Wyndham's
1945	*The Tragedy of Good Intentions*	Eric Capon	Liverpool
1948	*The Indifferent Shepherd*	Norman Marshall	Criterion
	Frenzy (adapted)	Murray Macdonald	St Martin's
1949	*The Man in the Raincoat*	Peter Ustinov	Edinburgh
1951	*The Love of Four Colonels*	John Fernald	Wyndham's
	The Moment of Truth	John Fernald	Adelphi

1952	*High Balcony*	Andrew van Gyseghem	Embassy
1953	*No Sign of the Dove*	Peter Ustinov	Savoy
1956	*Romanoff and Juliet*	Denis Carey	Piccadilly
	The Empty Chair	John Moody	Bristol Old Vic
1958	*Paris Not So Gay*	Frank Hauser	Oxford
1962	*Photo Finish*	Peter Ustinov and Nicholas Garland	Saville
1964	*The Life in My Hands*	Denis Carey	Nottingham
1967	*Halfway Up the Tree*	Peter Ustinov	New York
	The Unknown Soldier and His Wife	John Dexter	New York
1974	*Who's Who in Hell*	Ellis Babb	New York
1981	*Overheard*	Clifford Williams	Haymarket
1983	*Beethoven's Tenth*	Robert Chetwyn	Vaudeville

Also directed by Peter Ustinov:

1941	*Squaring the Circle*	Vaudeville
1949	*Love in Albania*	Lyric, Hammersmith, and St James's
1952	*A Fiddle at the Wedding*	UK tour

Appendix Two

Film

Date	Film	Director
1941	*One of Our Aircraft is Missing*	Michael Powell
	The Goose Steps Out	Will Hay/Basil Dearden
1944	*The Way Ahead* (also co-writer)	Carol Reed
1946	*School for Secrets* (also writer)	Peter Ustinov
1947	*Vice Versa* (also writer)	Peter Ustinov
1949	*Private Angelo* (also writer)	Peter Ustinov
1950	*Odette*	Herbert Wilcox
	Quo Vadis	Mervyn Leroy
1952	*Hotel Sahara*	Ken Annakin
1953	*Beau Brummell*	Curtis Bernhardt
1954	*The Egyptian*	Michael Curtiz
1955	*We're No Angels*	Michael Curtiz
	Lola Montès	Max Ophuls
	The Spies	H.G. Clouzot
	An Angel Flew Over Brooklyn	Ladislas Vajda
1960	*The Sundowners*	Fred Zinnemann
	Spartacus (first Oscar)	Stanley Kubrick
1961	*Romanoff and Juliet* (also writer)	Peter Ustinov
1962	*Billy Budd* (also co-writer)	Peter Ustinov
1963	*Topkapi* (second Oscar)	Jules Dassin
1964	*John Goldfarb, Please Come Home*	J. Lee Thompson
	Lady L (also co-writer)	Peter Ustinov
1967	*Blackbeard's Ghost*	Robert Stevenson
	The Comedians	Peter Glenville
1968	*Hot Millions* (also co-writer)	Eric Till

1969	*Viva Max*	Jerry Paris
1971	*Hammersmith is Out*	Peter Ustinov
	Big Truck and Poor Clare	Robert Ellis Miller
1974	*One of Our Dinosaurs is Missing*	Robert Stevenson
1975	*Logan's Run*	Michael Anderson
	Treasure of Matecumbe	Vincent McEveety
1976	*The Last Remake of Beau Geste*	Marty Feldman
1977	*Purple Taxi*	Yves Boisset
	Death on the Nile	John Guillermin
1978	*The Thief of Baghdad*	Clive Donner
1979	*Ashanti*	Richard Fleischer
1980	*Charlie Chan and the Curse of the Dragon Queen*	Clive Donner
1981	*Evil Under the Sun*	Guy Hamilton
1982	*Memed My Hawk* (also writer)	Peter Ustinov
1988	*Appointment with Death*	Michael Winner
1989	*The French Revolution*	Robert Enrico
1991	*Lorenzo's Oil*	George Miller
1993	*The Phoenix and the Magic Carpet*	Zoren Porisic
1996	*Stiff Upper Lips*	Gary Sinyor
1999	*The Bachelor*	Gary Sinyor
2003	*Luther*	Eric Till

Television
(A selective list of credits)

1957 *The Life of Samuel Johnson* (Emmy for Best Performance)

1966 *Barefoot in Athens* (Emmy for Best Performance)

1970 *Storm in Summer* (Emmy for Best Performance)

1973 *Jesus of Nazareth*

1979 *The Hermitage*
      Einstein's Universe
      Nuclear Nightmares

1984 *The Well-Tempered Bach* (Emmy nomination)
      Peter Ustinov's People

1985 *Thirteen at Dinner* (Poirot)
      Peter Ustinov's Russia
      Deadman's Folly (Poirot)

1987 *Murder in Three Acts* (Poirot)
      Peter Ustinov in China

1988 *Around the World in Eighty Days*

1990 *The Mozart Mystique*

1991 *Ustinov on the Orient Express*

1993 *Ustinov meets Pavarotti*

1994 *Inside the Vatican*
      The Old Curiosity Shop
      Haydn Gala

1995 *Ustinov in Thailand*
      Ustinov in Hong Kong

1997 *Peter Ustinov's Mendelssohn*

1998 *Planet Ustinov*
     Alice in Wonderland
2001 *Victoria and Albert*
2002 *The Salem Witch Trials*
2003 *Winter Solstice*

Opera Productions

1962	*L'Heure Espagnole*	Royal Opera House, Covent Garden
	Gianni Schicchi	Royal Opera House, Covent Garden
	Erwartung	Royal Opera House, Covent Garden
1968	*The Magic Flute*	Hamburg Opera
1973	*Don Giovanni*	Edinburgh Festival
	Don Quixote	Paris Opera
1978	*Les Brigands*	Berlin Opera
1981	*The Marriage*	Piccola Scala, Milan, and Edinburgh
1982	*Mavra* and *The Flood*	Piccola Scala, Milan
1985	*Káťa Kabanová*	Hamburg Opera
1987	*The Marriage of Figaro*	Mozarteum, Salzburg, and Hamburg Opera
1993	*Jolanthe* and *Francesca da Rimini*	Dresden Opera
1997	*The Love of Three Oranges*	Bolshoi Opera, Moscow

Phonograph Records

Mock Mozart – Ustinov as vocal quartet and full orchestra

The Grand Prix of Gibraltar – Ustinov as racing cars

Peter and the Wolf – narration, with London Philharmonia conducted by Herbert von Karajan (Grammy Award)

Nutcracker Suite – narration, with André Kostelanetz and orchestra

The Soldier's Tale – narration in French with Jean Cocteau, Igor Markevitch conducting chamber orchestra

Háry János – narration, with London Symphony Orchestra

The Little Prince – narration of fairy tale by Antoine de Saint-Exupéry

The Old Man of Lochnagar – narration of Prince of Wales's children's story

Grandpa – narration of original composition by Howard Blake

Babar and Father Christmas

Peter Ustinov Reads the Orchestra

The Donkey's Shadow – narration for Richard Strauss's last operatic fragment

Carnival of the Animals – narration for music by Saint-Saëns

Le Bourgeois Gentilhomme – narration and new third act

The Creatures of Prometheus – narration for Beethoven's ballet

Books

1960	*Add a Dash of Pity* (short stories)
	We Were Only Human (cartoons)
1961	*The Loser* (novel)
1966	*Frontiers of the Sea* (short stories)
1967	*Poodlestan Sketches* (cartoons)
1971	*Krumnagel* (novel)
1977	*Dear Me* (autobiography)
1983	*My Russia* (history)
1987	*Ustinov in Russia* (story of the TV series)
1989	*The Disinformer* (novella)
	A Nose by any Other Name (novella)
1990	*The Old Man and Mr Smith* (novel)
1991	*Ustinov at Large* (compilation of articles for *European* newspaper)
1993	*Still at Large* (further compilation of articles)
1998	*Monsieur René* (novel)

Awards and Honours

1957	Royal Society of Arts: Benjamin Franklin Medal
1961	Academy Award: Best Supporting Actor in *Spartacus*
1964	Academy Award: Best Supporting Actor in *Topkapi*
1967	Cleveland Institute of Music: Honorary Doctorate of Music
1969	University of Dundee: Honorary Doctorate of Laws
1971	La Salle College of Philadelphia: Honorary Doctorate of Laws
	University of Dundee: elected Rector by the Student Union
1972	University of Lancaster: Honorary Doctorate of Letters
1973	University of Letherbridge, Canada: Honorary Doctorate of Fine Arts
1975	HM Queen Elizabeth II Birthday Honours: CBE
1978	UNICEF: Award for Distinguished Service
	Prix de la Butte: French award for *Dear Me*
1979	Variety Club of Great Britain: Best Actor for *Death on the Nile*
1984	University of Toronto: Honorary Doctorate
1985	Commandeur des Arts et des Lettres, Paris
1986	Hashemite Kingdom of Jordan: Order of Istiqlal
1987	Order of the Yugoslav Flag
1988	Elected to Académie des Beaux Arts, Institut de France
	Georgetown University: Honorary Doctorate of Humane Letters
1990	HM Queen Elizabeth II Birthday Honours: Knight Bachelor
	City of Athens: Gold Medal
	Medal of the Greek Red Cross
1991	University of Ottawa: Honorary Doctorate of Laws
	Charles University, Prague: Medal of Honour

1992	University of Durham: Honorary Doctorate of Letters
	University of Durham: Chancellor
	World Federalist Movement: President
	BAFTA Los Angeles Branch: Britannia Award
1993	London Critics' Circle Award for Lifetime Achievement
1994	Brazil: Ordem Nacional do Cruzeiro do Sul
	German Cultural Award
	German Bambi for Lifetime Achievement
1995	UNICEF International Child Survival Award
	Pontifical Institute of Medieval Studies, St Michael's College, University of Toronto: Honorary Doctorate
	University of Brussels: Doctorate Honoris Causa
1997	German Video Prize for Lifetime Achievement
1998	German Bundesverdienskreuz
	Bayerischen Fernsehpreis for Lifetime Achievement
2000	National University of Ireland: Honorary Degree
2001	International University of Geneva: Honorary Degree
2002	Oesterreiches Verdienskreuz (First Class)

Bibliography

Ambler, Eric, *Here Lies Eric Ambler*, Weidenfeld & Nicolson, 1985

Benois, Alexandre, *Memoirs*, Chatto & Windus, 1960

Benois Ustinov, Nadia, *Klop and the Ustinov Family*, Sidgwick & Jackson, 1973

Bogarde, Dirk, *A Postillion Struck by Lightning*, Chatto & Windus, 1977

Braden, Bernard, *The Kindness of Strangers*, Hodder & Stoughton, 1990

Bragg, Melvyn, *Rich: the Life of Richard Burton*, Hodder & Stoughton, 1998

Coveney, Michael, *Maggie Smith*, Gollancz, 1992

Danischewsky, Monja, *White Russian – Red Face*, Gollancz, 1966

Daubeny, Peter, *My World of Theatre*, Jonathan Cape, 1971

Devlin, Diana, *A Speaking Part: Lewis Casson and the Theatre of his Time*, Hodder & Stoughton, 1982

Douglas, Kirk, *The Ragman's Son*, Simon & Schuster, 1988

Forbes, Bryan, *Ned's Girl: the Life of Edith Evans*, Hamish Hamilton, 1977

Gingold, Hermione, *How to Grow Old Disgracefully*, Gollancz, 1989

Grade, Lew, *Still Dancing*, Collins, 1987

Guinness, Alec, *Blessings in Disguise*, Hamish Hamilton, 1985

Millar, Ronald, *A View from the Wings*, Weidenfeld & Nicolson, 1993

Miller, Arthur, *Timebends: a Life*, Grove Press, 1987

Redgrave, Michael, *In My Mind's Eye*, Weidenfeld & Nicolson, 1983

Stamp, Terence, *Coming Attractions*, Bloomsbury, 1988

Stamp, Terence, *Double Feature*, Bloomsbury, 1989

Ustinov, Peter, *Dear Me*, Heinemann, 1977

Waldman, Michael, *Planet Ustinov*, Simon & Schuster, 1998

Warwick, Christopher, *The Universal Ustinov*, Sidgwick & Jackson, 1990

Willans, Geoffrey, *Peter Ustinov*, Peter Owen, 1957

Index

Works and performances by Peter Ustinov (PU) are listed under his name.

☐ **Audrey: Her Real Story** £6.99
ALEXANDER WALKER
1 85797 352 6

☐ **Callas** £8.99
ANNE EDWARDS
0 75284 844 5

☐ **Confessions of an Actor** £7.99
LAURENCE OLIVIER
1 85797 493 X

☐ **Doris Day** £7.99
ERIC BRAUN
0 75281 715 9

☐ **Elizabeth** £7.99
ALEXANDER WALKER
0 75280 579 7

☐ **Fatal Charm: The Life of Rex Harrison** £8.99
ALEXANDER WALKER
0 75284 901 8

☐ **Judi Dench** £8.99
JOHN MILLER
0 75284 894 1

☐ **Judy Garland** £6.99
ANNE EDWARDS
0 75280 404 9

☐ **Katharine Hepburn** £6.99
BARBARA LEAMING
1 85799 440 X

☐ **Marilyn** £6.99
GLORIA STEINEM
0 75284 372 9

☐ **Mrs Kennedy** £8.99
BARBARA LEAMING
0 75284 929 8

☐ **Orson Welles** £8.99
BARBARA LEAMING
1 85799 092 7

☐ **Streisand** £7.99
ANNE EDWARDS
0 75281 104 5

☐ **Up in the Clouds, Gentlemen Please** £7.99
JOHN MILLS
0 75284 449 0

☐ **Vivien** £6.99
ALEXANDER WALKER
1 85797 927 3

All Orion/Phoenix titles are available at your local bookshop or from the following address:

Littlehampton Book Services
Cash Sales Department L
14 Eldon Way, Lineside Industrial Estate
Littlehampton
West Sussex BN17 7HE
telephone 01903 721596, *facsimile* 01903 730914

Payment can either be made by credit card (Visa and Mastercard accepted) or by sending a cheque or postal order made payable to *Littlehampton Book Services*.
DO NOT SEND CASH OR CURRENCY.

Please add the following to cover postage and packing

UK and BFPO:
£1.50 for the first book, and 50P for each additional book to a maximum of £3.50

Overseas and Eire:
£2.50 for the first book plus £1.00 for the second book and 50p for each additional book ordered

---

BLOCK CAPITALS PLEASE

name of cardholder .... *delivery address*
.... *(if different from cardholder)*
address of cardholder ....
....
....
....
postcode .... *postcode* ....

☐ I enclose my remittance for £..............................

☐ please debit my Mastercard/Visa (delete as appropriate)

card number ☐☐☐☐☐☐☐☐☐☐☐☐☐☐☐☐

expiry date ☐☐☐☐

signature ....

prices and availability are subject to change without notice